W9-BYW-621

INDONESIAN POLITICS UNDER SUHARTO

After twenty-five years in power, President Suharto and his New Order government confront a crisis of renewal. The regime, which swept to power in the wake of a military putsch in 1965, has brought enduring stability and economic prosperity to the country, but has shown no inclination to pass the reins of power to the next generation. As a result pressures for political change are building up.

This book offers an informed and balanced analysis of Suharto's New Order as it approaches a crucial political juncture. Indonesia's remarkable political stability has for the most part kept the country out of the headlines. Quietly, Indonesia has moved into a strong position just behind other fast-growing economies in the region. Employing widely applauded liberal economic reforms and granting more freedom to the private sector, the government has transformed Indonesia's commodity-dependent economy into a nascent regional industrial dynamo. But now, economic success is running up against domestic political uncertainties.

The author reassesses the New Order's fiery origins and its military roots, and evaluates the considerable economic progress achieved under Suharto. He also analyses Suharto himself, a man whose low international profile and uncharismatic style have made him one of the least understood and most intriguing long-serving leaders.

Michael Vatikiotis is Bureau Chief in Malaysia and ASEAN correspondent for the *Far Eastern Economic Review*.

POLITICS IN ASIA SERIES
Edited by Michael Leifer
London School of Economics

ASEAN AND THE SECURITY OF SOUTH-EAST ASIA
Michael Leifer

CHINA'S POLICY TOWARDS TERRITORIAL DISPUTES
The Case of the South China Sea Islands
Chi-kin Lo

INDIA AND SOUTHEAST ASIA
Indian Perceptions and Policies
Mohammed Ayoob

GORBACHEV AND SOUTHEAST ASIA
Leszek Buszynski

INDONESIAN POLITICS UNDER SUHARTO

Order, development and pressure for change

Michael R.J. Vatikiotis

London and New York

First published 1993
by Routledge
11 New Fetter Lane, London EC4P 4EE

Reprinted 1993,
Revised 1994

Simultaneously published in the USA and Canada
by Routledge
29 West 35th Street, New York, NY 10001

© 1993 Michael R.J. Vatikiotis

Typeset in Bembo by Michael Mepham, Frome, Somerset
Printed and bound in Great Britain
by Biddles Ltd, Guildford and King's Lynn

All rights reserved. No part of this book may be reprinted
or reproduced or utilized in any form or by any electronic,
mechanical, or other means, now known or hereafter invented
including photocopying and recording, or in any information
storage or retrieval system, without permission in writing
from the publishers.

British Library Cataloguing in Publication Data
A catalogue record for this book is available
from the British Library.

Library of Congress Cataloging-in-Publication Data
has been applied for

ISBN 0–415–11701–1
ISBN 0–415–10707–5 (pbk)

For Janick

The people of Java are little different from the mountainous island on which they reside, a chain of volcanoes which at any moment can awaken to cough up a phlegm of burning lava.

(Y.B. Mangunwijaya)

CONTENTS

PREFACE

President Suharto has been in continuous political command in Indonesia ever since 11 March 1966 when he seized the reins of power from the incumbent President Sukarno. He was then a lieutenant-general, little known outside of the Republic. With the support of the Armed Forces, he proceeded to transform the country's politics and priorities. No less a nationalist then his flamboyant predecessor, his vision of the future stood in striking contrast. He explained, 'We shall only be able to play an effective role if we ourselves are possessed of a great national vitality.' To that end, a debilitated international pariah of a state was set on a course of rational economic development and regional co-operation, with the result that a quarter of a century later Indonesia has become a candidate member of the club of newly-industrialized countries. The intervening years have not been without turbulence in both domestic and foreign policy; nor have the fruits of development been evenly distributed. But President Suharto has concentrated and exercised power in a skilful and ruthless way, employing the forms of democracy to political advantage. In March 1993, close to 72 years of age, he secured re-election unopposed for a sixth consecutive term of office. That term may well be his last, with political succession a mounting issue.

Michael Vatikiotis has written a timely and authoritative study of President Suharto's self-styled New Order and of his legacy. In this paperback edition, he has carried his account beyond the presidential election of March 1993 to explore impending political change. It is well over ten years since one of his colleagues wrote a well-received assessment of Suharto's Indonesia. Since then, the country has experienced a number of significant changes below the level of leadership. Michael Vatikiotis addresses these changes, as well as the record of President Suharto's role, with intellectual rigour and clarity, demonstrating a profound understanding of the culture and dynamics of Indonesia's politics. This volume is the product of four years of close observation of those politics and related economic life. It provides a vivid comprehensive account of Indonesia at a turning point in its history, which is also exceptional in its ability to bridge the gap between the world of academe and that of the general reader.

Michael Leifer

FOREWORD TO THE
REVISED EDITION

When this book first went to print in late 1992, elections had been held (the previous June) and President Suharto was heading smoothly into his sixth term of office. Politically, the status quo remained much the same. In other respects, Indonesia was a much changed place from when I first sat down to write the first edition in 1989. Sustained economic growth has bred confidence and a greater sense of purpose – even ambition – among the country's ruling elite. The politicians felt the need for stronger political institutions, the businessmen wanted a more liberal business climate; educated intellectuals and professionals simply wanted more freedom to act and think for themselves. Yet, Indonesia remains entangled in the same web which prevented these urges being satisfied a decade or so earlier. For all the security offered by the country's growing economy and social stability, Indonesians felt politically insecure. The chief political problem was ensuring a smooth transfer of power from Suharto to his successor.

In this sense, I have felt no urge to tinker with my assessment of the New Order to date in the first edition. My hope is that it remains a relevant guide to Suharto's New Order and a primer for the political changes likely to occur in the next five years. I have succumbed, however, to the temptation of adding a final word in the form of a short chapter (Chapter 9) which takes in the 1992–3 election period and the political trends that emerged afterwards. The thoughts I have had on this more recent period developed in the course of several visits to Indonesia after my move to Kuala Lumpur in March 1991 – including coverage of the June 1992 elections.

In the process of making slight revisions to the existing text and compiling material for the new chapter, I am once again primarily indebted to my Indonesian friends and colleagues who have given me great encouragement from the start of this project. Their comments and constructive advice have always been as much an inspiration as they are a great help. I am also grateful to various Indonesian scholars, particularly those at Monash University who generously enabled me to attend the December 1992 Conference on Indonesian Democracy in Melbourne. Their tolerance of my views of a subject so complex is much appreciated. Of course, these views are entirely my own and are presented with the best of intentions.

Kuala Lumpur, November 1993

ACKNOWLEDGEMENTS

This book is the product of four years' stay in Indonesia, working as a foreign correspondent, mainly as bureau chief for the *Far Eastern Economic Review*. My first debt of gratitude is therefore to the magazine, and its former editor Philip Bowring, for granting me the time and resources to follow Indonesian affairs closely from 1987 to 1991. This was not always easy to do. A regional magazine can only offer limited space to one country, and with government sensitivities to what I wrote always weighing heavily, not all of what I saw was printable.

More essential, however, was the understanding and co-operation of the many hundreds of Indonesians in all walks of life and at all levels of society, who consented to share with me their thoughts and experiences under the New Order. The gratitude I owe them is inestimable. To list all of their names would be impractical, not only because it would fill a small pamphlet, but also because political life is such in Indonesia, that to be mentioned can damage careers.

I was, however, very fortunate to have access to all levels of the government, and a broad range of society. For all the criticism heaped on the government for its intolerance of the press, it must be said that foreign correspondents are treated more like diplomats than nuisances. The degree of courtesy and respect I experienced in Indonesia over four years far outweighed the moments of irritation. This undoubtedly helped foster my interest and contributed to my persistence. In this sense, I owe a general debt of gratitude to all those in government departments, institutions and organizations which I had cause to deal with, particularly in the Ministry of Information, Armed Forces, Defence Ministry, Ministry of Foreign Affairs, the Centre for Strategic and International Studies (CSIS), University of Indonesia, Gajah Mada University and LIPI.

The list of friends and colleagues who either helped or encouraged me in this endeavour is similarly long. I owe so much to my colleagues in the

Indonesian press for their patience, support and generosity. I would like to thank Professor Michael Leifer of the London School of Economics for his guidance in preparing the book. Hamish MacDonald edited much of my copy for the *Review* and shared my interest in Indonesian politics. Another of my *Review* colleagues, Rodney Tasker, made it all possible. C.P.F Luhulima, of LIPI in Jakarta, always warned me if I strayed too far off course. The Jakarta bureau secretary, Fanny Lioe, put up with my disorganized ways.

Special thanks are due also to: Mochtar Lubis, the late Slamet Bratanata, Nasir Tamara, General A.H. Nasution, Marsillam Simanjuntak, Aristides Katoppo, Brigadier-General Abdulkadir Besar, Tim Carney, Terry Properjohn, Terry Holland, John Florent, Manggi Habir, Nono Makarim and the Ronodipuro family. I was also fortunate to benefit from the wisdom of two of Indonesia's most inspiring thinkers before their death, General T.B. Simatupang and Professor Soedjatmoko.

Indonesia was not only an intellectual odyssey for me, but also the start of a new family experience. My two children, Chloe and Stefan, were born in Jakarta soon after I began the book. It is for them to judge later in life whether the final result begins to make up for the time I spent away from them in their earliest weeks. As for my wife, Janick, I can only say that without her boundless patience and encouragement, not one page could have been written.

Michael Vatikiotis
Kuala Lumpur

NOTE ON SPELLING

For the sake of consistency and ease of pronunciation by those unfamiliar with Indonesian names and terms, the author has tried wherever possible to avoid using the pre-1972 spelling of Indonesian words. This means that words which used to use the diphthong, *oe*, are now spelt with a simple *u*. Similarly *dj* is simplified to *j*; while *j* becomes *y*. Except in cases where a person's name employs the old spelling, the modern system is employed throughout the book.

INTRODUCTION

In a biting satire staged recently by the Indonesian playright, N. Riantiarno, a once powerful king lies sick and dying, surrounded by his children. Each of them vies for the ailing king's favour with shallow protestations of love and devotion, while beyond the palace walls chaos reigns as the competing royal progeny seek to destroy one another. The plot has a Shakespearean ring to it. However, the sense of confusion and chaos pervading the once prosperous and happy mythical kingdom, now facing impending succession, is something many Indonesians watching the play found uncomfortably familiar. Apparently, the authorities also felt that the play – entitled *Succession* – worked too well, and it was closed by the police before finishing its week-long run.

The play neatly captures, in allegorical form, the atmosphere in Indonesia as it headed into the 1990s. 'In these confusing times, a wrong word can be the end of you,' says a clown-like character at one point in the play. 'Therefore speak only in confused terms. The more one is confused, the safer we all are'. Indonesia in the late 1980s and early 1990s seemed to be in a confused state. Outwardly, healthy economic indicators gave cause for optimism and aroused outside interest in the country's enormous potential. Of all the states in South-east Asia, Indonesia was considered the most interesting to watch: a Muslim majority anchored to a secular social and political framework; a strong, assertive state apparatus which nevertheless allowed the private sector to operate with comparative freedom. Seen like this, Indonesia had the makings of a regional dynamo. Paradoxically, within domestic political circles, stresses and strains were evolving. After almost a quarter of a century of sometimes harsh but unquestionably constructive and stable rule, the New Order government, with President Suharto at the helm, faced a crisis of renewal. There was an understandable sense of pride in the achievements of the New Order, which over a twenty-five year period had ensured that material development was distributed in some measure over this vast and varied nation. But increasingly, demands for broader political participation grew more voluble. At the same time, there were concerns in elite circles about Suharto's receptiveness to the climate of change.

Suharto turned seventy in 1991. So far as anyone could judge, he had made no known plans for retirement. Supported by well-oiled bureaucratic machinery and a political culture given to pliancy, his leadership seemed securer than ever; and as elections neared, it was assumed he wanted to stay in power. There were few signs of widespread resistance to his continued rule except in limited but influential elite and military circles. Their principal concern was to ensure a smooth transition of power; one that demanded Suharto's co-operation. How was Suharto to be persuaded to relinquish a position which granted him supreme power, and which brooked no questioning of authority or political alternatives? At stake for the political and business elite was the preservation of order: the avoidance of chaos and a deep-seated fear in a society fraught with latent social, ethnic and religious tensions.

Half a century ago, the birth of Indonesia unleashed some of these tensions in a spate of uprisings which forced the infant republic to turn with ferocity on those who questioned the unity of the state. Twenty years later, an attempted *putsch* exposed the Communist Party to the wrath of its oppponents and resulted in another communal frenzy which threatened to tear the state apart. Indonesia's collective psyche is acutely sensitive to the destructive by-product of politicking. Another twenty-five years on, the portents are being read with particular care for fear that sudden political change in familiar partnership with mass acts of violence may be just around the corner. This book broaches no such apocalyptic scenario. However, focusing as it does on the latter period of the New Order under Suharto, it does reflect the fears of a political establishment uncertain of its future and divided over how to tackle it.

Indonesia has always fascinated regional specialists, faced as they are with the challenge of piercing the opaqueness of its political culture. The very size of the country, home to over 180 million people – the fourth largest population in the world – who live on 13,667 islands, spanning an area of 5.1 million square kilometres, offers a scholarly challenge. There is the allure of Indonesia's fragile unity; the very fact that it survives frankly impossible degrees of ethnic and regional diversity, and has absorbed remarkable socio-economic growth, makes it nothing short of a phenomenon.

Rather like North Americans, Indonesians possess a sense of continental insularity unusual for an archipelagic people. This developed in tandem with the potent nationalism that has underpinned the country's unity since independence was declared in August 1945. The confidence and self-assurance bred as a result – strangely untainted by overt arrogance – also invites scrutiny.

Yet, in common with other cultures which define national entities, such as the Thai and even the Japanese, the opinion of foreigners – if too critical – can provoke considerable resentment. Westerners employing the analytical tools of western social science are accused of misunderstanding local norms and values – a serious taboo in the tabernacles of Asian nationalism. In some cases, the accusation is more serious. How often is the western press accused by certain South-east Asian governments of 'deliberate' distortion of the facts, of being the tools of a 'neo-imperialist' plot to undermine the state? The analysis, argument and even the arrangement of narrative in this book, risks arousing such emotions, however objective the author has tried to remain.

What this book hopes to project is a sense of what the New Order is all about, stripped of value judgements, but reflecting wherever possible the opinion of Indonesians as well as those of the author as an objective outside observer. There is no political agenda lurking in the wings; no ideological conviction driving the analysis. The aim is simply to de-mystify and begin to understand the dynamics of leadership and power in South-east Asia's largest nation.

In the opening chapter, Suharto, the man who has led Indonesia through the second half of its independent existence, is examined in some detail. It is necessarily a sketchy biography, not least because of the scarcity of accurate biographical material, a heavy reliance on secondary source material, and the not always objective opinions of those who have served under him. Suharto's own recently published autobiography – ghost written by Ramadhan K.H. – offers a wealth of interesting, but often enigmatic insights into the man. These have played an illustrative rather than central role throughout the text. Chapter 2 focuses on what Suharto is perhaps best known for: the fostering of order and stability which have promoted steady economic growth. It charts pragmatic policies which have given the private sector a far bigger role than anyone considering the state-dominated economy of Indonesia just twenty years ago would have imagined possible.

Indonesia under Suharto has long been viewed from a distance as another of the region's military-led states. Consideration of the Indonesian armed forces as an institution in Chapter 3 offers an alternative view: that the military's own rather dogmatic view of itself as guardians of the nation has been eroded by the New Order's political success. Suharto's progressive dominance of the political scene has marginalized the military's once central role and forced some rethinking of their role in politics. A key factor underpinning the recent manoeuvring over the succession has been the army's realization of how weak they are as political players, followed by attempts to redress the balance.

Social engineering and the imposition of uniformity on society is most associated with Asia's more dogmatic regimes. Under the New Order, similar practices have been employed in the name of stability and order. What kind of society the New Order has fostered is the central theme of Chapter 4, where the social and political levelling of Indonesia's complex society is investigated. Because Indonesia is home to the largest Muslim population in the world, it was felt necessary to dwell on the role of Muslims in the contemporary social and political life of Indonesia. After the 1979 Iranian Revolution it became fashionable to predict the spread of Muslim fundamentalism, or more realistically to scan for signs of a renewed Muslim political consciousness. Fundamentalism – a much misunderstood term for Islamic radicalism – has not taken root in Indonesia, as Chapter 5 explains, but a number of social and political factors have conspired in recent years to allow Muslims to assert their majority status more forcefully.

From this point on, the book alters pace and style to track the more recent political turbulence created by the debate over succession. In a broader context, Suharto's position at the end of the 1980s was little different from other long-serving leaders in the region: facing a combination of old age and fast-altering social and economic realities, renewal was badly needed in order to shore up their position. Chapter 6 chronicles the emergence of pressure on the leadership and examines Suharto's apparent skill at countering the moves against him by tapping new areas of political support. But in Chapter 7, an assessment of Indonesia's political and economic strengths and weaknesses at the turn of the decade, set against the twists and turns of succession manoeuvring, hints at the potentially destabilizing forces Suharto may have unconsciously unleashed in the process of securing another term as president after 1993. It concludes that Indonesia sought to project an image of an emerging responsible regional power while at the same time domestic political dynamics conspired to project an uncertain future.

Conclusions are hard to draw because Suharto's grip over the New Order remains firm and the shadow he casts over the nation shows little sign of receding. In March 1993, Suharto was elected to his sixth term of office at the age of 72. Although the general election a year earlier indicated intensified pressure for political change, there was little sign of his grip on power weakening.

Ultimately, Indonesia's conservative leadership is being increasingly measured at home and abroad against a more liberal yardstick. Western governments have shed their ideological preoccupations and now pray at the altar of Human Rights. While Suharto's Indonesia was always rated highly in the war against Communism, it scores poorly in the new scheme of things. Chapter 8 attempts to place the problems posed by the new stress on Human Rights for Indonesia and its leadership in a regional perspective.

The 1992 elections and the presidential elections a year later conceded little to the liberal winds sweeping the region. Yet the elections demonstrated that doubts about the durability and stability of the New Order were also misplaced. Suharto may be criticized at home and abroad, but no viable alternative was on the horizon and Indonesians resigned themselves to five more years under the New Order.

But inevitably there was change. Suharto himself was adding new ingredients to the political pie. Some of these represented the growth of new political forces, others were created by Suharto to help shore up his position. The final chapter (Chapter 9) surveys developments after the June 1992 elections, highlighting the emergence of the Islamic lobby as a new political force and attempts by the armed forces to head off the threat the revival of Islamic nationalism seemed to pose to its entrenched position in the political order.

The story of Suharto's New Order may have some time to run, or be close to ending. It is tempting to search the region for a script or scenario; Marcos in the Philippines, or the Pro-Democracy movement in China spring to mind. Elements of both can be applied in a general way; a leader so wrapped up in his own sense of destiny that he is blind to the limits of his power, or a country which seeks to liberalize its economy without addressing the political change unleashed as a result. This study cannot possibly predict with any certainty what will be the outcome. But it does seek to influence how Suharto and the New Order should be regarded after a change of guard. In this sense, what follows attempts to provide an analytical backdrop to the next five year period, by which time, under new leadership, Indonesia may well have embarked on a new political course.

1

SUHARTO

I conjured up in my imagination the kings and bupatis of Java, mad
with their lust for power, making people bow down and crawl before
them, giving obeisance to them, do their pleasure. And no guarantee
that they would be better educated than those they ordered about.

(Pramoedya Ananta Toer)[1]

Indonesia emerged from the political turbulence of the immediate post-
colonial era more battered than most countries in South-east Asia. The
trauma of wrenching independence from the Dutch had only just been put
behind them in 1949, when Indonesians were plunged into a political
mayhem generated by competing power groups. The situation worsened
as Sukarno, the country's founding constitutional president, exploited
factional and regional divisions to assume executive authority. In July 1959,
Sukarno replaced parliamentary with 'Guided Democracy', wrapping
himself in the trappings of power. By the mid-1960s, he was on the verge
of allowing Indonesia's Communist Party, with over three million members, to arm themselves and neutralize the conservative army. Not
surprisingly, cold war warriors in the West saw this as Indonesia's first step
towards membership of a then ascending Communist bloc.

While the country struggled under the burden of triple-digit inflation,
Sukarno talked about revolution with politics as the commander. Finally,
goaded into action by a still unexplained coup attempt on 30 September
1965, the army moved in, effectively deposing Sukarno in March 1966
and ushering in a conservative military-backed regime steered by a relatively unknown general called Suharto.

The move left a trail of tragedy and a host of unanswered questions in
its wake, questions which continue to be posed even after a quarter of a
century of peace and stability. Yet the events of 1965 proved the exception
to generalized views about the inherent instability of coup-born

governments. Since then, the unitary basis of the state, with a powerful executive at its head, has remained intact and more or less unquestioned. While coup and counter-coup have plagued Thailand, and deep political and racial animosities have periodically afflicted Malaysia, Indonesia for the past twenty-five years has experienced comparative political tranquillity and steady, if comparatively sluggish, economic growth. Over the same period Indonesians have known only Suharto as president.

The extraordinary grip this man has maintained over such a large and diverse country continually amazes his own countrymen who, at the very least, consider him something of a political wizard – whom no one seems capable of outwitting. Any study of contemporary Indonesia must focus on this poorly educated, but determined farmer's son from Central Java, who became a general of the army and soon afterwards leader of South-east Asia's largest and most populous nation.

Suharto came to power in the confused and hitherto not fully explained aftermath of an abortive coup. Whether the events of 30 September/1 October 1965 were mounted by dissident soldiers against President Sukarno, or with the President's connivance against the army leadership remains to this day unresolved. The official explanation has always been that it was a Communist-inspired coup which failed. Every year to mark the anniversary the government shows a long feature film re-enactment of the events of those two days. In it Indonesians see men of the presidential guard round up six generals, who are later murdered by Communist Party members. The message is simple: Communists are barbarous and bad, the army is virtuous and good.

Objective assessments of the affair have yet to dislodge the primacy of the government's explantion that it was 'an attempted communist coup'. Still further suppressed – perhaps more instinctively than by design – is the fact that the events of that year and into the next, eventually cost the lives of possibly a million Indonesians, innocent of politics, and mostly in forgotten rural villages on the country's main island of Java.

Somehow, out of this chaos, the little-known General Suharto emerged on top. To this day contemporary observers insist that nobody knew very much about the man at the time. Yet he was confirmed as President in March 1968, and has been re-elected by a unanimous consensus of people he has appointed to the one thousand-member *Majelis Permusyawaratan Rakyat* (People's Consultative Assembly or MPR) four times since then.

Indonesia in the mid-1960s was ripe for political change. But it would be incorrect to assume that the country's founding President, Sukarno, was unpopular. As proclaimer of independence and great world leader in the eyes of his people, he commanded profound respect. The Javanese, who dominate Indonesia's tapestry of cultures, greatly respect authority and are hard pushed to question those who demonstrate a firm grip on power. Sukarno was, however, increasingly resented in ruling circles, and specifically by the military. Foremost among their grievances was Sukarno's apparent headlong tilt towards the Communist fold. The Indonesian Communist Party, which claimed some three million members, could count on some support from within the military – perhaps more than the army will ever be prepared to admit. By the 1960s, however, the bulk of officers were being trained by those under the influence of the US and its cold war warriors.

Sukarno's taste for wasteful displays of international diplomacy irked an inward-looking officer corps. Frustration was building up and, aided by development of a notion of the army's dual political and military role, many officers began to feel it was as much their duty to run the state as to guard it. Aid pouring in from the Soviet Union and China annoyed many in the intellectual elite and the army who saw their interests better served by the economically nascent West. Sukarno spoke of the need to continue the revolution that brought independence, mesmerizing the people with mass rallies and oratory laden with compelling rhetoric but little else. Meanwhile, what the people needed was stability, and to be fed. Yet despite the factors loaded against Sukarno, there is no convincing proof that there were a mess of plots against him. Sukarno commanded loyalty and respect. He was, after all, the man who declared independence; the country's paramount leader with a talent for demagoguery second to none.

Members of the Indonesian elite – many of them in the military – have begun to resent Suharto in similarly ambiguous fashion for almost the same reasons, but against a markedly different background. There is no easy comparison with the Sukarno period. Sukarno's Indonesia was bankrupt and starving when he was overthrown. Suharto's Indonesia is growing better off by the year as sensible economic policies bear fruit. Similarities between the two periods do exist, however. They provide compelling evidence of a political culture with one foot in the past; of a society resistant to change. One facet of this political culture is of crucial importance to understanding why Sukarno commanded popularity while people starved, why Suharto survives mounting pressure for more open government and criticism of his family's hydra-like business interests: that is the inordinate respect Indonesians have for firm, established leadership.

Like Sukarno at the end of his rule, Suharto is completely confident that he has the support of the people. Sukarno used to describe himself as *penyambung lidah rakyat* – literally the 'extension of the people's tongue'. Suharto, for his part, pins his legitimacy on a unanimous mandate from the people – a point he frequently makes in the course of his long and ratl.er dull public speeches. Increasingly, Suharto is also becoming aware of his international standing. Sukarno before him took pride in hosting gatherings of developing world leaders, basked in the regional controversy he stirred up, and took Indonesia out of the United Nations. Suharto is less brash, and far more circumspect when it comes to the outside world. But recent years have brought him awards and honours for achieving self-sufficiency in rice, and implementing effective birth control in the world's fourth most populous nation. The economic policies he has presided over have won plaudits overseas, and Indonesia is a model debtor country. Sukarno manipulated his overseas image in a showy and destructive fashion. Suharto is showing signs of wanting to use it to reinforce his mandate.

Suharto has always said that he is willing to be replaced at any time, if – and given Suharto's tight rein over formal political groups, this is a big if – anybody else can secure a unanimous mandate. To guarantee this unlikelihood, he rejected the notion that alternative candidates be allowed to campaign openly ahead of the presidential elections. Officially, one-tenth of the thousand-member MPR which elects him is directly selected by the president. But half the assembly is composed of members of the bureaucracy, armed forces and other social organizations. All its members undergo a rigorous screening procedure. In effect, less than 50 per cent of the MPR is actually composed of elected representatives.

By 1991 it seemed clear that Suharto, now in his seventieth year, was making no apparent preparations for a graceful exit. Rather, he appeared to be quietly and efficiently mobilizing support for his acclamation to another five-year term. While his colleague in Singapore, Prime Minister Lee Kuan Yew, seemed to have tackled the succession problem by settling for a step back (by assuming the post of 'Senior Minister') in November 1990, Suharto was talking about the need for his own generation to continue serving the nation and a 'New National Awakening' in 1993, which few doubted he wished to lead.

Like Sukarno, Suharto presents a paternal image to his people. Sukarno made a virtue out of his leadership of the 'revolution', Suharto since mid-1983 has been styled *Bapak Pembangunan* – the 'father of develop-ment'. The changes he has presided over are, by the developing world's standards, almost as revolutionary as Sukarno's achievement of inde-pendence in 1945. Poverty has been drastically reduced, the country is almost self-sufficient in basic foodstuffs, basic health and education facilities are available at every level of society. Quantitatively, Suharto has lent substance to that handiest of catchwords in the lexicon of third world politics: development. Development is his leitmotiv.

4

By the time he was elected to his fifth term of office in March 1988, a generation had come of age who knew no other president than Suharto. Yet muted criticism of his rule was being heard from young and old alike in educated circles. After almost a decade of inactivity on the nation's campuses, students in late 1988 began, in small numbers, to call for a change of leadership. By the middle of 1989, student protests – still in limited numbers and seemingly guided by the armed forces – were regularly reported in the press. In the course of 1989, the size and frequency of these protests increased, and some arrests were made to keep it all under control. The focus of demonstrations in the mid- and late 1970s had been on corruption. Now the 'corruptors' were singled out.

From the older generation came calls for renewal as well. They stemmed largely from a group of retired army officers, some of whom had been involved in previous moves against Suharto in the mid-1970s. But there was some evidence that these disgruntled men – characteristically of Suharto, more or less freely allowed to pursue their business interests – were being encouraged by the active military leadership. Their concern focused on the significant decline in the military's political power and their inability as a result to exert influence over the executive. Suharto's judicious use of divide-and-rule tactics over the previous decade has weakened and divided the ranks of the military. Though the cliché of military rule was still widely employed outside Indonesia, inside the country it was clear that only Suharto ruled.

In liberal intellectual circles, there was talk of the need to open up the system, give younger people a chance to take initiatives, and for the institutions of government to be more democratic. Some of these were old tunes, though now struck up with new vigour in harmony with the global wave of democratic and human rights awareness sweeping the new post-cold war world. Suharto became a target in this respect because of the role he played in the New Order's resistance to political change.

From the business community came grumbles about the president's wealth – an accusation never seriously hurled at Sukarno, who was more interested in what money could buy rather than the accumulation of riches. The youngest of his three sons and three daughters were still in their twenties, yet they had assembled fast-growing business empires and sizeable fortunes. Suharto insisted they were engaged in business for social and welfare-orientated ends. His eldest daughter, Siti Hardiyanti Hastuti Rukmana, even suggested that her father's position was a hindrance to her business activities. In reality, aided by a phalanx of sycophantic followers, the Suharto family was acquiring control over the fastest growing and most lucrative areas of the economy.

5

The web of profitable enterprises woven around his family and their mainly Chinese business associates was one source of Suharto's political strength. With an estimated $US2–3 billion tied up in ostensibly charitable foundations in his name, Suharto could draw on virtually unlimited funds for political purposes. There is no legislation governing these foundations save for their exemption from tax and auditing. By the late 1980s the scale of Suharto's family enterprise was so great that scarcely any large project could proceed without the involvement of one or another of the family's business groups. Government ministers came under pressure to channel tenders and projects their way.

For the most part, the family avoided any significant capital outlay on their own account, but received a hefty commission for the facilities they extended to enable the project to proceed. The principal facility employed was the use of the Suharto family name and the unequalled influence this brought to bear on the bureaucracy. Rather than sophisticated corporate strategies, what the family engaged in were essentially tollgate operations; a means of earning revenue Siti Rukmana applied literally by building several inner- and inter-city toll-roads on Java.

The behaviour of the young sycophantic entrepeneurs who were the children's business partners was criticized for the way in which they gambled with sizeable sums of other people's money for their own gain. Their business acumen was frequently none too good; their greed was seemingly unlimited. A newspaper editorial in September 1990 went so far as to ask if the near failure of a major private bank controlled by Suharto's foundations meant that the New Order 'was suffering from systematic fatigue by effected moral carelessness'.[2]

The issues are somewhat different, but the sense of creeping resentment disguised by apparently unwavering support and respect is reminiscent of the culturally driven sycophancy which gave Sukarno the illusion of power to the very end. Just as some of the fiercest criticism of Sukarno came from within bodies he set up, using the ideological parlance he insisted on; so with Suharto the banner of development is waved in his face. Members of the 1966 generation of students which helped bring Suharto to power, are today criticizing the New Order's failure to renew itself:

There is need to further cultivate responsible openness which is the key to political dynamism in society. Legal order based on Pancasila must prevail in the effort to create an image of the state based on the rule of law.[3]

In 1966 the New Order promised the rule of law. A quarter of a century later, many Indonesians feel that promise has yet to be fulfilled.

However useful comparisons with the Sukarno era may be with regard to the slow erosion of Suharto's popularity in the 1980s, the two leaders are about as far apart as possible in origin and background. Sukarno came from the upper classes of Javanese society and, like so many Indonesian nationalists, spent the first years of his life aspiring to acceptance by the Dutch civil service; acquiring a quasi-western education provided for the lucky few with the ability and the resources to obtain it.

Suharto's rural origins and military background set him firmly apart from Sukarno. Suharto typified what Harold Crouch so aptly described as the 'small town Java' types,[4] who dominated the new generation of Indonesians which inherited the mantle of power from the generation of Dutch-educated pioneer nationalists. Both Suharto's origins and early career are, if not shrouded in myth, subject to speculation. One thing is clear; the man who has held sway over the world's fifth largest nation for over a quarter of a century was, until he became president in 1966, no extraordinary person.

Suharto was born on 8 June 1921 in Kemusuk, a small hamlet or offshoot of the village of Godean in Argomulyo district 12 kilometres west of Jogyakarta in Central Java. By car today, the village is a twenty-minute drive from Jogyakarta, and given today's population densities in Central Java, is close to being absorbed by the city's outskirts. The surrounding ricefields have changed little, however. They stretch almost as far as the eye can see from the rear of the compound in which Suharto was raised; not an untypical perspective for a youth from this area to grow up with. His father, Kertosudiro, was an *ulu-ulu*, or minor village official with responsibility for the upkeep of irrigation works in the village rice fields. Suharto was Pak Kerto's third child. He already had two from his first wife by Suharto's own account. These were rude beginnings indeed for the future President, but they bear some examination.

The young Suharto lived in various homes away from his parents after they separated. His schooling, up to intermediate, or middle school level only, was in the Javanese language. His surroundings, from the rice fields of the village of Kemusuk in which he was born, to the aristocratic trappings of Solo where he lived briefly as a child, were steeped in Javanese culture and tradition. He had never travelled outside the area until he joined the Royal Netherland's Indies army (KNIL), in 1940 at the age of 19.

The student of psycho-biography might ponder over the separation of Suharto's parents and the frequent moves as a child. Before he was 2 months old, Suharto's mother, Sukirah, apparently fell ill and abandoned him, unable to suckle the young child. As a result, he was given to his paternal great aunt, the local midwife who attended his own birth, mBah

Kromodiryo. In his autobiography, Suharto claims to begin remembering his life at the age of 3 with mBah Kromo. What he remembers fits more or less the idyllic image of rural Javanese existence:

> I was often invited by mBah Kromo to the rice fields. Sometimes I was carried on the back of those turning the soil, or left to climb a bund. Happy on my own, I still remember how I would give orders to the buffalo to move forward, turn left or right. Then falling in the paddy, play in the water and the mud. If I felt tired, or hot, I rested at the edge of the field, or by the road.... I used to like looking for eels, which I liked very much to eat, as I do to the present day.[5]

It is not uncommon in rural Java for children to be taken in by other, related families and treated as offspring. Under these circumstances they are rarely treated as equals of the family's other children. In the Javanese language such children are known as *orang ngenger*, or 'foster children'. The term carries connotations of ill-fortune. Suharto's father took another wife and had several more children; Suharto himself was returned to his mother Sukirah at the age of 3 after she had remarried a local farmer. Later, when Suharto was 8, his father took him away again. Thereafter, the young Suharto began a peripatetic existence between town and village in Central Java. This must have been unsettling for him.

In his autobiography, Suharto talks of few close friends. Among his numerous relatives, Suharto makes out he was less well provided for. Describing an elder cousin, Mas Dharsono, who already wore a good shirt, Suharto says he felt 'humiliated'.

> At the time, I thought well, life's like that. I thought, we are from the same family, but receiving different treatment. Mas Dharsono already has a shirt, while I don't.[6]

The passage is illuminating. Suharto may be striving to give the impression of deprivation to make his subsequent achievement appear greater and more humbly accepted. Yet he betrays also a sense of bitterness over not being treated as an equal within his extended family.

It is perhaps not surprising, therefore, that Suharto's principal weakness in later life has been the indiscriminate promotion and protection of his own family's interests. One man who has observed him closely throughout his rule argues:

> Many people speak of Suharto's belief in Javanese values. But in his value system, the misery of his family background takes predomin-

ance. This explains the attitude towards his own children. Nothing is more important to him than this. He is serious about this.[7]

Shortly afterwards, at the age of 8, the young Suharto entered school. Referring to this period, Suharto talks about having to move several times from one relative to another, attending diferent schools in the area.[8] It may be that this peripatetic existence, shuttling between one relative and another, bred in the young Suharto, a deep respect of family values. It is hard, on the other hand, to meet a Javanese who believes otherwise.

Apart from the separation from his mother, much of Suharto's background is blandly normal in the Javanese context. There does not seem to have been an experience to inspire him to do things other men of his era did not. As his German biographer, O.G. Roeder, put it in the 1970 edition of *The Smiling General*:

Suharto did not rise to the highest rank in the state by an ardent zeal to save the nation and mankind. He was not obsessed by a sacred mission from boyhood and he did not formulate or develop a doctrinal ideology.... his rise to leadership was mainly the result of prevailing conditions and events.[9]

Indeed, Suharto's play on humble rural roots – steering buffalo and playing in the paddy mud – tells us something about the way he regards his current position as president, not how he achieved it.

Surrounded from the beginning of his rule by men of more education, status and indeed ability, Suharto has never pretended to be better than they are. Rather, he has always played up his peasant origins, enabling him to project proximity to the people and leave the experts isolated from him and easy to blame if things go wrong. He is clearly proud of his rise from humble farmer's son to President of the Republic, a transition brought into sharper focus when he is feted and awarded by outsiders. Significantly, perhaps, the first chapter of his autobiography opens with his receipt of a 'Ceres' Award from the Food and Agricultural Organization of the United Nations. The citation was for Suharto's contribution to Indonesia's self-sufficiency in rice. The ceremony, for which he travelled to Rome in 1985, was a proud moment, one he regards as a crowning achievement for the farmer's son from Kemusuk:

Imagine someone who more than sixty years ago was a child bathing in the mud, leading a peasant's life in Kemusuk village, stepping up to the podium and delivering a speech in front of assembled world experts, as a leader who has just solved the most important issue for 160 million mouths.[10]

9

Suharto's frequent and always televised dialogues with rural farmers appear to be events he genuinely enjoys. The fact that the farmers on these occasions address him with direct questions to which he gives long and expansive answers, reinforces his credentials as 'father of development'. Beside him, high state and local officials laugh nervously, made to look inferior by the fluency of the President's dialogue. At one such meeting with farmers in Bali, Suharto used this empathy with the farmers to blast his critics. An obviously irritated Suharto asked the astonished gathering in late July 1989, if the questions they were about to ask had been vetted. After being greeted with a chorus of 'noes', Suharto declared this proof that the nation's farmers could hold an open and frank discussion with their President.[11]

Suharto has remained conscious of his farmer's roots, while others around him – notably his wife – have periodically attempted to elevate his social origins to the ranks of the aristocracy. Suharto's ancestry has been raised from time to time in an attempt to link him to the royal house of Jogyakarta. Suharto has always emphatically denied these reports, preferring to present himself as a humble farmer's son. It is understandable in the Javanese cultural context that some among his subjects would like to link him with descent from the glorious Martaram kings. Given the vast extent of Javanese aristocratic genealogies, it is also more than likely that Suharto, as a pure Javanese, could trace some ancestry to the royal palace, or *kraton*.

Why then has Suharto resisted claiming royal descent? Perhaps because he judges it more valuable to identify with the *petani*, or farmer? Or is it, as some have suggested, because if played up, his links with the aristocracy might be shown to have some basis, but not high enough up the strictly hierarchical ladder to warrant anything more than retainer status within the *kraton*? There is said to have been oral confirmation from the 9th Sultan of Jogyakarta who died in October 1988, that the latter was the case, but this may have been malicious on his part. The two men never got along. As with many rumours about Suharto, however, it always remains difficult to separate the quantitative from the qualitative aspects of their content.

Suharto's marriage to Siti Hartinah, the daughter of a minor noble from the Mangkunegara royal house of Solo, has, if nothing else, established family links with the upper levels of Javanese society. In the late 1980s, it was rumoured, attempts were made to persuade the young crown prince of the Mangkunegara house to marry Suharto's youngest daughter. These apparently failed, and because Prince Djiwo already had a son from a previous marriage to one of Sukarno's daughters, it is widely believed Suharto decreed the prince could not take the title Mangkunegara X, when he was installed in January 1989. By allowing his wife to dabble in aristocratic trappings – such as the construction of an elaborate family mausoleum close to the Solo royal graves – Suharto has invited criticism from cultured Javanese circles. He, on the other hand has scrupulously upheld his humble origins.

After leaving school, Suharto tried his hand at various odd jobs, including that of a clerk's assistant in a village bank, or *Volks-bank*. Possibly maliciously motivated sources have subsequently told of Suharto's failure as a banker. Embezzlement of some of the bank's funds are said to have driven him from the job and the area. According to more charitable accounts, most of the time he was unemployed. Then in June 1940 at the age of 19, he was helped to join the Dutch colonial army by a friendly police officer, thus begining his military career. Within two years he rose to the rank of sergeant, serving in a battalion quartered at Malang in East Java. According to Roeder:

> His career was much discussed by his fellow soldiers, since men from Java were generally discriminated against in the KNIL, in favour of more loyal boys from the Moluccas and North Sulawesi.[12]

Suharto's loyal and obedient qualities as a soldier were also apparently noted by the Japanese after they invaded Java in 1942.

After the Dutch surrendered in March 1942, Suharto returned to his relatives in Central Java where, after a period of some months' unemployment, like many of his contemporaries he was attracted to the Japanese-run militia with its purportedly patriotic aim of helping Indonesians to achieve their own independence. In fact, the Japanese were more concerned to corral the youth into groups where they could expend their energies on the war effort.

Interestingly enough, here too, Suharto seemed to excel as a subordinate, and did not become a victim of Japanese retribution when Japanese-trained Indonesian officers rebelled in 1945.[13] In the Volunteer Army of the Defenders of the Fatherland, known as PETA, the young village boy received a rigorous military training and a large dose of Japanese propaganda – which he claims never to have swallowed.[14] When after the fall of Japan in August 1945 Indonesian nationalists declared independence, the young Suharto felt he had been 'called' to join the new People's Army.[15]

Suharto's official entry into the *Tentara Republik Indonesia*, or Army of the Republic of Indonesia, is dated 5 October 1945 in Jogyakarta. (Coincidentally or otherwise, 5 October is also the Armed Forces Day.) At that time, the nascent Indonesian army was little more than a collection of ragtag militia bands relying on weapons captured from the Japanese, with little formal leadership structure. Suharto's KNIL background and PETA training soon elevated him to the position of commander. His was not an unusual case. Many local commanders in Java could boast little more than their Japanese militia training and perhaps a local following based on less reputable pursuits as the Japanese withdrew. Suharto's lowly rural background and poor education later hindered his passage through the upper ranks of the military leadership, as those with a Dutch education or aristocratic status moved up after independence.

There is little we can garner from Suharto's military background which marked him out for what was to befall him later. Although he was said to be good with his troops, he was not such a remarkable leader of men. Nor, as far as anyone can tell, did his experience during the initial turbulent years of the revolution differ greatly from other young military commanders involved in the revolutionary struggle. The fact that he participated and, more providentially, commanded troops in an attack on Jogyakarta where the most celebrated action took place in 1949, can be seen – despite those who insist that his role was a minor one – as an important factor contributing to his later position in the armed forces.

Suharto himself attests to this, recalling, with apparent total clarity, conversations he had both with General Sudirman, Commander of the Indonesian National Army, and the Sultan of Jogyakarta, Hamengkubuwono IX, over matters of strategy. Certainly, photographs from the period show the young Suharto frequently at the centre of things; close to the army leaders – though always along with many others whose names have never become quite so well known subsequently. At one point, according to Suharto's own account, Sudirman even asks the young guerrilla leader's advice, referring to him in a familar way as 'Harto'.[16] For Suharto, even faint praise from a man as revered as Sudirman would have been a moment to treasure. The lean and consumptive general, who maintained a coolness and distance from the politicians and intellectual nationalists, appeared to possess all the classic qualities of the virtuous knight, or *ksatria* of the *wayang* shadow puppet theatre popular in Java. In fact, the two men shared humble origins, as Sudirman, once a teacher, is believed himself to have begun his military career as a local gang leader.

Much of modern Indonesian history has become embellished with myths bred of political expediency. Despite the collective nature of the republican military leadership in the late 1940s, Suharto claims it was his idea to launch the 1 March 'general attack' on Dutch-occupied Jogyakarta in 1949. The popular story is that Suharto, dressed as a peasant, took vegetables to the Sultan's kitchen before being led before him to discuss strategy.[17] Historians do not doubt Suharto's role in the 1 March attack, which lent credence to the nationalist struggle and helped turn international opinion against the Dutch, but are sceptical that the young officer could have influenced pre-eminent figures such as the Sultan and Sudirman. According to former Armed Forces Commander, General A.H. Nasution, the idea for the attack was a group decision taken at the guerrilla HQ outside the city.

> I was myself in central Java, commanding the whole island, and I received reports from all the divisonal commanders, of which Suharto was one. So I know very well what happened. The Sultan wrote a letter to general Sudirman saying that Jogyakarta must be attacked. Sudirman replied asking the Sultan to contact Suharto, who was the local commander. So in fact the Sultan always had a claim to responsibility for the attack. But later on Suharto chose to say he alone was responsible.[18]

Suharto's version of events during the heady days of anti-colonial struggle is certainly open to question. In any case, glorification of the period is a weakness shared by many of the generation of '45 who subsequently came to power. For the armed forces, the campaign against the Dutch in the years 1945–9 was, not to put too fine a point on it, a formative experience. Intellectuals of the Dutch-educated elite, or *priyayi* class, had dominated the ranks of the nationalist movement until the Japanese occupation. The struggle against the Dutch and the army's leading role after 1945 led to something of a division between the two groups. It boiled down to whether it had been the armed struggle or the negotiating skill of the civilian leadership which forced the Netherlands to give up its colony. The army maintained with some justification, that independence was achieved mainly through their efforts.

After the transfer of sovereignty to the Hatta government under Sukarno's constitutional presidency in 1949, Suharto, now a lieutenant-colonel, participated in a number of operations to mop up resistance to the new unitary state in the Eastern provinces. Suharto's troops, known as the 'Martaram Brigade', were among those sent to South Sulawesi in April 1950 to put down a revolt. Either the troops got out of control, or the methods employed by their commander were harsh, but it seems the Javanese soldiers behaved in an uncompromising and sometimes brutal fashion in order to quell the uprising.[19]

On his return to Central Java a year later, Suharto was also involved in the suppression of a Muslim uprising. Experiences like this impressed upon all the officer corps fresh from the struggle against the Dutch the fragility of the unitary state. Sadly, this imbued most of the same generation who subsequently went on to lead the nation with a deep-seated suspicion of non-conformity. The army leadership which took over in the mid-1960s, had an outlook similar to J. Edgar Hoover's obsessional mistrust of liberals in the US: anyone with a dissenting view became a suspect Communist or Muslim radical bent on the destruction of the state.

The period between Suharto's expedition to Sulawesi and 1959 was spent in his native Central Java where, in 1957 he became the region's military commander. These were formative years as far as Suharto's subsequent role in politics was concerned. Being divisional commander of what was known as the 'Diponegoro Division' lent him a certain amount of prestige. It provided him also with a pool of loyal subordinates, on whom he was to draw to appoint his key henchmen before and after 1965 in Jakarta.

While in Central Java he also developed the nucleus of the financial power base with which he was later to consolidate his control over the country after 1966. It was during this time that he met men like Liem Sioe Long, whose business skills satisfied first the quartermastering needs of Suharto's divison in Central Java, and later the acquisitive appetite of his family, members of which have subsequently become major shareholders in Liem's vast business empire.[20] By the mid-1980s the largest element of the Suharto family's corporate investments were equity holdings in Liem group companies.[21] By any measure, the web of Liem's domestic and offshore holdings made his the largest Indonesian-based business conglomerate, and one of the largest in Asia, a feat he owed in the main to Suharto's patronage. (By 1991 The Salim group's total turnover was estimated to be equivalent to 25 per cent of Unilever's worldwide turnover.)

Another Chinese businessman who financed Suharto's Central Java command in the 1950s, The Kian Siang (alias Bob Hasan), has also become a key Suharto business associate. In the 1980s Hasan frequently demonstrated the enormous influence he wielded in the presidential office by virtually writing government legislation favourable to his rattan and plywood industries.[22] Restrictions imposed, despite opposition from within the cabinet, on exports of raw rattan, and crippling taxes on sawn timber exports ensured that most smaller operations in this profitable area fell to his group of companies.

Given the contemporary prominence of men like Liem and Hasan, it is hard to underestimate the debts of obligation they feel. Being of Chinese descent, both were of course excluded from conventional national politics. But their ability to command substantial financial resources equipped them with more power than most cabinet ministers. Bob Hasan's involvement in charitable foundations owned by Suharto and various business ventures with his children constantly reinforced his links with the palace. By the mid-1980s Liem and Hasan had become Suharto's closest associates outside the immediate family, often spending more time on the golf course with the President during the week than any cabinet minister could hope to spend in a month.

Other key associates of Suharto's during his presidency were also men who worked with him in Central Java during this period. Two men dominated the scene until the mid-1980s: Ali Murtopo, his chief political strategist until his death in 1984, and Sœdjono Hœmardani, who served as Suharto's personal economic adviser until his death in 1986. It was Sœdjono's astonishing ability to organize military finances that brought army inspectors and the threat of corruption charges down on Suharto in 1959. A court martial was avoided, but Suharto lost his command of Central Java and, by some accounts, almost left the army. Clearly, the event was of more than passing significance in his life and bears closer examination.

Between 1957 and 1959, Sœdjono, aided by others, set up a number of companies in the name of Suharto and the Diponegoro territorial command. The capital for investment in these new companies came from two charitable foundations, or *yayasans*, that Sœdjono set up in late 1957. One was ostensibly for the economic development of the region covered by the Diponegoro command, the other for the assistance of retired military personnel.[23] These extra-budgetary funds originated from the seizure of Dutch assets in 1957, which left the military in possession of viable business concerns. There was also a need for the army to seek extra funding both because of the poor state of the economy and the rapid advances being made by the Communist Party in local politics. Sœdjono later defended his management of military smuggling operations in these political terms, saying the territory's organization under Suharto 'was perfect. The PKI [Communist Party of Indonesia] could not get its influence into it.'[24]

While warding off Communist influence, Sœdjono and his army financial team were conspicuously artful in binding the territory's economy to the military command. A contemporary account reported that:

> The money... was received by the territory IV development Fund Foundation from collections of donations such as those from kopra, salt, customs, sugar, telephone, electricity, lotteries, the Association of Indonesian Batik Co-operatives, cement, motor transport, radio, kapok, cloves, fertiliser auctions and others.[25]

According to the investigating officer sent by Army headquarters, the network of foundations run by Soedjono under Suharto's command to finance the troops was 'unique among all the territories of Indonesia'.[26] In many respects, Suharto's continued reliance on *yayasans* for political funding is proof of how effective a system he had hit upon. The fact that Suharto lost his job because the army at the time considered the system corrupt, appears to have had no effect on people's perception of the system as it is applied nation-wide today.[27]

Suharto was quietly removed from his position in Central Java in 1959 amid moves within the Army high command to clear up the worst excesses of the military–business relationship. But his good connections with a senior general staff officer, General Gatot Subroto, and Jogyakarta background ensured he was given an honourable transfer. In fact he was assigned to the Armed Forces staff college (SESKOAD) in Bandung, where – though not considered an outstanding student – he was exposed to many of the ideas he would later find opportunties for implementing as president.

As a young military commander with the bare minimum of training, Suharto may not have been privy to all that was going on around him, but he was certainly at the major centre of activity for much of the time. In the same way, Suharto's rise to power after the 1965 *putsch*, perhaps more than anything else, was a result of his being in the right place at the right time.

Suharto was a senior army officer in his forties in the mid-1960s. He was not particularly distinguished, but one of a group of officers from Central Java who had played a prominent role in securing the country from the Dutch in the late 1940s. He shared much in common with fellow Javanese officers of the time. His rural background and humble origins were not uncommon. His career had taken him from a regional command in Central Java to the Army's officer graduate school in Bandung, and subsequently to a staff position in Jakarta's prestigious Strategic Reserve Command (Kostrad). He was not considered among the military leadership who were growing restless under Sukarno – although this would not have ruled out his capacity to join in at a later stage. If Suharto's own view is to be believed, he was loyal to Sukarno – almost in awe of a man who for many Javanese possessed the hallmarks of a feudal Javanese king with supernatural powers. Then on the night of 30 September 1965, six senior generals were rounded up and brutally murdered by men ostensibly from the presidential guard. The action altered the course of Indonesian history.

For some years afterwards, Indonesian specialists outside the country and privately a number of Indonesians themselves, saw Suharto as a temporary phenomenon. Somehow this grubby little general from Central Java found himself at the top of the heap after the fray, and made good, they thought. It couldn't last. There was no substance to him. Former Army Chief of Staff General T. B. Simatupang described him as: 'not part of the intellectual circle in the armed forces'.[28] When one of Suharto's student followers approached the enormously influential Sultan Hamengkubuwono of Jogyakarta in early 1966 and asked if he would back the general, the Sultan reportedly laughed and asked if 'he was still in the habit of stealing'.[29]

The Sultan none the less lent Suharto support through his participation in the political triumverate which saw the transfer of power from the country's first President, Sukarno, and the eventual nomination of Suharto as President. He later served as Vice-President under Suharto from 1978 to 1983. However low people's estimates of the man were at the time, there seemed to be little will to oppose his rise to power. This is perhaps the central issue of any historical study of Suharto. How was a man whom no one in the military establishment particularly liked or respected, able to go so far?

Suharto's central role in the crushing of the October 1965 attempted *putsch* must be considered a factor that many of his opponents have subsequently tried to play down. Returning from command of Eastern Indonesia, where he commanded the successful campaign to wrest West Irian from the Dutch in 1962, Major-General Suharto joined Nasution's staff in armed forces HQ. Probably in order to balance General Ahmad Yani's promotion as army chief in 1962, Suharto, then 41, was given command of the Jakarta-based Army Kostrad. Nasution either disliked or mistrusted Yani, who was regarded as close to Sukarno – some even say he was being groomed to inherit the presidency, though this is unlikely. Given the personal nature of Army politics, Nasution probably perceived Suharto as a pawn – his pawn.

Kostrad was an elite, rapid deployment force designed to counter any insurrectionary moves by regional commanders. With feelings in the army running high over the murder of six generals on the night of 30 September, Suharto's decisive moves to restore order the following day earned him kudos he would have found hard to accumulate under normal circumstances. 'It was a sheer accident that he [Suharto] came to be the one', concluded a student leader who supported Suharto's rise to power in the mid-1960s.[30]

One view is that other contenders for power were reluctant to show their hand. The influential and popular Minister of Defence at the time, General A.H. Nasution, is widely believed to have backed away from the opportunity to seize power in the confusion that followed the *putsch*. A more recent and equally plausible view is that he fully expected power to pass to him after a few weeks once stability and order had been restored. In Indonesia, the conspicuous grabbing of power is regarded as unseemly.

17

There may even have been an informal agreement among the group of leading officers left after the *putsch*, whereby power would eventually be rotated among them. 'They all thought he [Suharto] would be malleable, colegial in his style of rule. They miscalculated'.[31] Certainly a number of this group, among them Dharsono, Kemal Idris and Sarwo Edhie Wibowo – three officers who played key roles in helping Suharto restore order after September 1965 – all later turned against him.

Major-General H. Dharsono, the most outspoken of the three, was removed from his position as Secretary-General of the Asean Secretariat in 1978 following a wave of army-backed student protests which were designed to force Suharto to step down – or at least persuade him to confer with his military peers. In 1984 Dharsono was imprisoned for speaking out against the military's tough repression of a Muslim riot in North Jakarta. He was released in 1990. Sarwo Edhie, the special forces officer who commanded the military operations which secured the capital in October 1965, died in late 1989 without ever publicly voicing his disillusionment with the New Order and opposition to Suharto, but it was reportedly considerable.[32] Kemal Idris, who commanded the special forces in 1965, was sent as an ambassador overseas after 1975, but has since returned to run a street-cleaning company in Jakarta. Were they all disappointed with their rewards after 1966, genuinely shocked at the way things developed, or did Suharto renege on some agreement?

A commonly heard view is that Suharto was thinking of standing down in the mid-1970s and passing the reins to – it was rumoured – General Surono. This never happened, and Surono was left a bitter and disappointed man. The same went for Kemal Idris:

> I never thought he would last so long. In 1971 I expressed the view that the president should only run for two terms otherwise his vested interests would take over. Even Suharto saw the sense in this by 1974, but those around him told him to go on.[33]

Those who regarded Suharto as a transient were, as it turned out, sorely mistaken.

Unanswered questions about the September 1965 coup still cast a shadow over the history of Suharto's New Order. The government has painted the murder of the six generals as an attempted coup mounted by elements of the military in collusion with the Communists. The Indonesian Communist Party is said to have set up a special bureau, acting without the knowledge of the party central committee, to foster ties with the military. This much was feasible. These were tumultuous times, politically. Sukarno was leading the country into the Communist camp and was in

18

poor health. The military was actively debating the future, and presumably positioning itself to seize power after he was gone. Sensing this, the PKI probably had feelers out to sympathetic areas of the military. But would party leaders have gauged support in the ranks sufficient to support a coup on their behalf?

The search for the the truth has focused on the controversial speculative paper written by Ruth McVey and Benedict Anderson a year after the event, in 1966. Their 'Preliminary Analysis' finds the official account that Beijing-backed Communists were involved untenable.[34] The two scholars propose instead that the coup originated with a move by officers loyal to Sukarno to prevent pro-western generals from conniving with the US and Britain to topple Sukarno. The coup attempt, which Anderson and McVey say deliberately implicated the PKI, was a botched job.

If so, the coup's failure is consistent with the army's poor track record of intervention. Riddled with internal factionalism, and divided above all over their role in the state, the Indonesian army lacked a sense of direction. Its spiritual leader, General A. H. Nasution, may have devised brilliant strategies for defeating the Dutch during the independence war, but in peacetime he was acquiring a record of indecisiveness. The army launched two coup attempts in 1952 and 1956, but they failed. In the '17 October Affair' of 1952, several senior officers attempted to persuade Sukarno to dissolve parliament. Instead, he had them removed. In late 1956, a former Army acting Chief of Staff, Colonel Zulkifli Lubis, made several abortive attempts to establish a military dictatorship. A year later, Sukarno created his own form of dictatorship under the guise of 'Guided Democracy'. Nasution was against the army's seizure of power. He demanded a role for the military in the state, but resisted going all the way, preferring instead to project the army as a professional force acting as the guardian of the state. The absence of a firm ideological position within the army increased the likelihood of polarization within its ranks. Senior officers were divided; some identifying closely with Sukarno, while others were disenchanted.

Contemporary reports from the US embassy in Jakarta, now declassified, shed little light on US attempts to goad the army into action and more on the army's confusion about what to do. A report by senior US diplomat, Ellsworth Bunker, in April 1965 stated:

> Sukarno is still the symbol for Indonesian unity and independence....
> There is little question of his continued hold on the loyalty of the
> Indonesian people, who in large measure look to him for leader-
> ship.[35]

By contrast, Bunker reported, the army had 'to concentrate on strengthening its own imperfect internal unity'. Bunker was perceptive, and saw the army locked onto the horns of a dilemma. The military leadership was dismayed by Sukarno's support for the PKI, which they saw as a threat to themselves and the nation's stability. At the same time, they saw their role as remaining loyal to the President. However, any chance of a decisive plan of action based on the circumstances was further diminished by uncertainty about who supported who within the ranks of the senior officer corps.

Attempts to implicate the CIA and other western intelligence agencies in a coup and counter-coup set-up have all sounded tantalizingly plausible, but consistently met stone walls. A tight clamp on information in Washington makes it unlikely that any more will be learned before Suharto leaves office. Recent probings have established that Washington was informally trying to persuade friendly elements of the military into some sort of action against Sukarno. But all the available evidence gives no positive proof of the CIA's involvement in the plot against the generals. In any case, it is now clear that the US State Department and CIA were by this time preoccupied by events in Vietnam. Experience of US foreign policy in South-east Asia has taught that it is rarely possible for Washington to be deeply involved in more than one crisis at a time.

When Suharto appeared on the scene in October 1965, no one in Washington knew who he was. Only after the Communists became the object of a national witch hunt did the US embassy swing into action, stirring up anti-Communist propaganda and providing logistical support to the army which expedited their ability to massacre PKI suspects.

The official version of what happened on that fateful night and thereafter has been given primacy for so long, many of the myths have become facts. Indonesians are resigned to and even relish the lack of any conclusive explanation. The multitude of riddles and rumours attending the birth of the New Order are wielded as a weapon by those who now oppose Suharto. Many still wonder why the coup plotters left Suharto off the list of generals they rounded up on the night of 30 September. As Kostrad commander, Suharto had access to a sophisticated nation-wide communications system at his HQ. He and the Jakarta garrison commander, Umar Wirahadikusumah, were the only officers in a position to control the capital, yet an attempt to secure Jakarta by military force did not try to neutralize them. Inevitably this has prompted the suspicion that Suharto was involved with the plotters. The government could have laid many of the unanswered questions to rest, but curiously a government white paper setting out a detailed explanation of the events of 1965, which was completed in the mid-1970s, has never been released.

Lurking behind the scenes is a hypothesis that implicates Suharto himself. Quite possibly he harboured a dislike for two of the targeted generals – Yani and Nasution. Yani himself is reported to have harboured no particular ill-feelings towards Suharto, often conferring on him the role of acting army chief of staff when out of town. But Suharto's dismissal from Central Java still wrankled. Nasution, considered a 'Mr Clean' in army circles, would have been apportioned part of the blame. Some say Suharto felt embittered. He saw his career going nowhere and was planning to resign and go into business as late as May 1965.

By far the most intriguing and as yet unexplained coincidence tying Suharto to the coup is that Suharto is known to have been visited twice by one of the key plotters – a Colonel Latief – once on 30 September shortly before the *putsch*. The story is that Latief came to warn Suharto about a plot to topple Sukarno being hatched by a council of generals. According to Nasution: 'If Latief told him maybe 20–30 per cent of what was going on, [Suharto] knew something, and he knew the situation was dangerous.' If Suharto knew, he chose not to act.

What strikes some as odd is why Latief reported to Suharto in the first place, since he was not, strictly speaking, Latief's superior officer. Latief was known to be fairly close to Suharto. They had shared experiences during the war against the Dutch. Significantly, Latief is the one leading actor of the alleged plot to escape execution. His survival has been held up as proof of Suharto's implication. Enigmatically, he languishes to this day in Jakarta's Cipinang prison, and was recently refused a pardon. Suharto also knew Untung, the chief plotter who announced the formation of a new government over Jakarta Radio the following day. Suharto was a guest at Untung's wedding. But perhaps this is not as significant a coincidence as its seems. As a senior officer in the presidential guard, Untung's company would have been much sought after. Access to those in power in Indonesia confers almost as much status on the individual as attaining power itself.

If Suharto had wind that something was up, why did he not report it to his superiors? Nasution argues that Suharto has always been indecisive in the field. He cites orders given to Suharto during the Dutch assault on Jogyakarta, which Suharto was slow to carry out. 'He was slow to implement orders, indecisive, never taking sides immediately, but wait-ing.'[36] Reflecting, a quarter of a century after the event, Nasution is unhappy with the notion that Suharto was the man who made the coup and that Communist involvement was a ruse. He prefers to cast Suharto as an opportunist, which does not in his view absolve him of responsibility for the deaths of the six generals.

The ease with which Suharto was able to put down the coup attempt and later assume command, though dressed up in a hestiant and spontaneous way by official accounts, certainly bears some of the marks of advanced planning. Why is it, for example, that when Untung's rebel troops formed up in Jakarta's Merdeka Square on 1 October, the only side they did not occupy was that formed by Suharto's Kostrad headquarters?

A more likely explanation, however, is that Suharto and a small group of supporters seized opportunties as they presented themselves without planning too far in advance. Kemal Idris, whose command of the special forces in Jakarta and role as deputy to Suharto put him in a key position, believes that ultimately Suharto pulled off something of a *coup d'état* when he sent a letter transferring powers from Sukarno to himself on 11 March 1966. In his view, Suharto was most likely acting on the advice of two other generals in the group – Basuki Rachmat and Amir Machmud who, along with Mohammad Yusuf, delivered the letter to Sukarno.

On 10 March 1966, Idris claims he gave the order for his troops to surround the palace where Sukarno and his cabinet were to meet the following day. Significantly, he recalls another general in the Suharto group, Maraden Panggabean, asking him to withdraw the troops. Umar Wirahadikusmah, Suharto's Kostrad deputy, went further Idris says, threatening to go to Sukarno and report Idris' insubordination. Idris assured both men the troops were there on Suharto's orders to arrest Sukarno's foreign minister, Subandrio. Subandrio was the military's chief target because he was suspected of helping to mastermind the September 1965 coup attempt. 'I offered to take responsibility', says Idris. 'The troops were meant only to capture Subandrio. It was Suharto's order. They were not sent to force Sukarno's hand'.[37] Idris insists that the 11 March letter authorizing the transfer of power to Suharto was never part of the military's plan, adding somewhat wistfully: 'If I had taken all my troops away as ordered, maybe history would have been different'.

Suharto himself, aware of the ease with which his actions could be considered precipitate, argues strongly in his autobiography that the 11 March letter should be regarded as an order to him from Sukarno to take over. Rather than amounting to a *coup d'état*, the letter was the 'beginning of the New Order's struggle'. Here the ease with which Javanese project appearances as reality is taken to the limit, but this is clearly what he expects people to believe. Suharto provides meticulous detail about the birth of the 11 March Order – what has since been known by acronym as *Supersemar* – demonstrating how Sukarno, as president, authorised the letter. In fact, it was an instruction from the president:

I never used Supersemar as an order to seize power. Neither was

Supersemar a tool for achieving a 'coup'. Supersemar was therefore only the beginning of the struggle for the New Order.[38]

In some respects it is fruitless to debate these issues here. Suharto's death, and the inevitable exorcism of his rule to follow, will generate a thousand versions in a flowering of introspection that could well reverse the bias – against Suharto. Of immediate interest, however, is the fact that this early period of Suharto's rise to power was marked first by his ability to marry compromise to personal advancement, and an extraordinary gift for subterfuge. The illusion of having greatness thrust upon him rather than seeking position and power for himself has been central to Suharto's own explanation of his rise to power. Suharto projects himself as remaining above the fray as various political forces swirled around him:

> I was pushed in an atmosphere of political conflict to step forward. Some politicians were impatient about a change of leadership to the point of proposing that I take over power just like that. I responded to this proposal at once; 'If that's the way things are, I'd better step down. Such a method is not good. Seizing power by military force will not bring about lasting stability. I am not going to bequeath a history indicating that there was once a seizure of power by military might'.[39]

Politics in Indonesia often seems to be burdened by passivity and acquiescence. There is a woeful lack of decisiveness or commitment on the part of political actors, who more typically wait to see which way things are moving before they jump. Reminiscent of the 'floaters', described by Ryszard Kapuscinski's Ethiopian informants from the court of Emperor Haile Selaisse in its final years: 'they don't think at all, but hope that like corks in the water they will float on the waves of circumstance, that in the end they will somehow settle down and they will arrive successfully in a hospitable port'.[40] The extent to which this passivity – whatever its roots are – has worked in Suharto's favour is an important component of his rule, and a generic feature of relations between the ruler and the ruled in Indonesia.

There are grounds to suspect that Suharto's position immediately after the 30 September *putsch* was extremely tenuous. 'In the period 1965–7 Suharto's was a frail shell of power. On the outside he appeared in control, but inside there was an empty void. Sukarno could have struck at any time'. The late Slamet Bratanata's reflection on the period is, like many of his contemporaries, part of a new attempt at reassessing the birth of the New Order – a genesis now heavily caked in official accounts and plain myth.

Suharto's reluctance to prosecute Sukarno after he had successfully rendered him powerless, demonstrates his ability to put political considerations before matters of principle. Equally, Sukarno's rapidly declining health and eventual death under virtual house arrest in 1970, suggests that depriving him of power was a more effective sentence than any concocted in a courtroom.

Suharto's actions also reflect the tenuous nature of his power at that time. There were grounds to suspect that some of the army would remain loyal to Sukarno because he was the mandated president. Suharto's show of strength relied on a group of radical students backed by units of the special forces under the command of Colonel Sarwo Edhie Wibowo. Along with other younger officers unhappy with the way things were going under Sukarno; Sarwo Edhie, Kemal Idris, Dharsono and others – whatever they have said subsequent to their defection – probably pushed Suharto into seizing power. These were the political realities of the time.

But there were others in the army, like Nasution, who preferred to uphold the law which they doubtless saw themselves as there to protect. 'Our principle is to uphold truth and justice', Nasution told the Consultative People's Assembly in 1966, 'in the judicial field our aim is to settle the responsibility of the person of the president for the crimes committed by him, in agreement with the spirit and provisions of the 1945 Constitution'.[41] In contrast, Suharto had argued before the same forum three days earlier that consideration of Sukarno's involvement in the coup attempt should not be based solely on legal principles, but should reflect the aspirations of all the people and avoid creating more social conflict.

The bending of principles in favour of *realpolitik* explains to a great extent why Suharto has been such a successful politician. It also sowed the seeds of his estrangement from many of his more idealistic contemporaries in the armed forces. Some have since accused him of violating the 1945 Constitution in his own interests.

Others are, however, ready to admit that when it came to confronting the complex social and economic issues of the past twenty years, Suharto's unschooled but pragmatic, flexible approach may ultimately have been to the country's advantage. Shortly before he died in 1989, former Armed Forces Chief of Staff General T.B. Simatupang mused that men thrown up by the independence struggle like himself could well have found themselves in the presidency – and to some extent possessed a more legitimate claim to it. However, he wondered whether the 'sense of moral right and wrong instilled in those officers with a Dutch-education' might not have hindered them, allowing hesitance and reflection to get in the way of the pursuit of power.

24

It is difficult to place Suharto in any commonly defined category of national leader. Because he assumed the presidency as a general, those least acquainted with Indonesia have painted his government as military and dubbed Suharto a dictator. This is too simplistic. The New Order government, as it has been constituted for the past decade, is made up of a mixture of retired military officers and western-educated technocrats. Only four ministers in the (1988–93) cabinet, including the armed forces commander, who holds cabinet rank, were military officers on the active list. Two of them never saw any active military duty, and were regarded with mistrust by the officer corps. In the new cabinet formed in March 1993, the number of military offices declined still further. The armed forces are still perceived as the most powerful political element in the country, but closer examination reveals the fact that the military's capacity for action independent of the executive has been progressively curtailed in the course of Suharto's presidency.

To say that Suharto is a dictator is again simplistic. Suharto has always defined himself as the servant of a state, which has never failed to endorse him with a mandate four times since 1968. He has argued that the 11 March 1966 order transferring power to him from Sukarno was not a *coup d'état*. Instead, after convening a special session of the the Consultative Assembly in 1966, Suharto spent almost two years working conspicuously through constitutional means to have himself appointed president. Apart from the fragile and tentative nature of his power in the months after October 1965, Suharto and those promoting him were also conscious of setting a dangerous precedent for the future by removing Sukarno by force.

Under the 1945 Constitution, which Sukarno reinstated in 1959, the MPR meets to elect the president once every five years – unless extraordinary circumstances persuade two-thirds of the lower house of representatives to call a special session. Under the New Order, the president has always been elected by arriving at a unanimous agreement on a single candidate. In practice, a consensus on who should be unanimously proclaimed sole candidate, and therefore the successful candidate, is arrived at well before the MPR meets through a series of declarations of support by major social and political organizations. These are usually engineered by Suharto's close supporters in advance.

Suharto has elaborated on this electoral college of sorts. Voters do not actually elect their president, but only half of those who constitute the MPR membership. The rest are composed of ministers, senior government and regional officials, prominent figures and military appointees. In most cases, the president approves their appointments to these positions. Should this fail to convince members of where their loyalties lie, all MPR members are carefully screened beforehand. The fact that such a large proportion of the body is composed of government officials tells us enough about the body's scope for action independent of the executive wishes. Even election of the vice-president is bound to the stipulation that the proposed candidate must be someone 'who can work with the president'. This effectively ensures the military can never install a potential challenger to Suharto. The system is virtually tamper-proof.

Just as the problem of deposing Sukarno delayed Suharto's proclamation as president, the Sukarno factor also dictated when Suharto felt secure enough to call his first election. It took Suharto three years after he was proclaimed president on 27 March 1968 before he held an election. Was he afraid people would still vote for Sukarno, as the former president boasted in late March 1966? Perhaps Sukarno's faith that if the 'people could only speak they would support him' was not entirely misplaced.[42]

Also questionable is Suharto's commitment to the liberal democratic views of his elders who, after wrestling independence from the Dutch, established a constitutional democracy in the newly independent republic. Devoting a chapter to the 1971 elections in his autobiography, Suharto explains in somewhat tortuous terms the balance that must be struck between the ideals of democracy and the need to preserve stability. Elections, he says, are necessary to 'create political stability'.[43] The implication is that elections serve less as an expression of the people's will and more as a prop to the legitimacy of the leadership. Significantly, perhaps, Suharto condenses the actual results of the 1971 election into a single paragraph.

In Javanese politics, appearances are everything. For Suharto, the mere fact that elections are held, and more importantly run smoothly with no significant show of dissent, is enough to prove the ideals of democracy are being served. Suharto never fully restored the country's parliamentary system to the position it enjoyed before 1957, yet Indonesia has held elections every five years since Suharto came to power. The substance, if not the fairness, of those elections is questionable by any democratic standards. All the same, democracy, in the strictly defined sense in which the term is employed in Indonesia, has been respected. Suharto cannot be easily accused of ruling by dictatorial fiat.

Similarly, as he approached the end of his fifth term in office, Suharto demonstrated the political sleight of hand required to deflect accusations that he is engineering a further term of office. Appearing to favour retirement, he calmly accepted declarations from political groups demanding that he serve another term. On the surface he is humbled by these pleas, playing the reluctant bride, yet always stressing his devotion to duty. As one editorial writer put it, the panegyric intentional or otherwise:

> If the people call him, or ask him to remain leader of the nation, he never refuses. He maintains that the bigger interest of the state must come before his own personal interests.[44]

If Suharto successfully camouflaged his rise to power and ability to stay in power with the trappings of constitutional democracy, he has been equally successful at hiding his charisma as a leader. The late Adam Malik, who served as Suharto's Foreign Minister and later Vice-President, boldly wrote in his 1980 autobiography that he considered Sukarno as charismatic: 'He towered over his colleagues and the people as no man can in the immediate future.'[45] Malik considered that while Sukarno led the country by force of his personality, 'his successors are doing their best to impose their will through a network of rigid hierarchy and stifling bureaucracy'. The main difference between Suharto and Sukarno, suggests a leading contemporary Indonesian political scientist, is that 'Suharto has established a system... with the army as the fulcrum of power'.[46]

Sukarno was a man of grandiose visions with a gift for making them seem tangible using the power of his oratory. Suharto has made pragmatism his hallmark, and, in contrast to the visionary rhetoric of his predecessor, has filled his speeches with simple goals and practical lessons. Suharto is a rather dull speaker. With very few exceptions he sticks closely to the text of his speeches, seldom looks up from the page and, because of long-sightedness, wears spectacles at the podium. He presents a fatherly image. His oratory is not meant to excite the people – the results are.

Suharto is known for his cold, steel-like glare, and a deep-voiced capacity for tongue-lashing those who have crossed him. For the most part, though, his style is passive. There are many stories of ministers who have mistaken Suharto's effusive nods and smiles for approval, only to discover to their cost that this was far from the case. The smiles mask his emotions, for Suharto is not a man to betray what he thinks, a skill he has fashioned into a considerable political asset. Distance and passivity are regarded as traditional qualities of Javanese kings.

In his autobiography, Suharto relates an alleged conversation he had with Sukarno in 1966. With students demonstrating in the streets calling for his downfall, Sukarno asks Suharto: 'Is it true you want to replace me?' Respectfully, Suharto denies this is the case:

> Bapak President, I am but the son of a poor farmer. But my father always told me to respect my elders. I am always reminded of this in

order that [and here he employs a Javanese proverb *mikul dhuwur mendhem jero* meaning:] outwardly I can respect their highest qualities, while keeping to my inner self their shortcomings.[47]

The passage reveals something of Suharto's belief, steeped in Javanese tradition, in the value of discretion and clever subterfuge. Suharto has employed both qualities to overcome intermittent but potentially dangerous threats to his position. Faced with strong resistance in military circles to his standing for another term after re-election in 1988, Suharto chose not to react openly. Instead, he worked quietly behind the scenes to undermine their case, and finally emerged with a potentially stronger mandate, having seized the higher ground on many of the issues his opponents hoped would bring him down.

Given this inscrutable passivity, there is much debate over Suharto's actual qualities and abilities as a leader. A perceptive younger minister in the cabinet described what he called Suharto's 'strategic sense':

He pays attention to what he considers the most important aspect of politics. He decides for himself what is important or not. When you push too hard, he baulks. It is a mistake to think he is weak.[48]

Conversely, General Nasution, who has known Suharto since the 1940s, argues that strategic thinking is beyond the man. 'He has an excellent grasp of tactics, he never thinks strategically.'[49] Backing up this opinion to some extent is Kemal Idris' view of the man:

Suharto is a man who makes decisions only in accordance with his own interests. In the past, people like myself would tell him, no, look at it from all the angles and you will see that you are wrong. Then at the last moment he would change his mind and follow what other people had suggested.[50]

Both comments, from men who knew Suharto well – even if they have lost admiration for him – point to Suharto's skill at preserving his own interests.

Suharto has always demonstrated a dogged perseverance,in attaining his goals. Those who have worked with him speak of his diligence in learning facts and figures which, coupled with a reputedly photographic memory, has enabled him always to appear on top of the material in any given situation. Policy-making is clearly not all his own work, but in the system he has fashioned, ministers can never appear to have been the source of inspiration for an idea. Advice must be offered to Suharto in such a way as to confer the wisdom of a decision on him alone.

After twenty-five years in the job, Suharto has brought a dull but relentlessly dutiful image to the job of president. He is constantly pictured wearing a simple safari suit, a fashion closely followed by his ministers. By his own account, he rises between 4.30 and 5.00 a. m. 'as is normal for either a farmer or soldier'. He prays, reads the Koran and drinks coffee. By 8.30 he is in his office, the Bina Graha building, a thoroughly untasteful example of 1970s bureaucratic baroque next to the old state palace, whose stately halls he has shunned for all except formal state occasions. (This useful display of humility probably has more to do with the fact that Suharto has never used any of the residences or offices built or inhabited by his predecessor, Sukarno.) At 2.30 in the afternoon, Suharto claims he returns home – to pray again and rest.[51] For most of his tenure, he has lived in what, from the outside looks like a modest home in the central suburb of Menteng. Those who have been to the Jalan Cendana residence, however, say it stretches back in a seemingly endless configuration of buildings. The entire street, though not closed to public traffic, is heavily guarded. A diplomat who happened to live on the same street told of gifts of food and cigarettes from the Suharto houschold being placed at his doorstep during festive holidays.

The apparent simplicity of his existence, passive style and belief in homespun Javanese philosophy has not lent much colour to his rule. Charisma of sorts is definable in the indigenous context. Suharto's actions aspire to classical Javanese values of refinement and humility. The island of Java, the most important component of Indonesia in cultural and demographic terms, possesses a tradition of kingship which survives to the present day in two cities of the province of Central Java, Solo and Jogyakarta. Suharto grew up in the 1920s in the shadow of one of the last semi-divine monarchies in South-east Asia. The courts of the Sultans of Solo and Jogyakarta – divided remnants of the medieval kingdom of Martaram – wielded no effective political power under the Dutch, but the strictly hierarchical court society was – and still is – considered the crucible of Javanese cultural refinement; a vestige of a glorious past which the Dutch preserved in aspic, as it were, to enhance control over their subjects.

Suharto's perception of Indonesia is conceivably that of a kingdom modelled closely on the independent polities of pre-colonial Java. Critics say the style of his rule is feudal. While observing the 1945 Constitution and the notionally sovereign representative institutions enshrined within it, Suharto brooks no dissent from below. The loyalty and obedience he demands from his ministers and officials is absolute and uncompromising. One of his homespun proverbs states: 'Whoever forgets the favours of others is like an animal'. To be made a minister in the New Order must be considered a potentially lucrative favour. Paid a minimal basic salary, an Indonesian minister none the less has the potential to accumulate wealth through a plethora of allowances, donations and the power of patronage. The principle, if not the precise model, is almost identical to the parcelling and allotment of revenues and authority whereby the Sultans of Java controlled their feudal retainers.

Another estimate of Suharto's qualities as a leader can be made from an examination of the political edifice he has erected. Adam Malik could well have been referring to Suharto obliquely when he described the bureaucracy as the new apparatus of control. Suharto has formed a succession of governments over the years, drawing on a small circle of close military associates from the pre–1965 period, mingled with a few of the former student leaders of 1966, packed around a small core of western-trained technocrats. Together they have constructed a system of rule which, though constitutionally correct, allows the goal posts to be moved at will.

For much of the early, formative part of his rule, his old Central Java Command associate, Ali Murtopo, virtually ran a small state within the state, the aim of which was to promote and protect the New Order's aims using extra-judicial or illegal means if necessary. Murtopo's *Opsus* (special operations) group is credited with organizing finance, masterminding intelligence and building up key contacts with the oustide world in the early years of the New Order. Murtopo may also have saved Suharto from downfall in 1974, when a group of generals plotted to have him removed.[52]

Using his special powers, Murtopo was able to conceive of and then smash putative anti-government plots to help preserve the regime's security. Murtopo's scheming lay behind a rash of Islamic radicalism which swept Java under the improbable name of *Kommando Jihad* in the late 1970s. Some even speculate that the dramatic hijacking of a domestic airliner by Muslim radicals to Bangkok in 1981 was orchestrated by Murtopo to discredit Muslim political forces before the 1982 elections.

Murtopo and his Opsus team were the regime's fixers and troubleshooters; their methods beyond the law at times. Meanwhile, labouring hard to erect the New Order's legal and constitutional structure as a body of laws and decrees was another group of aides, led by the former army lawyer, Sudharmono. It was this group that fashioned a system based on the 1945 Constitution, but with significant elaborations governing the relationship between the MPR and the executive. The effect was to make the former beholden to the latter.

The fact that no one is credited by Suharto in his autobiography for any of the regime's achievements, tells us something else about Suharto. Another of his close advisers, the mystic Sœdjono Hœmardani, was fond of a Javanese proverb which states: 'there is no need for friends or enemies, just the truth'.[53] Suharto himself is quoted as telling his children: 'No friend is worth [more than] high and useful knowledge'.[54] By this reckoning, Suharto has felt no urge to recognize those around him since his actions – the truth – spoke for themselves.

This highlights one essential difference between Indonesia's two presidents. Sukarno, for all his bombast, was a man who took refuge in foreign learning. He himself had no benefit of an overseas education, but he was surrounded by those who had. He believed in the power of ideas. In sharp contrast, a prominent general of the 1945 generation described Suharto as 'an unsophisticated regional commander with little time for Western ideas and even less for those around him who espoused them'.[55] Suharto's reference points – the historical and cultural experiences that have coloured his views – are relatively easy to define. Culturally, his Central Java origins have imbued in him the region's pre-eminence in the country's past and recent history. He participated in the struggle against the Dutch, upon which the new nation built a strong sense of nationalism. Then he bore the brunt of the excesses and neglect of the Sukarno era, culminating in the September 1965 coup attempt which posed a threat to national unity.

These themes have combined in specific ways to mould Suharto's thinking. Unlike Sukarno, therefore, who was influenced by a variety of half-learned European ideas and set out to defeat imperialism in all forms, Suharto projects himself primarily as a man of his people and a product of its culture and recent history. In many ways these represent more potent qualities. They have certainly helped Suharto serve the nation well in terms of fostering a stable environment for the growth of the economy and dissemination of social welfare. But they also imply a degree of innate conservatism, a resistance to social and political change. Suharto is fond of saying that change must be executed without disturbing the *status quo*. After so long with Suharto as the epitomy of that *status quo*, meaningful political change can perhaps only occur when he himself becomes the object of change.

2

ORDER AND DEVELOPMENT

Bad times make good policies.

(Mohammad Sadli)

In a rambling section of his autobiography 'As told to Cindy Adams', Indonesia's first President, Sukarno, claims to have 'mentally talked with Thomas Jefferson', with whom he felt 'friendly and close'. He also asserts he discussed George Washington's problems with him and – more remarkably 'relived Paul Revere's ride'. With a grounding such as this, Sukarno asks, how could he be unfriendly towards the United States?[1]

Metaphysically acquainted as Sukarno may have been with America's founding fathers, their descendants in Washington had little or no time for him. The Sukarno government of the mid-1960s presented all the proof one needed of the domino theory so fashionable in the corridors of power at the time. It was corrupt, bankrupt, anti-capitalist, maintained close relations with China, and – with over three million members – had the largest Communist Party in the developing world outside China.

So when in the early hours of 30 September 1965, members of the Indonesian armed forces intervened and lit the short fuse to the end of Sukarno's rule three years later, many governments in the non-communist developed world were privately relieved (once Suharto moved to restore order), in spite of the carnage that followed, to see Indonesia join the ranks of the non-communist developing world. 'Perhaps because it was Communists who were being killed,' wrote John Legge in his 1972 biography of Sukarno, 'the conscience of the outside world seemed comparatively undisturbed by what must rank, in any assessment, as one of the bloodiest massacres in modern history.'[2]

Nobody knew anything about the shy man with a wide smile who stepped into Sukarno's shoes. To many diplomats working in Jakarta at the time, Major-General Suharto came across as little more than a cheerful but reserved general who enjoyed fishing. Once in power, though, he set about restoring order and embarked on a realistic campaign to develop the economy. Sukarno left the country with a negative growth rate, 600 per cent inflation, no foreign reserves to speak of, and a national debt of over $US2 billion. It is scarcely surprising then that Suharto and his army colleagues could safely place economic above political development.

Order, fostering stability, generating growth and development; these have been the buzzwords of the Suharto years. Sukarno peppered his long emotional speeches with talk of maintaining the revolutionary spirit which helped achieve independence. He offered his people rhetoric instead of rice. Suharto and his men were pragmatists who quickly saw that solid political legitimacy could only be achieved by putting the country back on its feet.

Yet the New Order had to tread carefully, avoiding a total break with the past. The army was still dangerously divided between loyalties of the old and new order. By upholding the 1945 Constitution and the vague unitary philosophy of *Pancasila*, Suharto's men found a neat way of preserving the ideals created at independence. The New Order was presented as a no more than a 'correction' of what were considered to be deviations from the 1945 Constitution perpetrated by Sukarno's Old Order.

In fact, the leaders of the New Order came to power with no grand strategy for political renewal and reform. Those who saw the end of Sukarno's rule as an opportunity for radical political reform were frozen out from the beginning. The students and anti-communist urban intellectuals who provided the political energy fuelling Suharto's rise to power in 1966, found their breathless ideals for the restoration of democracy fairly hastily shoved aside. Very few of these people were rewarded with senior positions in the government until the 1980s – in part a reflection of military mistrust of civilians, partly also product of Javanese cultural resistance to conferring responsibility on those below the age of 40. Many of them subsequently became disillusioned, and by the late 1980s could be considered outsiders.

Though often overlooked today, the prelude to re-establishing order and the reconstruction of Indonesia's economy was a brief but bloody period of further turmoil. The New Order exploited the highly polarized state of society left by Sukarno to dispose of its opponents and provide an outlet for some cathartic bloodletting. Tens of thousands of artists, intellectuals and civil servants who had made the mistake of either joining the Communist Party or tagging along to benefit from its patronage, were arrested and classified by their degree of involvement with the PKI. Many thousands ended up on Buru island, a remote prison camp in the Moluccas. Though officially no longer a prison camp, Buru island serves to remind Indonesians of the violent debut Suharto and his men made.

In what must warrant as one of the bloodiest inaugurations of a new regime anywhere in the world, hundreds of thousands of rural Javanese were reportedly mown down by the army in the early months of 1966 on suspicion of being PKI cadres. In many instances old scores were settled on a communal basis. The weapons to do so were provided by the army. The scale of the killings and the unimaginable brutality with which they were carried out, is hard for even those who witnessed them to describe. Oddly, there is little material evidence in the form of film or photographs of these atrocities. Some may have been exaggerrated accounts given by zealous anti-Communists. Indeed, it says something about the instrinsic relationship between rulers and the ruled in Indonesia, that residual feelings about this period have not coloured popular perceptions of Suharto's rule.

Arguably, memories of the repression and carnage of 1966 have faded in the light of the New Order's successful strategy of national development. The programme of national development, or *pembangunan nasional*, became a slogan with a mesmerizing effect on Indonesians and outsiders alike. There was a reason for this. Within a decade of his coming to power, Indonesia stabilized, joined the exclusive ranks of oil-producing states and was using the revenue from oil to implement an extraordinary programme of development. It was a turnaround too remarkable by Third World standards to argue with. Indonesia, the nightmare of US foreign policy analysts in the 1960s, suddenly became burning proof that not all regimes born out of the barrel of a gun are bad.

The new regime's rapid implementation of macro-economic stabilization saved the country from economic disaster. New policies aimed at reviving the economy laid the basis for more rapid industrial growth. The foreign trade regime was liberalized, allowing better access to the raw materials and capital goods the industrial sector badly needed. There were early signs of the New Order's intention to foster the private sector. A new investment law pushed through in 1966 was hung with import and tax concessions making Indonesia more attractive to foreign investors. The combination of better conditions, under-utilized capacity and high domestic demand ignited industrial growth early on in the New Order's stewardship of the economy.

Indonesia, not to mention Suharto, was also lucky. With the upward surge of oil prices in the 1970s, one of Indonesia's traditional commodities suddenly became almost literally a pot of gold. In 1972, Indonesian crude sold for less than $US3 a barrel. By 1980 a barrel of oil sold for over $US30.

In the period 1970–81, export revenues from oil increased at a rate of 45.5 per cent. Oil and gas accounted for 37 per cent of total export revenue in 1970; by 1981 this proportion had climbed to 82 per cent. During this period the country's growth rate (GDP) averaged 7–8 per cent per year.

The oil sector was dominated by the state, and it was principally oil revenues which paid for the rapid infrastructural development of the 1970s and early 1980s. Encouraged at last, overseas investment, particularly from Japan, poured in. In 1967 Japan had just two investment projects in Indonesia, at a value of $US6.7 million. Two years later this number had risen to seventeen projects, with a total value of $US132.3 million.[3] Today Indonesia is the second largest recipient of Japanese investment in the world.

As foreign investment and lucrative oil revenues flowed in, much neglected services and infrastructure were installed. Widespread poverty, estimated to have afflicted 60 per cent of the population in 1967, began to recede. Per capita income began to rise above the $US260 it was in 1970 and by 1980 was over $US500. The infrastructure of basic health and education facilities began to fan out from the centre, laying the basis for one of the highest primary school enrolment rates in the developing world (93 per cent in 1987). Perhaps the most crucial of these improvements was the beginning of an intensive food-production programme, one that set Indonesia on a course to basic food self-sufficiency by the early 1980s.

Indonesia under Suharto has been held up as something of a model of Third World development. A net show of growth, comparatively little social unrest, and the absence of tanks in the streets is enough to qualify for laurels in many regions of the world. In Indonesia's case, state-managed economic development since the 1970s has, against considerable odds, steadily improved the welfare of the majority of Indonesian people. Specifically, Indonesia has been singled out for deploying ground-breaking programmes of population control and food self-sufficiency.

Production of rice, the staple food, has grown at a rate unparalleled in Asia over the past twenty years. Between 1960 and 1980 per capita production of rice and other food crops increased from 95 kg to 142 kg per capita. Rice production has increased 50 per cent since 1970, and in 1989–90 increased by over 3 per cent to over 30 million tonnes, despite a run of prolonged dry seasons. Suharto took particular pride in declaring self-sufficiency in rice in the mid-1980s. For many years the country was the world's largest rice importer. But the drive towards self-sufficiency was heavily supported by government subsidies on fertilizers and pesticides, which the government is under pressure to curtail as part of a broader international effort to regularize international trade under the Gatt. The diminishing size of land holdings and higher input costs may persuade many farmers in future to revert to higher-yielding cash crops. The government's reluctance to sanction open importation of rice has led to logistical problems when, as in the past few years, a run of long dry seasons cuts domestic output. In 1991, a prolonged drought in Java forced the government publicly to sanction rice imports.

Nevertheless, the rice intensification programme is an achievement the government is proud of. A recent World Bank comparative study on the effects of the oil boom on the economies of Indonesia, Nigeria, Venezuela, Ecuador, Algeria and Trinidad showed that Indonesia was the only oil-rich country in which agricultural output expanded.[4] Tradition, perhaps more than the wisdom of those in power, dictated prudence in the face of all the temptations to squander petrodollars. Indonesian, specifically Javanese society, has traditionally responded effectively to rapid demographic change by finding ways to increase food production, a phenomenon the American anthropologist Clifford Geertz called 'agricultural involution'.

Demographically speaking, Indonesia is a nightmare. The 1990 census determined Indonesia's total population to be 179.3 million people, making it the fourth most populous country in the world. Growth in the density of population per square kilometre is exceeded only by China and India. By the year 2000, Indonesia's population will have exceeded 200 million, and may still be growing at over 1 per cent per year. Though the projections seem alarming enough, demographers argue that the rate of population growth has already been curbed by family planning and birth control programmes implemented since the 1970s.

Helped by an extensive village-level voluntary organization, a staggering 18.5 million women have accepted government sponsored birth control, though at least 24 million will have to do so in order to hold down the current population growth rate by 1995. Projections calculated by the University of Indonesia show that the average number of children borne by each female is declining, and will be below three by the turn of the century. Other factors such as improvements in the child mortality rate, have of course worked against reducing growth in the population.

Alarming projections of demographic growth, even with the progress made so far in family planning, mean that the government can never relax its attention on this area. Some parts of Central Java will boast urban-like densities of up to 1,000 per square kilometre in the next decade. The pressure on resources in Java, where 60 per cent of the total population is concentrated, is now considered a serious threat to the environment. The island's rich volcanic soils have up till now contained the Malthusian population explosion triggered in the colonial period. Today, however, serious damage to watershed forests and heavily polluted water supplies, pose a serious threat to the island's ability to support a population over 100 million.

By way of illustration, the twelve million or so residents of greater Jakarta are dependent on a single river, the Ciliwung, which flows off the mountains of West Java, for their water. The fact that upwards of two million people have already used this water before it reaches the city gives some idea of the scale of the problem. The lack of adequate supplies of fresh water is a considerable drain on household expenditure in low-income areas. Clean water must be bought for a price, which eats into already pitifully low incomes.

Despite the demographic pressure on resources, qualitative improvements to the well-being of ordinary Indonesians have been the hallmark of Suharto's rule, and most observers agree that the benefits brought to the country by the New Order almost overshadow the social and political side-effects. All the same, increasing the standard of living of most Indonesians has also meant exposing them to a larger and more embracing state apparatus. For as well as fuelling remarkable national growth, the oil bonanza allowed the state to grow at an alarming rate. In the period 1974–83, the size of the bureaucracy mushroomed at double the rate of population growth – from 1.67 million to 2.63 million civil servants. Oil revenues were used to finance the growth of state enterprises, which together with the bureaucracy made the state the biggest single employer. By 1983 state enterprises accounted for 25 per cent of GDP, contributing almost 50 per cent of the total corporate taxes paid to the government alone.

The larger the state became, the more prone it was to mismanagement and corruption. Some of these side-effects began to make themselves felt in the mid-1970s. The near disastrous financial scandal of 1974, involving the state oil company Pertamina's inability to pay an estimated $US10 billion in debts, exposed enormous levels of corruption, but made little dent on the regime's credibility in the eyes of hungry foreign investors and their governments. Suharto grudgingly fired his Pertamina chief, Ibnu Sutowo, whose embezzlement and greed landed the company in such desperate straits, but he only did so under pressure. Sutowo, for his sins, was later made chairman of the Indonesian Red Cross. Today he owns a string of companies including the Jakarta Hilton and, through the president's family, still brings influence to bear on his former patron.

The latter half of the 1970s was marked by protests aimed at the regime's increasingly corrupt image. In 1974 and 1978, student demonstrations targeted the corruption of Suharto's business cronies, the extensive business interests of his wife, and relentless Japanese investment. In response, Suharto was forced to adjust investment laws to provide for more native ownership and tone down the excessive displays of wealth his rich friends had become accustomed to. Henceforth all new foreign investments were to be joint ventures, involving the transfer of equity to Indonesian partners over a specified period. Running up against a potentially dangerous threat to his rule, Suharto showed he was able to adapt fast. A more remarkable feat of escape artistry was required after the price of oil on world markets took a nosedive in the early 1980s.

Recession in the oil market set in during the 1982–3 financial year. Overproduction by Opec members and a glut on the European market finally pulled the rug from underneath the mighty petrodollar. The impact on Indonesia neatly reversed the strong upward trends established during the oil boom. In the period 1982–86, export revenues declined from $US14.7 billion to a little under $US7 billion, decreasing by 16.4 per cent per year, as oil prices plummeted from $US30 per barrel to under $US10. The national growth rate was cut by half, and reached as low as 2 per cent in 1985. The crisis cut deeply into the country's foreign reserves, which slipped from $US4.15 billion in December 1982 to $US3.07 billion by March the following year. By 1987, per capita income had fallen below the $US500 level it had reached in the early 1980s.

The body blow to the economy dealt by the oil crisis forced the government to realize two things. First, oil was a fortuitous but unreliable source of growth and that diversification of the export base was essential. Second, that a much more efficient basis of economic growth was required; less reliant on the state and more on market forces. 'We knew that economic growth required export growth to pay for needed imports and to service the debt,' reflected senior economic minister Radius Prawiro:

> Without foreign exchange from oil, it would become necessary to expand dramatically the range of non-oil export products which would be competitive internationally. To do this would require an efficient, low cost and productive economy – this meant creating the conditions for a competitive market.[5]

Having grapsed these realities, the government set about adjusting to and making good the situation with admirable precision and, remarkably, with a minimum of disturbance to society. While the general assumption in other parts of the world is that forced economic change rains hardship on the less advantaged in society, in the case of Indonesia figures show that forced austerity did not drastically cut into public spending, and as a result

38

per capita income increased by some 15 per cent during this adjustment period.[6]

Pragmatic, flexible policies and a well-directed programme of fiscal austerity account for some of the success in the face of adversity. The government's initial reaction was to cut energy and food subsidies at the risk of provoking social unrest. On the fiscal front, hard though it was, the government was able to administer the bitter medicine of two currency devaluations and stave off intervention from the International Monetary Fund. Cushioning the economy against the effects of this heavy dose of fiscal austerity has been the huge amount of foreign aid, which reached annual totals in excess of $US4 billion by 1989. Channelling this aid into the development budget – which in some years has consisted almost entirely of foreign aid – meant that public spending on development could be maintained throughout the oil recession. In fact, it increased by 6 per cent per year.

Suharto's western-trained economic technocrats knew that austerity and retrenchment were only stopgap measures. The key to longer-term survival was to broaden the revenue-generating base of the economy by improving in particular the performance of non-oil exports. To do this, the private sector had to be granted more freedom. But this required the political will to reform the country's economy. In the first place, the ideological underpinning of the New Order had somehow to be sidestepped. This meant drifting away from the organization of production under state control on what was supposed to be a strictly equitable basis, towards a more autonomous private sector driven by market forces. Second, the bevy of import-substitution monopolies, which had accumulated under Suharto's indirect or direct patronage, was a burden for the domestic manufacturing sector and a heavy bias against exports.

In the initial period after the collapse of the oil boom, protectionist sentiments intensified. Non-tariff barriers multiplied. Monopolies on the import of essential raw materials for light manufacturing, such as tin-plate and plastics, were distributed to 'approved distributors' in the shape of cronies and members of Suharto's own family. The justification of these concessionary import monopolies was that they ensured a fair price for local producers. In fact they mostly served the private interests of public officials and, while they contributed handsomely to extra-budgetary coffers, they acted as a considerable brake on domestic investment by the private sector.

Since the late 1960s, the state has facilitated the emergence of a powerful domestic corporate sector using policies of subsidy and protection. Access to the market has in most cases been determined by state officials, and almost always at a price. But in the harsh light of economic reality, and with the main prop to his legitimacy provided by development threatened by the loss of oil revenues, Suharto was persuaded to give his approval to a programme of economic 'deregulation', which began in earnest after 1985.

It is a significant, but not always recognized, fact that liberalization of Indonesia's over-regulated economy was forced on the regime by the decline in oil prices which set in during the mid-1980s. 'Bad times make good policies' was a favoured adage. Leading technocrats later saw the oil shock as a blessing in disguise. Inefficiencies wrought by blatantly protectionist import policies could be ignored while the economy floated on a large lake of oil revenues. Only when the petrodollars stopped flowing, could the technocrats obtain leverage over the vested interests.

The technocrats opened their campaign with tentative measures to liberalize the trade and import regime. They employed a team of foreign economists, mostly from Harvard or the University of California at Berkeley, to formulate policy behind the scenes. The so-called 'Harvard Group' was low key, since nobody wished to advertise the role of foreigners and provoke nationalist sentiment. In reality, these foreign economists, in conjunction with a dedicated team at the finance and trade ministries, worked intensively to restructure the economy.

Initially, complex licensing procedures were cut down to one or two steps. Investment incentives, such as tax concessions, bonded trade zones, and access to domestic distribution for foreign concerns were gradually introduced. Many of these reforms looked good enough on paper, but implementation lagged. There was concentration on reform of the financial sector, and less emphasis on the real sector, where monopolies controlled by business interests closest to Suharto remained untouched.

Nevertheless, the chief aim of stimulating non-oil exports was achieved. The share of non-oil exports as a percentage of total exports increased from 31 per cent to 50 per cent in the period 1978–87. By 1990, there was no longer talk about Indonesia's reliance on hydrocarbon exports. Instead, garments and shoes, the symbols of incipient Newly Industrialized Country (NIC) status in Asia, were stalking western markets with some success. GDP growth, which had fallen as low as 2 per cent in 1985, bounced back as high as 6 per cent in 1988–9, and exceeded 7 per cent in 1989–90. On this basis, 5 per cent growth targets set by planners for the five year period beginning in 1988–9, were confidently expected to be met, if not surpassed. In short, the Indonesian economy by the late 1980s looked more like that of a neo-'NIC' than at any time before. Despite recession brought on by a fall in oil prices, Indonesia had managed a thorough restructuring of the economy and avoided crippling fiscal side-effects. In 1970 manufacturing accounted for just 8 per cent of GDP against agriculture's 45 per cent contribution. By 1990 the balance was more even, with manufacturing accounting for 19 per cent, against the agricultural sector's 20 per cent share.

There was a measure of luck, but in the main it was the skilful management of the economy that enabled macro-economic restructuring to proceed in the face of adversity. Resisting the temptation to control persistent capital flight the government stuck firmly to a free foreign-exchange regime. While this applied the brake on domestic savings capacity, it meant overseas investors turned a blind eye to high interest rates and the heavy-handed role of the state. Foreign investors began to flock in even greater numbers to Indonesia after a package of reforms in October 1988 opened up key areas of the financial system for growth which had long been held back by bureaucratic red tape.

Sweeping liberalization of banking regulations contained in the October 1988 reform package, cleared the way for a radical restructuring of the banking sector. The banking market was previously dominated by state banks, which were prone to inefficiency. The new regulations gave private national and foreign banks considerably more space to operate, thus further boosting business confidence and the scope for domestic investment. The reforms breathed new life into the retail banking sector and expansion was rapid. Just two years after the October 1988 reforms, over forty new private banks had been granted licences. Savings on deposit doubled from a little under $US10 billion in 1987, to over $US30 billion by the end of 1989.[7]

Large Chinese business groups fell over themselves to obtain banking licences, and launch gimmicky savings schemes. But many of them were expanding so rapidly that foreign banks extending them generous credit lines began to worry about the soundness of their asset base. In September 1990, these concerns were lent some substance when the country's second largest private bank, Bank Duta, sustained a massive loss on a foreign-exchange position held on behalf of a major client with the National Bank of Kuwait. Bank Duta was not the only bank risking large sums of its own capital on the forex market, but with 73 per cent of the bank's shares owned by three of President Suharto's charitable foundations, it was effectively the President's bank, and therefore a favoured vehicle for the high-risk financial chicanery of his children.[8]

With credit freely available through the banks and equity easily multiplied by issuing shares in the revived bourse, private-sector growth was extraordinary. In 1988, Jakarta's tiny stock market took off. Listing just twenty-four companies in 1988, by July 1990 ninety-six companies were listed on the board. The share price index more than doubled in the first three weeks of December 1988, and by late 1989 the value of daily trading had increased to $US2.3 million a day from the average $US100,000 a day done on a good day a few months earlier.

A string of highly oversubscribed share issues by large companies raised over $US1 billion in the course of 1989, spurring on further capitalization. The value of listed shares was a puny $US250 million in 1988. By July 1990 it was put at $US5 billion. Finance ministry officials, though surprised and often alarmed by the market's growth, none the less pushed for institutional savings such as pension funds to invest in stock to mobilize considerable funds held in static-time deposits. Finance Minister Johannes Sumarlin faced criticism from some of his colleagues, principally former Economic Minister Ali Wardhana, for risking the nation's credit rating with the bourse. In late 1989, he pushed through a regulation allowing foreigners to buy up to 49 per cent of a domestic company's stock in the face of staunch nationalist opposition. His ultimate goal:

> to use this vehicle to really mobilize resources, primarily long term resources badly needed by our industry. In the past, our manufacturing sector was dependent on bank funds, which are mostly short term in nature.[9]

Export-driven growth elsewhere in the region seemed to be slowing down by the close of the 1980s, and Indonesia loomed as Asia's newest growth miracle by comparison. The growth rate in 1989–90, at 6.5 per cent, equalled that of South Korea.[10] Foreign investment – much of it from South Korea, Taiwan and Japan – steadily increased, exceeding $US4.7 billion in 1989. In 1990 total foreign investment since 1967 was valued at over $US33 billion, with Japan accounting for 8.2 per cent of the total value.[11] Indonesian wage rates, practically the lowest in the region, were partly responsible for all this interest. In 1991, even Vietnam could not undercut Indonesia's $US42 weekly basic wage. Political uncertainty in the Philippines and rising costs and saturation in Thailand was persuading Koreans and Japanese that Indonesia was at last living up to its potential.

To some extent this was the case. At long last, the suffocating role of the state was recognized and offset by moves to devolve more decision-making to the market. The private sector was given air to breathe. Profits habitually siphoned offshore by the Chinese business groups were being cautiously ploughed back – though in part attracted by high interest rates (averaging over 18 per cent in 1989–90). The rupiah was depreciating at a steady 5 per cent per year by the early 1990s, and the government's promise not to devalue stood firm. For the first time there was an improvement in tax compliance, long one of the lowest in the region. As the investment flowed in, the government recognized that a major weakness was the country's poorly developed infrastructure.

The vested interests, represented in the bureaucracy and large conglomerates with close links to the president, have not always been happy with the pace of reform, which challenged their monopolistic ways. The technocrats had to move slowly and stealthily, sometimes barely touching core interests. There was a 'blue-smoke and mirrors' approach to reforming some of the most protected areas of trade. When lucrative areas were affected, crony businesses were sent rushing upstream to build the only capacity for raw materials now freed from import monopolies.

For example, in November 1988, the government, to many people's surprise, at last attacked the controversial steel and plastics import monopoly. To counter this move on their cosy financial fiefdom, Suharto's two sons active in business, Bambang Trihatmodjo and Hutomo Mandala Putra ('Tommy'), moved smartly from monopolizing import licences for plastics to licensing petrochemical complexes making the same material in Indonesia to be built by Japanese and German companies.

In July 1990, British Petroleum, Mitsui and Sumitomo formed a joint venture with Suharto's eldest son, Sigit Harjojudanto, to build a ployethylene plant in West Java valued at $US800 million.[12] Sigit presided over a monopoly importing raw materials for the plastics industry that the new plant planned to serve. Like other members of the Suharto family, Sigit translated the loss of his import monopoly into essentially a 'tollgate' operation. This involved lending their name to projects to be built with little or no equity participation by themselves. Sigit has a 9 per cent stake in the polyethylene project. The cost of lending their considerable sway to the investments was usually the sole right to market domestic output.

Gradually, the private sector, even those at the receiving end of government favours, grew happy with the reforms. One view is that bargaining with technocrats anxious to erode artificial barriers to growth set up by monopolies, had in fact left them in a prime position from which to benefit from the new liberal economic environment. A senior executive of one prominent Chinese conglomerate revealed that powerful business interests were always consulted by the relevant economic ministries before the reforms were made public.[13] It was, perhaps, the only way to secure their compliance in a system where the president's business cronies wielded as much power as his ministers. Even without prior knowledge of what was coming, awash with capital earned from their lucrative monopolies, well-connected conglomerates were often in the best position to exploit the economic reforms. Overall, the concentration of reforms in the financial sector preserved many monopolies in the real sector and simply opened up new areas of expansion for the larger business groups.

One after the other, Mochtar Riady's Lippo Group, Eka Tjipta Widjaya's Sinar Mas Group, and the better respected Soeryadjaya family's Astra group all launched ambitious expansion into new fields. All these conglomerates began life in trade associated with military or government-granted concessions. Obtaining choice opportunities from the government's reform programme was merely patronage in another guise. Lippo concentrated on retail banking freed up by the October 1988 reforms. Sinar Mas moved off its commanding position over edible oils to try to become the region's biggest pulp and paper producer. Astra accelerated diversification into agribusiness, banking and real estate. Most of these major groups had already begun investing overseas in the region and beyond. The tooling of this expansion, principally via the capital market, was newfangled, but their domination of the domestic market and ability to cut corners continued to be assured by carefully nurtured political links.

Another reason the vested interests could go along with deregulation was their ability to persuade the reformers to hive off some areas over which they presided into newly protected, re-regulated bastions. As Indonesian economist Hadi Soesastro points out:

> The strong drive for non-oil exports seemed to have induced in some government quarters a tendency towards new regulation or re-regulation either by restricting or totally banning the export of a range of products, primarily unprocessed or semi-processed goods.[14]

Thus key New Order supporters and financiers, many of whom had been granted forestry concessions in return for political favours, were more or less untouched by the reforms. Export bans on logs, sawn wood and unfinished rattan could easily be dressed up as beneficial to the nation's downstream wood and rattan industries. In reality the export bans were of questionable economic – not to mention environmental – soundness. They ultimately benefited the strong export associations set up to channel exports on their behalf. Rattan and timber bans, reinforced after 1988, forced many secondary producers in outlying areas of Kalimantan to go out of business. The self-styled king of the rattan and timber industry, Suharto's old friend from Central Java Command days, Bob Hasan, headed the export associations which collected a levy on all exports and determined who could and could not be in the business.

Worrying for some was Suharto's apparent inability to recognize the obstacles close cronies and his own children posed to the reform programme. Well-connected firms, for example, could easily tap state banks for low-interest funds using Suharto's name, thereby reducing the availability of resources for credit programmes Suharto himself was sponsoring. Instead of holding up Bank Duta as an example of financial mismanagement, Suharto quietly had two of his close business cronies, Liem Sioe Long and Prayogo Pangestu, bail the bank out.

In 1991 state banks were persuaded to back Tommy Suharto's strategic clove stock fund, which bought up raw clove stocks at a little over Rp 3,000 per kilo and sold the crop to *kretek* cigarette manufacturers at almost four times the price. Observers saw the move as a glaring setback for the progressive liberalization of Indonesia's economy. Tommy (Hutomo Mandala Putra, Suharto's youngest son) told a senior editor in Jakarta that in the age of deregulation there was no need for rules.[15] By 1991, the government's forced backing for the clove fund had brought private cigarette firms, once considered among the most profitable private enterprises in the country, virtually to their knees. While Suharto continued publicly to endorse deregulation for the sake of foreign donors and investors, he was at the same time urging the private sector to support the monopolistic schemes of his children. Defending themselves, the children cited the country's development as their goal; harnessing the very core of the New Order's legitimacy – national development – to the private interests of the New Order's leader and in the process exposing him to political risks.

Partly because of the way in which the country has adapted to and even reaped fortune from adversity, it is often hard to examine New Order policies and the climate in which they were developed objectively. Indonesia's record flew in the face of the experience of Latin American countries where overarching debt, weak economies and dubious policies were fuelling social and political crisis. 'The success of Suharto's economic reforms has strengthened his popularity' trumpeted one foreign financial analyst's report in 1989. Who wants to nay say such a remarkable record of survival? But the reality is rather more complex.

Indonesia has demonstrated a knack for survival which masks many other shortcomings. Economic growth has relied heavily on revenues earned from the export of primary commodities, and the industrial and manufacturing base remains narrow and constrained by tariff and protectionist barriers to the most lucrative markets. It is no oversimplification to say that Indonesia has grown primarily on the back of its trade in raw materials with the outside world since the Dutch founded the Dutch East India Company (VOC) in the latter part of the seventeenth century. Commodity exports still account for the bulk of export revenues, and the

45

mercurial hydrocarbon still accounted for 39 per cent of those exports in 1990.

A major factor explaining why the economy has weathered various global economic crises to which it was particularly susceptible is shrewd management unencumbered by the baggage of accountability to anyone but a strong, pragmatic executive. Equally important, though, has been the uninterrupted flow of foreign aid. The outside world moved quickly to endorse Suharto's leadership by bankrolling it.

The mid-1960s saw Communism in Asia reach a high-water mark. America's entry into the Vietnam war in earnest after 1965 generated a plethora of what now seem half-baked theories pushing the notion of a Communist advance and the need for a pro-western 'shield' in the region. In 1967, a group of thirteen western donor nations, Japan, and multilateral lending agencies formed the 'Inter-Governmental Group on Indonesia' (IGGI) – principally at Washington's behest. After rescheduling the national debt, the group pledged a swath of new loans to help restore the country's shattered economy. The group has met every year since then, and in 1991 pledged a record $US4.75 billion in new grants and loans. For Indonesians, IGGI is a convenient way to mask the fact that western nations and Japan are pumping so much aid into the country. The very use of a body like IGGI, and the fact that the Netherlands, not the US or Japan, heads the group, is typical of Indonesia's skill at manipulating appearances.

Equally important in explaining the ease with which Indonesia has attracted massive influxes of aid, has been the country's avoidance of a major external debt crisis. This is all the more remarkable given the potential for disaster caused by the oil boom. High oil prices in the early 1970s encouraged the government to borrow huge sums on the commercial credit market. By Latin American standards the maturity structure of the burgeoning debt was more prudently managed, with less than 15 per cent of the total comprising short-term loans in 1981.

The Pertamina crisis taught the government an early lesson in debt management, and after 1975 state enterprises were denied access to commercial overseas loans. Nevertheless, in common with other oil-rich countries, Indonesia's tax base remained woefully narrow, the non-oil export base was underdeveloped and capital flight was endemic. Some economists believe cogent management of the exchange rate, involving timely currency devaluations in November 1978, March 1983 and September 1986, was the major reason Indonesia averted a debt crisis in the mid-1980s.[16]

Today Indonesia manages Asia's largest debt – estimated by the World Bank at $US58 billion in 1989 [including undisbursed loans] – with the blessing of major donors. By persuading donors to lend a portion of their aid in local currency, Indonesia has staved off the worst effects of currency fluctuations. Even so, by 1995 the government will be paying back more to the donors than it receives from them, but there is no sign that key donors like Japan are about to staunch the flow of aid. External factors also play a role. The IGGI aid consortium is regarded as one of the most successful of its genre, and few members are in a hurry to dismantle it.*

Sukarno may have read the Madison Papers and De Tocqueville, but the man who read mostly fishing magazines has earned the title 'father of development'. This simple contrast raises many questions. Sukarno was a leader of men, a brilliant orator and polemicist. His economic policies were disastrous. Suharto is a reserved, self-made man; barely educated, his only professional skill is soldiering. Yet, his policies have shown vision and borne fruit. Why?

A key reason was the trust he placed early on in a small group of western-trained economists, most of whom taught at the economics faculty of Jakarta's University of Indonesia. Led by Berkeley-trained Professor Widjojo Nitisastro, this band of technocrats laid before their new master a plan to set the country back on its feet. The plan aimed to allow in foreign investment, loosen the tight reins of the state's hold over the economy, and encourage the West to extend much-needed credit to the country. In hindsight, it is difficult to judge just how much more important these ideas were than the soon to be tapped wealth from oil and gas, or the harnessing of capital and entreprenurial skills accumulated by the country's wealthy Chinese businessmen. All the more so because, relatively speaking, foreign investment is still under-represented; the state continues to dominate the economy – which still depends heavily on foreign aid and loans. Suharto's acceptance of Widjojo was undoubtedly important in determining the influence of the technocrats. Suharto was exposed to Widjojo's teaching while he attended the army's staff college in Bandung at the end of the 1950s. Given the young colonel's minimal basic education, this period spent at the army's most prestigious educational institution must have been abnormally formative for the impressionable Suharto. Once the tables were turned, and it was Suharto's turn to impress, it is commonly accepted that Widjojo's diplomatic skills prevented the new president from suspecting political motive or ambition within the economist's group. As a testament to this, they have survived. Widjojo has held no cabinet position since the

---

* In fact, reinforcing the point that IGGI was a vehicle favoured by the donors was that the body's eventual demise in April 1992 came on Indonesia's instigation after Dutch insistence on tying aid to human rights proved too much for Jakarta to stomach.

early 1980s, but continues to exert considerable influence from behind the scenes.

Without doubt, this enduring primacy the technocrats have enjoyed in managing the economy has ensured the uninterrupted flow of foreign assistance to Indonesia. A visiting risk analyst once remarked that the biggest blow to Indonesia's credit rating would be dealt by the demise of Ali Wardhana – at that time (1987) co-ordinating Minister for Economic Financial and Industrial affairs. While other developing countries responded to crisis by turning inward and dragging up nationalist issues to distract attention from the core problems, Suharto took refuge in a group of people who were unashamedly indoctrinated by the West.

The faith entrusted to this handful of western-trained economists has been great enough for western governments to turn a blind eye to their more usual obsessions in the region; wider political participation and the prevalence of corruption. The more sophisticated among them will no doubt have noticed that it was precisely Indonesia's non-participatory system which has given the technocrats so much latitude, enabling them to implement policies by decree or presidential instruction – few of which have been given a solid basis in law. In the final analysis, with billions of dollars of foreign aid flowing in, the donors were grateful for the stability a strong government guaranteed. The New Order's obsession with order has been one of its best selling points in the corridors of western finance.

The technocrats proved particularly skilful at blending a elements of the free-market economy with an essentially indestructible state sector at its core. Despite the extensive reform of the financial and trade sectors of the economy, the sword of state intervention dangles constantly overhead. Key, or 'strategic' industries remain under state control, including oil, steel, and the high-technology ship and aircraft industries controlled by the influential Minister of Technology, Professor Dr B. J. Habibie.

The need to appease opponents of economic liberalization may be the reason why none of the reform measures have any concrete standing in law. Most measures have been introduced through the mechanism of presidential decree and have yet to be enacted as laws. As presidential decrees they are subject to reversal by presidential decree. Legislation is a slow and cumbersome process in Indonesia. Because each department in the bureaucracy has to be consulted, the scope for deadlock over issues perceived as depriving the government of its power over resources or decision-making is endless.

The legal system itself is now considered the area most in need of urgent reform. The World Bank's 1989 annual country report described Indonesia's legal structure as falling 'far short' of a 'well functioning legal system that is an important prerequisite if the shift towards a less government-regulated environment for the private sector is to be successful'.[17]

Ironically, legal reform was a major aim of the New Order, when it came to power. Arbitary intervention by the executive in the courts was common practice under the Old Order. Under the New Order, attempts have been made to improve judicial procedure and the criminal code, but old attitudes and most of the old Dutch statutes on which the law is based, remain entrenched. The fact that the Dutch laws were designed by the colonial authorities to enhance administrative power and control has perpetuated their usefulness. Use of Dutch precedents has by all accounts increased under the New Order.[18]

It would be false to assume that the New Order has set Indonesia on an irreversible course towards becoming a fully liberalized economy. Rather the reforms of the 1980s should be considered a measure of the New Order's pragmatism. They were necessary adjustments, not acquired principles − at least as far as the bulk of the state apparatus is concerned. The more the economy shows the resilience to survive further external shocks, the more pressure there is likely to be to revert to the ideological purity demanded of the New Order by its strict adherence to the 1945 Constitution. This theme will be explored again and set against the political problems confronting the New Order in Chapter 7. Altogether, it suggests a regime quick to adapt but slow to change.

Statism has always been prevalent in Indonesian economic development − from the period under Dutch rule to Suharto's era of order and development. The role of the state in important areas of the economy is written into the Constitution and is therefore difficult to circumvent. Article 33 states that all areas of the economy of crucial to the welfare of the people must be controlled by the state. Not even the the crusading zeal of the technocrats has been able to make a breach in this oft-quoted article. Article 33 ensures that key economic decisions are made by the government − either its bureaucratic or military arm − rather than by the private sector, whose growth is therefore subject to tight control. Policies tend therefore to represent less the product of lobbying from the market place, but compromises between the competing elements within the ruling elite. In order to obtain what it wants, the bridled private sector is beholden to that elite, thus preventing its members from uniting in their own interests − further retarding the assertion of the nascent middle class. As a thumbnail sketch of the country's political economy, this may seem simplistic, but there is merit in precis when, as in Indonesia, complexity is so often used to strew obstacles in the path of analysis.

The hope is that momentum generated by the economic reforms since

1986 will guarantee there is no turning back on the road towards a *laissez-faire* economy which allows the market the greater say in decision-making. One way the technocrats have been able to get around Article 33 is to persuade Suharto that unprofitable state enterprises should be sold to the private sector. The problem here was their inability to act directly. 'I never use the word privatization,' remarked Finance Minister Johannes Sumarlin, 'it gives a bad connotation in some quarters of society'.[19] Privately, Sumarlin admitted to pressures on the technocrats from nationalist quarters. Suharto himself professed commitment to the role of the state. Yet by the middle of 1990, those state companies that had been privatized were sold to his son's companies at giveaway prices involving significant government write-down of their debts.

With respect to the economy, Suharto presents a baffling array of contrasts. He has chosen wisely from among the country's top foreign-trained economists to run fiscal policies which are held up as an example by commercial bankers and multilateral agencies alike. He has given this small group of technocrats virtually a free hand in running the economy. Yet he has also placed his closest cronies, and lately members of his own family, in positions which have enabled them to rake off astonishingly large profits. The astonishing wealth of his family has earned Suharto criticism at home and a degree of disapproval among overseas investors. Suharto defends the activities of his family by pointing out that his critics have said he favoured the Chinese too much in the past; at least his children are not Chinese. The web of financial interests erected around Suharto is so extensive that he is, in theory, a massively wealthy individual. Estimates of the size of Suharto's family assets are in the $US2–3 billion range, but any calculation is at best guesswork. Examination of this aspect of Suharto's influence over the economy is no less astonishing, only a good deal more negative.

The reason why Suharto patronized a small circle of mostly Chinese businessmen is rooted in the Indonesian army's traditional quartermastering links with Indonesian Chinese traders in the 1940s and 1950s. Political expediency also played a role in their meteoric rise under the New Order. Old Order business interests were left either financially weak, or politically discredited by the events of 1965–6. On the other hand, Indonesian Chinese businessmen were feeling vulnerable after the anti-Chinese sentiment any period of upheaval in Indonesia gives vent to. They were thus in a position to have their capital exploited in return for protection.[20]

If this was the case, the Chinese did extraordinarily well out of the deal. One of them, Indonesian Chinese businessman Liem Sioe Long, is now ranked among the forty richest men in the world and runs a business empire that stretches from the west coast of the US, across South-east Asia and into Europe. In 1988, the top 300 large business groups, most of whom owed their wealth to Suharto's New Order, boasted an estimated total sales turnover of Rp 70,000 billion, or nearly three times the Rp 28,983 billion allocated for the 1989–90 state budget.[21] By the end of the 1980s, economic liberalization highlighted the wealth and success of the Chinese business community to such an extent that it was becoming a sensitive political issue. The threat this posed to Suharto's position forced him, as a later chapter will show, to distance himself publicly from the Chinese.

As well as mastering the art of patronage, Suharto has pioneered the institutionalization of personal wealth. While the Marcoses in the Philippines were content to fritter their wealth on property and material goods at home and overseas, Suharto has erected an imposing financial edifice which puts the money to work – both on his and the nation's behalf. The web of Suharto's investments through holding organizations and 'charitable foundations', or *yayasans*, is wide, encompassing the country's most profitable enterprises, but also funding some of the lowest levels of society.

Through a network of such foundations Suharto and his family hold stakes – and a share of profits – in a dozen large enterprises, including the fourth largest private bank (Bank Duta), an insurance company (Asuransi Timur Jauh) and rice, textile and flour milling concerns controlled by Liem Sioe Long. The important point to note is that the *yayasans* are not subject to auditing, do not return profits to the government or pay taxes, and therefore cannot be called into account. Ironically, the *yayasan* became a popular vehicle for fund-raising during the colonial period. The foundations were a loophole in Dutch law, and it was soon realized that by exploiting them, nationalist organizations could collect funds for ostensibly charitable purposes without interference from the colonial authorities.

Today *yayasans*, as non-profit welfare organizations, attract donations – mostly in the form of company equity – and are not liable to tax. A great many powerful men invest their wealth in such foundations. In late 1989, deposits made by such foundations in state banks alone amounted to Rp 1,695 billion against Rp 755 billion held by limited liability companies. The Jakarta phone book lists four closely printed pages of *yayasans*, covering a range of activities from pension funds, hospitals, and religious activities to those with more specifically political aims.

The foundations are a remarkable vehicle for those with excessive personal wealth, since they provide both a means of accumulating riches and disguising or atoning for the fact by doing good works. 'They are the creation of a captive market mentality', argues Sjahrir, a noted economist in Jakarta. 'Their social symbolism not only attracts funds, but also ensures that contracts can be obtained.' Using *yayasans* as a way of marshalling wealth under a philanthropic banner, Suharto docks as much as Rp 500 a month from every one of the country's four million civil servants as a compulsory contribution to a mosque-building foundation he heads. The estimated Rp 200 million a month this nets goes unaudited.

Suharto argues in his autobiography, that the money in these found-ations has come from contributions and is only employed for the social good. He adds that they run off earned interest, and that the money – wherever it is – is never touched. Perhaps one reason criticism of the system has been mute for so long is because a similar fund-raising system is employed by others in the establishment, specifically the military. But with the growing realization in military circles that Suharto has employed his wealth to undermine their political influence, this level of tolerance has been weakening. Efforts to establish more rigorous legal guidelines to govern foundations have persistently met with no success. How do you legislate the President's wealth?

Suharto's fund-raising machinery is not only efficient, it has been developed at the expense of competing foci of financial patronage. Throughout the 1980s, Suharto's loyal State Secretary, Sudharmono, worked assiduously to wrest control over lucrative government tenders away from the military, turning them over instead to close civilian business associates of the President. Presidential decision No.10 decreed that portions of government contracts over Rp 200 million had to be approved by a special team in the state secretariat. The ostensible purpose of this device was to ensure contracts were awarded to non-Chinese business interests. In practice it meant Sudharmono steered business towards his business cronies and received sizeable kickbacks in the process.[22] Because the military used mainly Chinese businessmen to handle their business, the decree struck at the heart of their revenue generating capacity.

These and other practices which tied the economy closely to sources of patronage in the bureaucracy and the executive office, persist in spite of the economic reforms of the 1980s. The reforms and their effect on foreign investment overshadowed the continuity in other, important areas of the economy. Thus payments out of Suharto's own purse continued to be made to all senior officials. Presidential aid for all districts in Indonesia continued to bypass regional governments. Funding for the government's political organization, Golkar, remained sourced almost exclusively to three *yayasans* controlled by the President. For there is a sense in which the secret of Suharto's grip on power is less the power of the gun and more that of the purse.

Those who have worked closely with Suharto find it hard to decide whether he possesses a strategic sense of where the country is headed, or that his approach is primarily reactive, and driven by the needs of power. Attempts to move analysis of Suharto's New Order out of the realm of personal politics into the broader social and economic context have all drawn heavily on western neo-classical theory, with predictably unsatis-factory results. Summarizing these, Robison argues that attempts to explain the New Order in 'structural-functional' terms, in apolitical 'end of ideology' terms – even by applying 'dependency' theory, all fail because: 'it is instead the consequence of a protracted and complex process of social and economic, and political conflict'.[23] However, Robison's own explan-ation is also suspect. His marrying of the state and capital accumulation, though tempting, underestimates the egalitarian idealism of 'development ideology' as conceived by the New Order strategists.

The New Order's 'development ideology' is a curious blend of two seemingly incompatible positions – economic growth and social justice for all. The latter has roots in the strong anti-foreign, anti-capitalist views of the country's pre-independence nationalist movement. The Dutch created a system in which capital was carefully kept out of the hands of the indigenous population. Only the Dutch and Chinese, who were granted legal protection as 'non-native orientals', had the power to accumulate capital. This bred in the early nationalists a deep suspicion of capitalism which has been passed on more or less unaltered through the country's Constitution. For all the anti-communist rhetoric of the New Order – not to mention its more recent supplication before the altar of free market economics – it draws heavily on the quasi-socialist ideals of nationalist leaders like Sutan Sjahrir. His vision of Indonesia in the 1940s and 1950s was of 'an industrialized economy, an egalitarian society, and an activist welfare state'.

Sjahrir and others of his generation were influenced by their liberal European education, and also by the invidious inequalities bred by the colonial system. They decanted these feelings into the 1945 Constitution which, after suspension in the 1950s, was reinstated by Sukarno in 1959 and has remained in force ever since. Article 33 of the Constitution makes it clear that the state must control all means of production which 'affect the people'. Paragraph 1 of the same article describes economic activity as for the benefit of society rather than for the individiual.

In practice, the growth imperative in development has fairly occluded the ideal of social justice. Given a choice between social justice and growth, the New Order's ideology of struggle argues that economic growth has priority in order to pave the way for future generations to enjoy a better deal. Thanks mainly to the stability, or security priority of key New Order architects like General Ali Murtopo, political development – whereby demands for social justice might be more effectively articulated – was consciously set aside. The system born out of Murtopo's convictions was 'a belief system which, in practice, justifies short term political hardship for the people and legitimises military activities in political, economic and social affairs'.[24] The latter in turn, gave the technocrats a free hand so long as they kept an eye on the vested interests the system was designed to preserve.

For all the praises heaped on Suharto's policies for the way in which they rescued Indonesia from the jaws of disaster and established a climate for sustained economic growth, it is hard in the final analysis to detect any meaningful social concepts behind them. The provision of basic needs and infrastructure preserved order in the state, but was all this really intended to stimulate popular participation in political decision-making, or broaden access to the means of production?

The New Order generals and their acolytes differed significantly from the generation of nationalists who governed Indonesia in the early years of independence. The latter, with their liberal Dutch education, overseas university degrees and grounding in European political thought, might have envisaged social and economic development leading ultimately to the kind of social democracy provided for in theory by the 1945 Constitution. But their roughly educated, less travelled military successors were more imbued with traditional notions of social order. In their world – primarily the rigidly structured feudal culture of Central Java – the people have always to be guided from above. Wisdom is the monopoly of the rulers, ignorance is a burden the people must bear relieved only by the generosity and charity of the wise and powerful. Corruption is regarded as a prerogative of the elite.

Co-operatives may originally have been conceived as a way of enfranchising the native with the means of production after the departure of the Dutch, but under the New Order co-operatives are less a vehicle for developing the entrepeneurial skills of the farmers, and more a framework for channelling the state's largesse down to the lower strata. Strict control of co-operatives by the state ensures that members can have no control over their own funds. This essentially feudal approach to government comes with an assorted baggage of excesses, the least of which – petty corruption – has steadily increased in intensity throughout the last quarter century.

The political economy of Indonesia can be examined as the neo-Marxist economists do by dwelling on the emergence of a powerful Chinese and indigenous proto-capitalist class fostered by and bound to a powerful state.

But developments since Robison propounded his thesis in the mid-1980s make it difficult for some to identify the march of capitalism. More recent studies of the region stress instead the 'fragile, corrupt and speculative' nature of South-east Asian economies.[25] Japanese economist Kunio Yoshihara argues persuasively that capitalism in South-east Asia is better described as imperfect or ersatz capitalism, bereft of the rationality and integrity normally present in capitalist theory. 'South-east Asian capitalism is ersatz because it is dominated by rent-seekers', Yoshihara explains, 'What they seek is not only protection from foreign competition, but also concessions, licenses, monopoly rights, and government subsidies.... As a result, all sorts of irregularities have flourished in the economy'.[26]

In Indonesia, a powerful state has throughout history manipulated the levers of patronage and tradition to enhance the wealth of its 'patricians', distribute enough to maintain legitimacy and oil the wheels of patronage, and then – over-extended and a victim of its own ends – gradually decline. The dualism inherent in Suharto's approach to economic development approximates this model. Development is regarded both as a stamp of his legitimacy and the cornucopia out of which patronage and personal gain can be pulled at will. Viewing pre-independence Dutch East Indies and independent Indonesia as one long continuum of political and economic development reveals something of this pattern. The Dutch imposed a harsh system of colonial rule designed primarily to reap the rich harvests of Java's volcanic soils. Java was the 'rice basket' and 'timber yard' of the Dutch East Indies Company. Social and political development of the populace was pursued only at the end of the Company's long rule, to stave off revolt and ease the burden of administration.

While the British in India struggled with their consciences to impose the principles of common law on the feudal remnants of Mogul India, the Dutch simply created a dual system; one law for them, another for us. It was the Dutch who first recognized the principle of *adat*, the observance of regional cultural traditions among Indonesia's diverse societies. The legal system they created, with its emphasis on separateness, inequality and strong central control, passed more or less unchanged into the hands of the newly independent Indonesian government.

After independence, early experiments with a parliamentary democracy gave way by the late 1950s to Sukarno's characteristically flamboyant form of autocracy, termed 'Guided Democracy', which drew on Dutch colonial statutes to enforce strict state control. In both cases, the end of empire, so to speak, took root in the elite. Under the Dutch, the early nationalist movement sprung from the ranks of Dutch-educated youths destined for the native civil service. Under Sukarno, an unlikely coalition of students and restive military officers eventually deposed the nation's 'proclamator' of independence. Beneath the unquestionable success of Suharto's rule in economic terms, lurks a disturbing sense of malaise similar in some key respects to the last years of Sukarno. At first sight this is not easy to detect. Western observers have always – and will continue to be – accused of interpreting or judging Indonesia by western standards. Arguably, though, western moral principles as applied to political behaviour have been most glaringly flouted by those westerners who are happy to see Indonesia flourish economically, while its people remain politically backward, if not wholly repressed.

As the New Order approaches a quarter-century in age, a key question is whether the order and development fostered by Suharto is enough to sustain the system he has created. Or will he – or his successor – be forced to match development and economic progress with democracy and political progress? The model is familiar to those who have watched developments in China, the Soviet Union and Eastern Europe. Yet it may not be so easy to apply to Indonesia.

There are indeed signs that having stabilized the economy, the government is willing to fall back on the socialistic principles inherent in New Order ideology for expressly political purposes. Suharto has made equity a key theme of his speeches since 1990. In his budget speech of January 1990 Suharto surprised his economic advisers by urging them to make 'co-operatives one of the main pillars of the national economy'.[27] High up in their ivory towers, the technocrats poured scorn on the national co-operative movement which seemed good for little else except the pocket-lining of local officials. None the less they faced a dilemna. Pushed to do so, the technocrats strove to find a formula which synthesized the necessary tolerance of overseas Chinese-dominated corporate growth in the private sector with the need to share the benefits of that growth more equitably. They termed it 'Economic Democracy'.[28]

The struggle for economic maturity – or 'take-off' – and inherited suspicions of capitalism dance an awkward tango on the New Order's political stage. On the one hand the Suharto government has promoted Chinese-run private enterprise to underwrite the state's weak capacity to accumulate capital. At the same time, the government has consistently denied the private sector untrammelled use of market forces. Politically, the state cannot afford to abandon its commitment to cooperatives, small credit schemes and other public displays of disdain for capitalism triumphant. The more so, if political pressures from below remind it of the ideals and values on which its legitimacy is based, namely the equitable distribution of the benefits of development.

It should also be remembered that before the oil crisis forced radical adjustments, the domination of the economy by the state, inherited by Sukarno from the Dutch colonial system, was in fact strengthened under Suharto in the 1970s. In the period 1968 to 1983, the percentage of GDP accounted for by the state sector increased from 13 per cent to 41 per cent. The oil windfall helped make the state financially self-sufficient, and insulated it against the pressures of inefficiency and corruption. The overseas-educated technocrats brought in to liberalize trade and investment did so in order to attract foreign capital and free up commodities for export needed to rehabilitate the economy. The liberalization of the foreign-exchange regime, interest rate adjustments, and investments in infrastructure provided a basis for growth, but fell well short of a commit-ment to *laissez-faire* capitalism.

For a time, foreign investors were required to set up joint ventures with state enterprises. They are still required to do so with private domestic private companies, though divestment is loosely enforced. All foreign oil companies are still obliged to enter into production-sharing contracts with the state oil company Pertamina. Opportunities for profitable domestic investment were offered primarily to a group of Indonesian-Chinese entrepeneurs who had brokered business deals with Suharto during his army days in central Java. Even so, the quid pro quo for the lucrative trading monopolies of men like Liem Sioe Long, was their heavy investment in manufacturing under state ownership. The presence of foreign investors was a price the government had to pay to secure easy credit from overseas donors.

Yet, for all the inconsistencies of the system, in two significant areas, real progress has been achieved. First, Indonesia has industrialized under the New Order, and joined the ranks of Asia's dynamic economies. Second, the effect of this growth on the economic position of Indonesians has in overall terms been positive. Lacunae of neglect remain and disparities have altered, not disappeared entirely. In parts of Central Java, dire Malthusian predictions were made in the 1960s. Far from facing a threat of famine, today the area as a whole comes near the top of the scale in provincial prosperity tables. However, less densely populated eastern Indonesia, parts of which were comparatively better off at a lower level of overall devel-opment, are now being left behind. A 1990 World Bank report on poverty in Indonesia, recorded zero or negative growth rates in per capita income in five eastern provinces, while Jakarta's estimated increase in per capita income was as much as 5.33 per cent in the period 1981–7.

A recent US AID-funded study of employment in Java showed how the growth of urban centres in Java have significantly relieved the pressure on rural areas.[29] But urban growth has naturally enough promoted income disparities, while new agricultural techniques have exacerbated rural unemployment and landlessness. Many of these problems are coming to a head; land issues – specifically reform of land-ownership regulations – were a hotly debated topic in the more politically charged atmosphere after Suharto's re-election in 1988.

For all this, the majority of Indonesians have achieved a higher standard of living under Suharto's New Order. The World Bank calculates that poverty had declined in absolute terms from about 40 per cent of the population in 1980 to 21 per cent, or thirty-seven million people living below the poverty line in 1987. Problems of equity and distribution are only now beginning to manifest themselves, arising primarily as by-products of growth – a greater concentration in urban areas and the rising expectations of the better educated. With the labour force growing by over two million a year, the government faces an uphill struggle finding them jobs. About 600,000 university graduates could not find employment in 1988–9. Over 60 per cent of the labour force between the ages of 15 and 19 with a high school education were looking for work in the same year.[30]

A simple and deterministic view of the New Order might argue that the growth and basic improvements in living standards it has fostered have prevented too much questioning of its legitimacy. For the majority of Indonesians, at least superficially, this is the case. The New Order has overseen the transformation of a nation which in 1965 had few roads, was mired in poverty and hunger and at war with its neighbour, Malaysia. By contrast Indonesia today is perceived as an incipient Newly Industrialized Country. It has roads, fine airports and even plans for monorails in the capital, Jakarta.

For the ordinary Indonesian with time to pause and reflect, Suharto has done much good for the country. The elite can share much the same feeling. Chinese businessmen have prospered, bureaucrats grew rich with impunity and, until recently, the military had the lion's share of power. But power breeds competition for power, and Suharto's leadership has been questioned at several stages in his long rule, mostly by those who helped him achieve it in the first place. He is facing even more political pressure in the 1990s just as the prudence of his policies is bearing a second crop of fruit. Contenders for political leadership in any given situation may need economic malaise to provide combustible material for their cause, but never for the germ of a challenge to establish itself. Among Suharto's key talents has been his ability to defuse threats to his rule and then mostly to co-opt those responsible. Suharto's command of the money required to buy off political challengers is far greater than anybody else's. The genius of the system he has created is that it embodies legal channels for accumulating financial clout that would make a US politician green with envy. The beauty of Suharto's brand of development is that most of what the people see of it flows directly from him. The firm but flexible role of the state guarantees order. The question asked by many is whether he can continue to hold the centre using guile and cash alone.

The focus of debate in Indonesia at the close of the 1980s, and Suharto's first quarter-century in power, was how to achieve a smooth succession. There were those, of course, who wanted a change of leadership sooner rather than later. Others were concerned about the impact on stability if Suharto departed the scene too soon. At the risk of pressing the point too far, all the major upheavals in Indonesia this century were born of the failure of those in power to perceive the exhaustion of their own mandate. The Dutch, unlike the British in India, had no plans to decolonize after the Second World War. Sukarno persisted with his impulsive policies – an attack against Malaysia, withdrawal from the UN, and support for the PKI – despite the alienation they sowed in the ranks of the armed forces.

Suharto too has alienated key sections of the armed forces on whose backs he rode to power. Among his own generation of fellow officers, most of whom supported his rise to power, the gap between their ideals and the course of Suharto's presidency has grown steadily wider. Their sense of idealism has increased sharply as Suharto has chosen to confer the fruits of power more and more on a limited circle of close associates and family members. More recently, Suharto has shown signs of exploiting divisions in society for political ends, cutting right across the integrating, stabilizing effect of his economic policies. The question this raises is whether the achievements of the New Order are now in danger of being dashed against the rocks of political expediency.

3

TWO FUNCTIONS, ONE PURPOSE: THE INDONESIAN ARMY IN POLITICS

There are no soldiers and non-soldiers, just good citizens and bad citizens.

(General L. B. Murdani, August 1989)

If there is one institution in modern Indonesia which towers above all others in importance, it is the armed forces. The Indonesian armed forces (*Angkatan Bersenjata Republik Indonesia*, or Abri) constitute an institution that is far more than a standing force with a command structure; it is the soul of the nation and the largest political organization in the country. Prodigiously pompous as these definitions may sound, they reflect the perception both of the officer corps, and, to some extent, the civilian population.

Perceptions of military involvement in politics have changed in many parts of the world, and especially in South-east Asia. Military-backed, or military-run governments, with some notable exceptions, have become more sophisticated. The image of overweight and odious generals in fancy uniforms riding roughshod over their people is fading. Emerging in its place is the image of clever, executive-suited generals oozing diplomatic charm, a grasp of international affairs and the ability to project populist or nationalist causes.

A number of factors, ranging from the growing debt obligation these countries have accumulated to the difficulty of avoiding global approbrium for human rights excesses, have contributed to what is perhaps more an adaptation rather than fundamental change. For the power motive remains as strong as ever, but modern government requires complex linkages with the outside world – the non-military world in particular – something that generals who want to remain in power must adjust to.

Among Asean countries, neither the Thai nor Philippine armed forces possesses a strong ideological or legal framework to support a permanent

60

role in government. Consequently, military intervention is intermittent, and never tolerated for long. In Malaysia, reflecting the British colonial heritage, the armed forces are under the authority of a civilian minister of defence, and play almost second fiddle to the strong internal security function of the police force, which falls under the authority of the home ministry.

Indonesia's armed forces are the only military organization in the region with a solid legal and ideological basis for their role in civilian affairs. Through what is known as the 'dual function', Abri plays both a civilian and military role, which is enshrined in law. Abri's institutionalized role is envied in other countries. The Thai army, for example, has seen its generals enter politics in 'civvies' and turn soft, or go into business and squabble. One general even termed this 'parliamentary dictatorship'.[1] Ironically, some Thai officers have a high regard for Indonesia's dual function.

The irony doubles back, however. Younger officers in the Indonesian army are showing signs of frustration with their legally determined dual role and yearn for something akin to the less formalized situation in Thailand. Some of them are dissatisfied with the way in which involvement in politics has hindered the development of a professional army. The army's social and political role dominates academy curricula and leaves little time for modern war-games and the study of hi-tech tactics. At a lecture given by an Australian officer to senior staff college students in 1989, his remark that the Australian army had no dual military and political role was greeted by Indonesian officers with a round of applause.

Conversely, their elders – who for the time being remain firmly in the saddle – are concerned that a weaker political role will only hasten their redundancy. Though no one likes to admit it, this difference of views has opened dangerous fissures within the army. Younger officers say it is time to re-fashion the army's political doctrine to fit contemporary conditions – not necessarily do away with it. As reflected in the conclusions of a recent army seminar, they sense that a better educated, more prosperous Indonesian society is likely to be more critical and demand a greater say in government. The older generals grumble about the younger generation of officers, saying they are a disappointing lot, not responsible enough to lead the country. Of course, whether the military does in fact lead the country is also open to question.

The demilitarization of Suharto's New Order has gone so far it is barely recognized as a military-led government. In many ways it is not. The current cabinet is dominated by civilian technocrats and retired officers. Compared with the cabinet's composition in 1980, when there were eleven military personnel against thirteen civilians, those still on the active list are a smaller minority. In 1988, they consisted of the Armed Forces Chief, a four-star general; a serving general in the unimportant Transmigration portfolio; the State Secretary, a major-general; the Mines and Energy Minister, who held an air force rank; and the Attorney-General.

Oddly enough, the purely military function of Indonesia's armed forces is poor and underdeveloped. There are all told 533,000 men in Abri, which includes the police force.[2] Yet for size of the country – and compared to smaller regional neighbours – the army, air force and navy are small and under-equipped. Abri manpower strength amounts to just 0.15 per cent of the total population, compared with the Singapore armed forces' figure of 2.06 per cent, or Thailand's 0.46 per cent, or even Malaysia's 0.68 per cent. Abri's budget as a percentage of GNP is similarly small by regional standards, totalling 1.96 per cent of total GNP, compared with Singapore's 5.48 per cent, or Thailand's 3.26 per cent. The army fields over a dozen infantry brigades, and possesses no more than 100 heavy tanks and 160 light tanks. Special forces and the strategic reserve (Kostrad) undertake most overtly military operations, while the regular army is mostly occupied with its 'territorial' or internal security role.

The military's internal policing function is overdeveloped. In this respect, the army is the most important service. For the army is represented at every level of Indonesian society by means of a territorial structure which places a member of the army – as well as police and local militia – in every settlement down to the smallest hamlet. The system was developed early on when the army faced regional insurrection and Communist-led revolt against the newly independent republic. Fitted to a rigid chain of command, such a system theoretically ensures almost total control of the population. Every Indonesian citizen is recorded against an address. If he or she moves, non-notification of a change of address is an offence. In this way, it is possible in theory for almost anybody to be picked up simply by lifting a phone and passing the order down the chain of command to the rural or urban village level. The political arena may no longer be the army's exclusive preserve, but their ability to influence the grass roots of society remains unquestioned. To understand how this finely tuned and fiercely defended system of territorial rule evolved, something of Indonesia's military history must first be explained.

The army's essential military strategy is based on a doctrine of Universal People's Defence, or *Sishankamrata*, a concept which has more bearing on the relationship between the army, society and the state than most modern military analysts would allow it has on principles of modern warfare. Because of this, the general literature on military politics is less helpful at the outset than the Indonesian military's own theoretical explanation.

Every national army dwells on its traditions; the Indonesian army is ruled by them. 'All of us must recall', reads the preamble to a draft bill on soldiership presented to parliament in late 1987:

The struggle to defend and maintain Indonesian independence from 1945 to 1949, first against the Japanese, then the British and eventually the Dutch. Though short on equipment, supplies and tactical as well as technical aspects, through the people's war spearheaded with a guerrilla warfare we ultimately were able to cause the Dutch military adventurism to meet a deadlock by removing their expectation to win the war. We succeeded in forcing them back to the negotiating table and in making them recognize the idependence and sovereignty of the Republic of Indonesia. It is clear we did not gain victory by conventional means. Our independence war is an unconventional war now called 'universal people's war', a form of war based on the people's armed resistance, that is, the people who did not recognize occupation and who spontaneously rose up to bear arms to offer an armed resistance by refusing to surrender. Such a way of waging war was later on developed into a state defence system which we call 'Universal People's defence'.[3]

The important point to notice here is that the notion of the army relying on spontaneous people's resistance is not simply a hallowed relic of regimental history; it remains at the core of Abri military strategy. Foreign students at the senior officers staff college in Bandung, West Java [SESKOAD], attest to the army's continued teaching of people's defence as the major element in tactical exercises involving an external threat. One foreign student described how Indonesian officers during a theoretical exercise were taught to clear a minefield employing local villagers instead of sappers, without considering the sophistication of modern mine-laying technology.[4] Here is how it was put by the SESKOAD commander:

The development of Abri cannot evade the fact that Abri was born of the people during the struggle for independence which sprang forth with youthful passion to fight for national independence in 1945. Based on this historical perspective we realise that the strength of Abri is based on the strength of the unity of Abri and the people, and that the development of Abri cannot ignore that fact.[5]

Behind Abri's continued faith in the idea of Total People's Defence lies the more complex belief of the military's role in the state.

The Indonesian army sees itself as quite different from other armies in the world, because it was never created as an instrument of the state, but was itself involved in the creation of the state. Thus the military considers itself the embodiment of Indonesian nationalism. In theory, it remains above the state, and technically does not consider itself answerable to the government of the day, although in theory, the president is supreme commander of the armed forces. Abri's decisive role in the defence of the Republic during the 1945–9 period, when it came under Dutch attack provided the military with the basic justification for wielding political power. 'The government may change every day; the army remains the same,' General Sudirman, the army's first and much revered commander, said in 1947.

In the eyes of military officers, the army has saved the state from catastrophe on several occasions – something the army will not let Indonesians forget. On 18 September 1948, a group of Communists declared a 'Soviet Republic' at Madiun in East Java. They did so just as the Dutch returned to re-take their colony, an unforgiveable act of treachery which was paid for in blood. The Madiun revolt was put down and the seeds of hatred for Communists planted deep in the hearts of the officer corps. A few weeks later, on 19 December 1948, the civilian government, led by President Sukarno, surrendered to the Dutch as they advanced on their first capital in Jogyakarta. The army, led by General Sudirman, refused to comply with the surrender and waged a guerrilla war against the Dutch.

Both events, albeit subsequently amplified by army historians, act as essential props to Abri's doctrine. At the core of this doctrine is the implicit justification for the army's role in politics. This was above all a product of early tensions between the civilian led government of the republic and the hastily organized and fractious army. The army, led by Sudirman, fell out with the government over its policy of negotiating with the Dutch. Then, when the civilian government fell back in the face of the advancing Dutch, the army opted to carry on the national struggle using guerrilla tactics. When a soldier takes his oath he swears to uphold principles exemplified by the crushing of the treacherous Communists at Madiun and the heroic decision of General Sudirman to continue the armed struggle. This historical perception of Abri's decisiveness set against a weak though probably prudent civilian government is embedded deeply in the Indonesian political psyche.

On 30 September 1965, the murder of six generals and the declaration of a revolutionary government took the Republic to the brink again, this time with the assumed – but never proved – threat of a Communist take-over. The prompt suppression of the uprising by Major-General Suharto once again saved the Republic, and brought the military to power for the first time in its history. Explaining the strength with which these events have made themselves felt in Abri doctrine, the eloquent former Army Commander, the late General T. B. Simatupang wrote:

> The basic challenge for national security during the first 21 years after independence... was to defend the Unitary Republic... against threats from colonialism, from federalism linked to semi-colonialism, from various forms of separatism, from fanatical muslims and from Communists.[6]

The deep sense of purpose imbued in the Indonesian military is something western analysts find easy to ignore. Conventional approaches to the military in politics dwell heavily on the personal ambitions and vested interests of the individual officers who come out on top. The assumption that armed might breeds power-lust and greed is not easily dislodged – nor can it be dismissed entirely in the case of Indonesia. Yet the full-blown macho-military stereotyope typified by some Latin American states sits awkwardly on reality in this case.

Yet, through most of its forty-five-year existence, Abri has been plagued by shortcomings which have denied it the chance to completely dominate the political scene. An attempt to force Sukarno to dissolve parliament and hold elections failed in 1952. Sukarno's own declaration of martial law in 1957 arguably offered the army an opportunity to seize power, but they were divided over the issue and ill-equipped to match the political skills of the nascent Indonesian Communist Party. Eight years later, when the opportunity to rule again presented istelf, the army once again fell victim to divisions of opinion in the senior ranks. The more sophisticated, Dutch-educated officers wanted to share power with a civilian government; others, like Suharto, with more humble backgrounds, probably favoured more traditional models of power, based on a clique headed by a strong leader – not necessarily distinguishing between the army and the state.

The image projected by the title of David Jenkins's 1983 monograph, 'Suharto and his Generals', is perhaps intentionally chilling, but the thrust of his arguments reflect these deep divisons within the army on which Suharto has played in order to maintain his pre-eminent position.[7] The contrast is all the more compelling today. Rather than a coterie of jackbooted, overweight men behind dark-glasses which some of the photographs in the Jenkins book suggest, the contemporary impression is more one of a group of old men sitting on a park bench, remembering better times and wondering whatever happened to principles.

Abri, like the Republic itself, was fashioned out of a series of compromises that had to be made in view of all the complex social ethnic and religious components of the nascent state which clamoured for a greater say. There was also the question of loyalty. Towards the end of their rule, the Dutch built up a considerable native fighting force known as the Royal Netherland's East Indies Army (*Koninlijk Nederlandsch-Indische Leger*, or KNIL). The natives were usually selected from certain regions and deployed in areas where they could be relied upon to bear the most antipathy towards the locals. A majority of the indigenous troops in the KNIL were Ambonese or other eastern islanders. Few were trained as officers and even as late as 1940 there were less than a dozen natives in all who had attained the rank of captain. Only two had been promoted as far as lieutenant-colonel. When the Japanese occupied the Dutch Indies after 1942, they set up their own armed force, known as the PETA (*Tentara Sukarela Pembela Tanah Air* or 'Volunteer army for the Defence of the Fatherland'). The Japanese styled the PETA as an embryonic independent army to attract young Indonesians, many of whom regarded the Japanese as their liberators.

The collapse of the Japanese brought confusion to the Indies. Civilian nationalist leaders had to be pushed into declaring independence which they thought the Japanese would arrange for them. The PETA and other ragtag militia were poorly armed and badly organized. More disturbingly, few of the civilian nationalist leaders trusted them. Thus divisions between the army and the state have early antecedents. Barely three months after declaring independence, the country's first Defence Minister, Amir Syarif-fudin, spoke out against the PETA and said the KNIL could not be trusted. 'So,' concluded General Nasution's biographers, 'in one breath the minister had managed to insult practically the whole Indonesian officer corps'.[8]

In the first years after independence the army, which was formally organized on 5 October 1945, engaged in a series of operations to quell regional rebellions which erupted in response to the new state's first steps towards centralization of the old fragmented Dutch empire. In some of these, like the *Permesta* revolt of the late 1950s in Sumatra, army officers were involved, thus highlighting the potential for disunity. At the same time, the experience of putting down regional revolts in West Java, South Sulawesi and the Moluccas in 1950s, reinforced Abri's perception of itself as defender of the unitary state and began to strengthen their political role. To some extent this heavy emphasis on internal security was already imbued in those officers who had served in the Dutch colonial army, where the ever-present threat of insurrection underpinned military training. But, as Sundhaussen points out, the internal security role played by the military in the first years of independence dragged it deeper and deeper into politics:

Neither the military nor the civilian leaders at the time seem to have been aware of the fact that using the military in internal security operations involved them in making political choices, and thus inevitably to make political friends and political enemies as well.[9]

This very quickly became apparent as plans to modernize the armed forces ran up against political obstacles which forced senior officers to take sides. On one side, senior military leaders such as the young T.B. Simatupang, and A.H. Nasution, envisioned a leaner, more disciplined force, essentially along European lines, reflecting their Dutch educational background. According to Simatupang, there was a strong reluctance and a feeling of scepticism about the army's expanded security role felt by some senior officers. As they saw mounting political instability around them, 'They were haunted by the spectre of creating what was perceived then as a Latin American situation in Indonesia'.[10] But their caution and plans for rationalization were not necessarily shared by the more roughly educated officers who had been trained by the Japanese. They also alienated more radical politicians, particularly on Indonesia's emerging left, who saw the fractious guerrilla army which defeated the Dutch as the nucleus of a politically inspired people's army.

The left regarded Abri as the tool they needed to establish a Communist state. They in turn received some support from officers in outlying regions who regarded the Simatupang/Nasution reforms as a threat to their authority.[11] Matters came to a head on 17 October 1952, when a group of reformist officers elected to press Sukarno to dissolve parliament and adopt greater power which would make him more dependent on the military. The ploy failed, and the military suffered the first of many blows to its political prestige.

Matters grew steadily worse with Sukarno's cultivation of the Indonesian Communist Party in the 1960s. It is hard today to imagine how powerful the PKI was, and to judge just how close Indonesia came to joining Vietnam as a socialist bloc state in the region. Again it is also difficult to say to what extent the political passivity of Indonesians and the ease with which they become one thing or another for the sake of gaining access to patronage also explains the PKI's success. However, external concerns demonstrated by debate in Washington about whether to mount covert operations to destabilize Sukarno were matched by mounting internal concern, most of it rooted in the military.

Attempts to combat PKI influence taught the military a good deal more about playing politics. They began to cultivate anti-left groups in the press, on campuses and in literary and intellectual circles. Like the group of writers and poets who later declared their opposition to the PKI under the banner of a 'cultural manifesto,' there was plenty of anti-left sentiment for the army to cultivate. The Javanese are prone to shows of intense jealousy towards one another. Any group which achieves success at the expense of another is ensured of a host of sworn enemies.

Seeing the need for an institutional bulwark against the PKI's influence, and with encouragement from US intelligence advisers, the military participated in the formation of social organizations with anti-PKI leanings. These groups formed the basis of Golkar, the election-winning organ of the New Order which gave the military a concrete stake in the Suharto regime. The military's campaign against the PKI in the early 1960s taught them how to mobilize civilian groups against political targets and deepened their mistrust of civilian politicians. It also sowed seeds of disunity within the ranks and between the services. Interestingly enough, similar methods and their by-products were evident in Abri's political role under the New Order.

The deeper the army was drawn into politics, the more uncomfortable its officers felt about their relationship to the mandated leadership. For unlike the case of Thailand, where military intervention is a determining factor in the change of government, Abri has never successfully launched a *coup d'état*: a fact the army is proud of for reasons made clear above. It is important to stress this, because whatever else about the events of September/October 1965 is eventually unearthed, it was certainly a disaster for the military high command. Not only were six senior staff officers murdered, but Lieutenant-Colonel Untung's declaration of a Revolutionary Council on the morning of 1 October 1965 also marked the clearest attempt by the army to usurp power.

Moreover, early emergence of opposition to Suharto's rule from officers who had played key roles in his rise to power, like Nasution, Kemal Idris and Dharsono, suggests that not everybody in the army felt their interests were served by Suharto's resolution of the 30 September affair. It also shows how quickly the unity forged within Abri by the traumatic murder of six generals dissipated. Suharto trod carefully where Sukarno was concerned, but he was unwilling to listen to respected military peers, like Nasution, over whom he prevailed in the Provisional People's Deliberative Assembly. Nasution urged the strict application of the law under which Sukarno was liable for prosecution. Suharto wanted to protect Sukarno and, as already suggested, avoid setting a dangerous precedent of impeachment. Nasution also advocated that Abri co-operate with the civilian establishment, not dominate it. Suharto argued that conditions dictated that the army must take the lead. Subsequently, the methods by which Suharto sought to build a solid basis for power in the late 1960s and early 1970s drew as much on countervailing civilian sources as they did on the military. In the process, Abri began to lose power from the moment it was obtained.

Suharto gathered around him a group of men who were not of the military mainstream, or elite. In the months before September 1965, Suharto drew together close associates from his days in Central Java, building up a core of trusted deputies. Ali Murtopo, his trusted territorial assistant in Central Java, became his intelligence chief in Kostrad. Yoga Sugama, another of his trusted deputies from the 1950s, was recalled from duty overseas to join Suharto in Jakarta in March 1965. According to Sugama, the three of them began working as a team again in early 1965, making moves to counter PKI influence.[12] Nasution recalls that in the course of 1966, Suharto began taking advice from people who were from outside the mainstream military leadership.

> We [the Army] had no plans. In this sense the army more or less faded away in its influence on Suharto. Sarwo Edhie was against this. So he was sent to Medan in 1968. Kemal Idris was sent to Makassar. Dharsono as ambassador to Bangkok. The three kingmakers were eased out – finished.[13]

Compelling as it is to conceive the Indonesian military as a mighty concentration of political power backed by the threat of armed force, an objective assesement of Abri's fortunes during the New Order it spawned leaves one with the impression that it has served the ends of power while at the same time losing its ability to curb the real power-holders.

By the end of the 1980s, with Suharto's popularity among the elite in slow but perceptible decline, senior military figures, both active and retired, had begun working quietly to seek his removal. There was no question of doing so by force. This would cast Abri as usurpers and threaten their legitimacy in the eyes of the people. On the other hand, three years after Suharto's re-election in 1988, there were no obvious signs they had come up with a workable political strategy. An examination of Abri's 'dual function' partly reveals why this was the case.

The genesis of the dual function was a speech delivered by then Army Chief of Staff, General A. H. Nasution, on 11 November 1958 at the army's officer training collage at Magelang in Central Java. Hemmed in on one side by increasingly leftward leaning civilian politicians close to Sukarno, and threatened on the other by the rash of regional revolts, Nasution felt the time had come to define clearly the army's role in the state.

Nasution called for the military to be given a role not just in cabinet, but in every state institution, from ministries to the diplomatic service. His insistence that the armed forces act neither as political activists nor mere spectators later earned the label 'middle way' (*Jalan tengah tentara*). Describing the early evolution of the doctrine General Simatupang wrote:

> The political instability and tensions or even antagonisms between the political parties forced the army leadership to look seriously into the problem of how such a stabilising role could be performed without falling into the pitfall of a Latin American situation.[14]

Having laid the basis for the dual function, Simatupang argues that many senior officers (among them himself) felt uneasy about expanding the army's role any further.[15] This prompted a series of army seminars at which, despite the reservations of some, the dual function was formalized and refined. Interestingly enough, these seminars, one in April 1965, the other in August 1966, straddled the transfer of power to Suharto in 1966, by which time active military officers had already begun moving into key political positions. They clearly needed the ideological justification for what had already become reality.

The main thrust of the new doctrine was that henceforth the armed forces would formally play a role both as a military force and a socio-political force. Abri would have two functions and the term *dwi-fungsi*, or 'dual function', was adopted. Unlike other armies entering politics, Abri made no pretence at the temporary, contingent nature of its intervention to protect the state. Its was a birthright as co-founder of the state; the logical extension of its position above the state and alongside the people. But as David Jenkins points out in his seminal monograph on Indonesian military politics, while the basic principle of the dual function was unquestioned, the acceptable parameters of military intervention in society have always been controversial.[16]

In the early years of the New Order, the dual function was employed more or less as a means of extending total military control of the instruments of state – and to some extent the economy – by replacing civilian personnel with military men under the *kekaryaan* system – a term which loosely translated means 'cadre-ization'. This involved the transfer of active military officers across to the bureaucracy in large numbers. Abri justified its bureaucratic role by arguing that because the people had placed their hopes in the army, there was a need for Abri to participate fully in all aspects of government. Of course this hindered the development of a strong civilian bureaucracy.

By the late 1970s, half the cabinet and over two-thirds of the regional governorships were military appointees. At the district level, 56 per cent of district officers were military men. In the bureaucracy, 78 per cent of director-generals and 84 per cent of ministerial secretaries were Abri appointees. Even in the diplomatic service, almost half the country's ambassadors were from the military in 1977.[17] In the early 1980s, a former US diplomat estimated that active and retired military men occupied half the positions in the 'higher central bureaucracy'. More importantly, the military dominated the affairs of every cabinet department. Some of these appointments, especially to the diplomatic service were favours granted to retiring officers. The majority were on the active list and valued the wider publicity and greater opportunities for renumeration offered by their posts.

With the passage of a bill entitled 'Basic Provisions for the Defence and Security of the Republic of Indonesia' in 1982, *dwi fungsi* became enshrined in law. Typically of the New Order, legal enshrinement of the political edifice it was erecting was slowly and cautiously undertaken. However, with this law and an array of emergency decrees sanctioning the continued existence of the Special Command for the Restoration of Order (*Kopkamtib*), it is hardly surprising that Suharto's government has been styled a military regime. But if things were this simple, Suharto would have been replaced by another general long ago. For while Abri officers justified their presence in the ranks of the civil administration as a means of correcting the swing to the left perpetrated by Sukarno and his men, Suharto himself worked the system as a means of distributing patronage to his supporters and silencing his critics.

Military influence extended into the economy too. The early years of the New Order saw the consolidation and expansion of Abri business interests, which had their origins in the ultra-nationalist policies of the Sukarno period. The military was forced from the beginning of the republic to raise revenue by milking local business activities or by imposing tolls and taxes in operational areas. Martial law was declared in 1957, and soon afterwards nationalist furore over the campaign to wrest West Irian from the Dutch resulted in the expulsion of all Dutch companies. Using its martial law powers, the army seized all the assets of the Dutch companies, most of which commanded dominant positions in the country's profitable oil, mining, agribusiness and banking sectors. Most of these companies subsequently became state enterprises run by military-dominated boards with the help of Chinese businessmen close to Abri.

Drawing on his own profitable experience of the system in Central Java, Suharto actively encouraged military participation in the economy as soon as he came to power. He hived off large and profitable areas of the state sector and awarded them to Abri – one unit which became particularly active in business was Suharto's old command, Kostrad. He allowed

71

manipulation of export credits and the award of state contracts to Abri, or to their clients. Suharto knew the importance of controlling profitable business enterprises to the articulation of military power – a relationship which seems to hold throughout South-east Asia. The military's ability to participate in business is regarded as an essential prerequisite to weilding political power. For having their own financial resources enables the generals to circumvent central government attempts to limit their power by budgetary means. Internally, the material benefits accruing to officers in business gave them a bigger stake in the *status quo* and helped ensure their loyalty. In the specific case of Indonesia, Abri's expanding role in business also tended to clear up doubts within the ranks about the military's dual function. It simply became too profitable to question.

The immediate beneficiaries of this redistribution of the means of production were those units and their commanding officers close to, or in the Suharto group. Many of them had already become involved in business through the Financial and Economic (Finek) sections Abri had established in the 1950s to run its smuggling and other business interests at the provincial level. Now these 'financial generals' were given access to lucrative export and import monopolies, forestry concessions and Indonesia's black gold; the oil industry.

The strength of the relationship between the executive and Abri interests ensured it took relatively little time for the military to achieve a dominant position in the economy. Ibnu Sutowo, a military colleague of Suharto's, was appointed head of a new state oil company, North Sumatra Oil Exploration, in 1957. By 1968 he was head of the Pertamina company, under which all state oil companies had been incorporated. By the height of the oil boom in the early 1970s, Pertamina had become not only the major source of Abri funding, but accounted through tax payments for almost 40 per cent of domestic revenue.

Immune to the normal processes of accountability and, under a law passed in 1971, answerable only to the president, Sutowo presided over the oil sector at the height of the oil boom. All drilling and processing concessions were channelled through Pertamina, which became the most profitable Abri-run enterprise. When a payments crisis erupted in 1974, the ties that bind were so strong, Suharto was reluctant to dismiss Sutowo, even under intense domestic and international pressure.

It was precisely this kind of issue which, from the mid-1970s, began to divide Suharto and his men from other officers. Those who felt uneasy were at first mostly sidelined or retired senior officers, who felt Suharto was strengthening the military's role in society at the expense of the development of civilian institutions. The best known, and perhaps only genuine proponent of this view was Simatupang. He clearly saw the dual function as something temporary. 'To be successful', he used to say before his death in 1990, 'the dual function must work towards its own elimination'.

Others went along with Simatupang after they fell from Suharto's grace and began to seek the means to attack Suharto. To many in Jakarta, for example, the social democratic bleatings of a man like retired General Sumitro in 1989, jarred too much with the image of Sumitro a decade before as the all-powerful security czar until his implication in the January 1974 Malari disturbances brought him, some say literally, to his knees. 'It was never the army's philosophy to perpetuate the crisis situation that prevailed in 1965,' Sumitro said in early 1988:

> The intensity and involvement of the army in political life is completely dependent on the political situation of the moment. If we feel it is no longer needed, we have to release all the jobs to civilians.[18]

Yet, as security chief in 1972, Sumitro had rejected Nasution's proposal to alter the stress on 'stabilization' to 'dynamization' within Abri's doctrine.[19] In Indonesia, it seems, officers become more democratically minded after they have fallen from grace.

The character of this opposition is significant, because those who began to form up against Suharto were among those who helped bring him to power. There were four so-called kingmakers of the New Order – men whose actions after the September 1965 coup enabled Suharto to come to power: Lieutenant-General Sarwo Edhie Wibowo, the special forces officer who carried out key operations to restore order in Jakarta in September 1965; and H. R. Dharsono, Kemal Idris and Amir Machmud, all three of whom had a hand in the elaborate bluff which enabled Suharto to wrest supreme authority from Sukarno in March 1966. Among them only Machmud subsequently remained loyal to Suharto. Idris and Dharsono made their feelings known in the late 1970s, and Dharsono – the most outspoken – was eventually imprisoned in 1984 after being implicated in a Muslim riot in North Jakarta.[20]

Sarwo Edhie's story is instructive, because the extent of his opposition to Suharto only became widely known after his death in November 1989. As commander of the special forces, Sarwo Edhie was called upon by Suharto to crush the 30 September movement in the first days of October 1965. Having done so, in mid-October, Sarwo Edhie was sent to Central Java to eliminate supporters of the coup – presumed to be members of the PKI. Later, Sarwo Edhie admitted his participation in the killings of thousands of villagers in rural Java accused of Communist sympathies. The following year, student protests and military intimidation orchestrated by Sarwo Edhie and his special forces, helped persuade President Sukarno to invest Suharto with authority to govern the country by the 11 March 1966 Order. In sum, Sarwo Edhie is credited with spearheading Suharto's drive to power.

Not surprisingly, Sarwo Edhie's death on 9 November 1989 was the occasion of considerable comment on his role (amazingly enough, none reflecting the less savoury tasks he undertook). The press chose to play up the fact that Sarwo Edhie never enriched himself from his position. The respected daily *Kompas* described him as a man 'whose actions matched his words'. 'Sarwo Edhie always gave his thoughts to the interests of the people', said a former student leader of the 1966 generation. 'Kingmaker', 'idealist', 'hero' were all terms used to eulogize the former commando whose subsequent career never saw him rise above inspector-general at the foreign ministry.

Judging from Sarwo Edhie's career after 1966, Suharto clearly mistrusted the man. He was sent to be regional commander of North Sumatra in 1968. (Regional commands off-Java are not considered influential.) His post as commandant of the prestigious army academy at Magelang was cut short in 1974 (after the Malari affair) and he was subsequently sent to be ambassador in South Korea. Sarwo Edhie never openly voiced his misgivings about Suharto, preferring instead in typically Javanese fashion to place respect of those in authority above his own feelings. Other assessements were less charitable. 'He was nothing but a robot,' remarked one senior government official. The tough commando's loyalty and patience held until 1988, when he resigned as a member of parliament. His action, extremely rare for those in public office, was construed as a protest – most likely because he objected to Suharto's choice of Sudharmono as a Vice-President after his re-election in March that year.[21] Sarwo Edhie's enigmatic opposition to Suharto illustrates the deep cultural inhibitions which, exchewing open disloyalty or opposition, may have prevented Indonesia falling victim to an endless round of military-inspired coups and counter-coups.

Instead of rewarding the 'kingmakers' with key positions after 1966, Suharto fell back on a group of officers with whom he had worked closely during his years in the field. These included men like Major-General Alamsjah Ratu Perwiranegara, with whom he had worked in army headquarters since 1960. Ali Murtopo, Sœdjono Hœmardani and Yoga Sugama were fellow officers from his days in Central Java. Benny Murdani and Sudomo were with Suharto during the West Irian campaign in the early 1960s. This raises the question of whether the men who are credited with bringing Suharto to power anticipated the results of their handiwork, and also why they never lifted a finger to do anything about it.

Ironically enough, the nature of Suharto's ties with Abri are not easily divined from his own military background. For years, it was asssumed that Suharto was part of a group, and as such could count on the loyalty of its members. In reality, Suharto has always fostered relations with individuals rather than groups, playing one off against another and forcing those close to him to expend a great deal of energy spying on or conniving against one another. Indonesians have coined the acronym 'Kiss', or *Ke istana sendiri-sendiri*: 'to the palace one by one' to describe his style. In crude terms the system worked best of all if two individuals were given different or even conflicting orders and were left to squabble between themselves. They inevitably destroyed each other. Looking at the large number of retired officers who now sit ranged against him – even though they mostly mouth ineffectual insults with barely disguised bitterness at their failure to retain influence – it is hard to understand why Suharto chose to so deliberately alienate rather than foster links among the ranks.

Competition between Murtopo with his pervasive intelligence network known as 'Opsus' (Special Operations), and General Sumitro, who commanded the powerful internal security command known as *Kopkamtib*, resulted in a showdown in early 1974 which has never been satisfactorily explained. Loyal members of Murtopo's group have tried to paint Sumitro, the overweight but canny former internal security chief, as a man who had ambitions to succeed Suharto. They are probably not far wrong. Sumitro employed his considerable power to stir up student protests, prompting mass demonstrations and the burning of cars during a visit by Japanese Prime Minister Tanaka in January 1974. Murtopo, so this version goes, won the day for Suharto and had Sumitro effectively fired. Significantly, even the downfall of a man as powerful as Sumitro prompted no backlash against Suharto from within the army.

With Murtopo dead (he died of a heart attack in 1984), and Sumitro at large in business and media circles, it could not be too long before the man many referred to as the 'thinking general' began propounding his own view on the 1974 'Malari' incident and other, more pressing, contemporary issues. Sumitro launched his new image as a concerned member of the older Abri generation shortly after Suharto's re-election in 1988. In calling for the proper implementation of the Constitution, more democracy and a fair contest for the presidency in 1993, the near-explicit message was that it was time for Suharto to go.

In the course of 1989, and into 1990, the ebullient former security chief received many visitors in his office in the southern suburb of Kemang – where he ran a small business. Here, first the Vice-President's, then the President's portrait disappeared from the wall behind his desk. From this desk he wrote leading articles for the newspapers, calling for more openness. He lobbied Abri leaders, bombarded them with letters on all manner of political issues, and by his own testimony openly discussed ways of 'ensuring a smooth transition of power in 1993'.[22] Such isolated instances of open defiance were at odds with Abri's respect for the Javanese cult of obedience, yet it was as if these were fissures leading to obviously much larger pools of discontent beneath the surface.

The source of Sumitro's opposition to Suharto dated back to the mid-1970s, and his belief that Suharto should step down after two terms. Later he blamed Suharto's advisers for persuading him not to listen to Abri and stay on. Like many other serving Abri officers at the time Sumitro would have been incensed at the informal freedom of action granted to Murtopo. Murtopo was an intelligence officer and was therefore viewed with suspicion by the regular army. But his power was considerable. At its peak in the mid 1970s, foreign ministry officials were at a loss to explain why Indonesia was apparently forging links with intelligence services in Taiwan, the military in Laos and operating undercover in Papua New Guinea. Murtopo was a perfect tool for Suharto because he used informal and ultimately expendable channels. In fact, some years after a rash of mysterious killings that swept Java in the early 1980s, knowledgeable sources were of the view that many of the victims were probabably members of Murtopo's shady intelligence network – ordered terminated after Murtopo's death – as well as the petty criminals they were presumed to be at the time.

With hindsight, it seems clear that Suharto never felt at ease with the Abri hierachy after he came to power. In the first place, he was not considered a member of the army's inner circle, most of whom met their end on that fateful night at the end of September 1965. A recent biography of one, the late General Ahmad Yani (by his daughter Amelia), revealed that Suharto had never been considered 'a friend' of her father.[23] Suharto was forced instead to rely on lower-ranking intelligence officers and men with whom he had worked in his previous commands outside Jakarta. Naturally this rankled other senior officers of Suharto's generation. More importantly, it meant that more reasoned, objective approaches to the army's role in society were marginalized along with the intellectual elite which helped formulate Abri's doctrine. As Jenkins points out, the New Order has been characterized by two distinct approaches to the military in politics: one essentially committed to complete domination of all the institutions of state, and close to Suharto; the other, increasingly question-ing the degree of Abri involvement in politics, and at odds with the president.

Once firmly at the helm, another of Suharto's tactics was to shore up his position by constantly pitting the generals against each other. This was facilitated by the creation of intelligence bodies (civil and military) which, aside from their stated internal security role, provided ample access to knowledge of what the military itself was up to. In Nasution's view, this has been Suharto's major accomplishment regarding Abri: to weave an intelligence network so intricate that the officer corps is mistrustful of one another and incapable of uniting against him. In frequent contact with younger officers, Nasution often heard of their fear of speaking up in the military academy or staff college in case the all-pervasive 'intel' later used their views to hinder their promotion. Rather than a hierarchical chain of command typical of military administration, Suharto fostered a more arbitrary system based on personal loyalty, which allowed officers to come from nowhere into senior positions, thus further hindering the unity Abri has always found so elusive.

The principle was also applied to Abri's broader structure. Under the New Order the importance of regional commands and the divisional loyalties they bred has declined. The regiment-like titles given to these commands; *Diponegoro* (for Central Java) and *Siliwangi* (for West Java) have passed out of official usage, replaced by less inspiring numbered commands. At the same time elite units under central command, such as Kostrad, and the Koppassandra special forces have assumed much greater operational importance. The confinement of operational capability and mobility to a relatively small number of troops located in the capital is a generic aspect of military organization in the region, and is consciously or otherwise a form of insurance against military-led coups.

Also with the benefit of hindsight, Abri's major problem under the New Order has been the need to maintain the relevance of its political role. During the early years of the New Order, with memories of how close the country had supposedly come to Communist rule still fresh, no one questioned the *dwi-fungsi*. Abri provided the key players in politics, organized the groups they led, and when election time came, got out the vote. In each of the four elections Suharto has held, support from the armed forces has ensured a hefty majority for the government's Golkar party. Abri's territorial network has proved as effective an electoral machine as any. As proof of this, in the 1987 general election Abri for the first time decided to lend tacit support to one of the two minority parties, the Christian-backed Indonesian Democratic Party (PDI). Abri-organized PDI

77

rallies in Jakarta resulted in spectacular electoral gains for the party in the capital.

Golkar itself is Abri's creation. As already mentioned, the marked swing to the left under Sukarno eventually forced the military to form a civilian counter-force. A range of organizations known as 'functional groups' were founded under Abri sponsorship in the 1960s for this purpose. The most prominent of these, SOKSI, was a quasi-trade union organization composed of workers in military-owned state enterprises. Its chief purpose was as a mass-based political organization to counter the PKI. Abri's more or less open backing of SOKSI proved to be the only way to forge unity among anti-communist groups and, more importantly guarantee their protection.[24]

Organizations like SOKSI and Sekber Golkar, the forebears of Golkar, placed Abri at the centre of institutionalized politics and opened up a pandora's box of troubles. Some officers believed that fostering an organization like Golkar was taking Abri's political role too far, and that the purity of Abri risked political pollution. Once the PKI had been defeated, powerful civilian groups, notably Muslim activists, began to resent Abri's contribution to the secularization of politics through its role in Golkar. This drove another wedge into the officer corps, dividing Muslim from non-Muslim, and laying the basis for future political divisions. The Abri-Golkar nexus, and the perception of Golkar as a ruling party, meant that Abri increasingly became associated with – rather than positioned above the state – as the doctrine preaches. That certain officers were concerned about this state of affairs became clear within a decade of Suharto coming to power. It certainly fuelled concerns about the value of the dual function

Strange as it may seem for an army which lives by doctrine, Abri has undergone several periods of introspection and reorganization in the past twenty years. Initially, a rash of army seminars clustered around the birth of the New Order confirmed the military's central role in the government of Indonesia. 'All the people's hopes for well-being are focused on the armed forces in general and the army in particular,' declared the published product of the second army seminar in August' 1966. By the time of Suharto's third election in 1978, there were those who had become convinced that Abri's continued overt support of the government was a betrayal of the people's hopes and the sanctity of Abri.

This polarization of views crystallized around two papers written between 1977 and 1980 which dwelt extensively on the role of Abri in politics. The 'Seskoad Paper', written in 1977–8, took the view that politics was corrupting Abri's spirit and therefore hampering its social function and defence of the Constitution. The paper recommended that Abri remain above groups: 'the politics of Abri are those of the 1945 Constitution, not the politics of a group or the politics of Abri as a group'. The implication, according to the paper's author, Brigadier-General Abdulkadir Besar, was that the concept of the dual function should not be viewed as a vehicle for the accumulation of power by the military: 'military officials should only be appointed to political positions as they are needed, and then only with the approval of the people'.[25]

Clearly this view implied a distancing of Abri from the current regime. Suharto and his group responded by formulating their own version of Abri's political philosphy, which was that Abri must choose sides, and cannot remain above all groups. In one of his infrequent but periodic emotional outbursts, Suharto lashed out at Abri at a commanders meeting in the Sumatran town of Pekanbaru at the end of March 1980. Against a background of disagreement between Muslim political groups and the government over the implementation of the state political philosophy of *Pancasila*, Suharto urged Abri to 'choose partners, friends who truly defend Pancasila, and have no doubts whatsoever in Pancasila'.[26] Suharto was clearly demanding Abri's unwavering support for Golkar in the 1982 election, and the Seskoad paper, together with some of the people who backed it, were quietly shelved.

A short while later a massive rejuvenation of the officer corps, involving the transfer of command posts to a younger generation of officers, began to occur. In the first six months of 1983 close to a hundred senior command positions were changed as many of the older generation came up against limits to their one year extensions after the mandatory retirement age of fifty-five.[27] For the barely trained older generation of officers which had come through the struggle for independence and been rewarded with status and position as the backbone of the national elite, the prospect of yielding to a more numerous, professionally trained body of men emerging from the military academies of Central Java, rankled. Set against the academy graduates who began passing out in the early 1960s, the ragtag militia roots of the old revolutionary paled. Would the new professionals show their seniors the respect they were owed? Would they try to reduce the army's involvement in civil affairs? If there was the slightest risk of either of these two possibilities, how could the elders retain their power and influence?

Loyalty to Suharto was one of the best options. So long as the country was led by a '45er', there was a place for them among the ranks of the leadership. In 1982, the 1945 generation retained a near monopoly of military *kekaryaan* positions in the higher central bureaucracy. This solid control by the Generation of 1945 persisted despite the fact that all those in Abri born by 1925 had retired from active duty status. There is something obsessional about the way the 45ers have clung on. The organization of retired officers in veterans organizations like *Pepabri* was imbued with almost as much status as the active officer corps. Stress was laid on projecting veterans as important senior figures; as *pejuang*, or 'fighters', whose presence was required to keep the spirit of the revolution alive. The successor generation crisis, as some have styled it, has never really been resolved, and although no longer even in the government, retired generals like Nasution and Sumitro continue to assert senior status over their juniors in active command positions.

Against this background in March 1983, Abri began a far reaching reorganization of its structure. The ostensible rationale for this reorganization was to advance Abri's professionalism and at the same time curb costs. Behind it lay the vision of Abri's new commander, General L. B. Murdani. Murdani's background as an intelligence officer, and perhaps also his Central Javanese upbringing taught him the value of strict centralized control at every level of the armed forces.

This was reflected in the main elements of the reform programme, which tightened central control over territorial (provincial-level) commanders (*Kodams*) by eliminating intermediate regional-level commands (*Kowilhans*) and made *Kodam* commanders directly answerable to Jakarta. Murdani's strong belief in Abri's socio-political role, resulted in more *sospol* (socio-political) officers being assigned at the *Kodam* and *Korem* (sub-provincial) levels. Also included was the scrapping of regional air and naval territorial commands, with a resulting strengthening of army authority in the armed forces. 'It adds up to an intelligence man's vision of how an army should be organized; very much on the alert at the micro-level, but always plugged into macro-direction at the top,' commented one observer at the time.[28] Subsequently, the reform programme became a useful vehicle for Murdani to place his intelligence cronies and subordinates in key command positions, which they held until Murdani's operational influence began to wane after 1988.

Murdani was faced with the task of finding jobs for a slew of army officers emerging from the academy. The more streamlined command structure was designed in part to offset their numbers and potential fractiousness by limiting the number of powerful commands. Abri was also under pressure, as always, to trim costs and at the same time preserve political influence. The elevation of the *Sospol* function achieved both ends admirably. As in previous reorganizations, form took precedence over substance, and no one doubted that for the next few years Abri policy would be a function of Murdani. The reorganization helped; under the new defence and security structure the posts of minister of defence and Abri commander were split up, conferring ministerial rank and overall command of troops on the latter, leaving the minister of defence a pale shadow by comparison.

Murdani has occupied the minds of military and political analysts in Indonesia for almost a decade. In Suharto's Indonesia this is something of an achievement, as most potentially powerful men saw their careers shunted into comfortable but shady sidings almost as soon as they fell prey to the mentioners. Murdani stands apart from other Abri commanders in this respect. He survived both as an aggressive and unpopular Suharto loyalist and, after falling out with the President in early 1988, as an outspoken independent operator who by 1990 was still considered an important factor in the power equation. Even after he left the cabinet in March 1993, many Indonesians refused to dismiss Murdani as a political player.

Like some of the so-called 'bridging generation' which immediately followed the '45ers', Murdani had gained some important combat experience. As a young officer in the 1950s he saw action in operations against rebellious Muslims in West Java, the 1957–8 *Permesta* revolt, and also participated in operations against the Dutch in Irian Jaya in 1962, where his exploits as a paratroop officer first brought him to Suharto's attention.

Murdani joined the army before finishing high school in 1950. He was one of the few officers trained at the army's first formal training centre (P3AD) in Bandung in the 1950s. Only 18 years old and the centre's youngest student, Murdani was apparently diligent. 'He was one of the most hard-working and would stay up at night studying. He was very fond of reading books both on military science and general knowledge', recalled a classmate.[29] All the same, not having attended a formal military academy, Murdani was never credited with a sophisticated military background; something he made up for using his wits and a considerable flair for intelligence work.

Murdani's stern looks masking a lively intellect and sense of humour, earned him popularity among his seniors and fear among those below him. A Javanese, born the son of a railway official in Cepu Central Java, Murdani came from a strong Catholic background. Murdani's trace of European ancestry (his mother was a Eurasian) marked him apart from other Javanese generals. He could play both insider and outsider in the cultural context. His ten years overseas, at Fort Benning in the US, and in the diplomatic service from the mid-1960s, polished his ability to deal with outsiders and understand broader strategic concepts. His close links with Singapore, Malaysia and South Korea (where he served as consul-general in the 1970s) have proved particularly helpful in strategic defence matters. In the

1988–93 cabinet he served as Foreign Minister *ad interim* when Ali Alatas was overseas – as he frequently was.

Murdani was propelled through the ranks under Suharto's wing. He was the youngest lieutenant-general of his generation. He played a leading role in the 1975 invasion of East Timor, where he earned a less savoury reputation. His promotion from the staff post of intelligence assistant at Abri HQ to Abri commander in 1983 was unprecedented, and almost certainly resented. Insiders say the president treated him like a son, and certainly the early 1980s saw Murdani as a member of the inner circle, advising Suharto and acting as something of a mentor to his children. But his reputation among the troops was never as good. Unlike General Mohammad Yusuf, his predecessor as Abri commander, Murdani was not one to occupy his time with the welfare of his men. He had favourites, and these men were promoted into a circle of 'golden boys' resented by other officers. He employed the intelligence apparatus he created as a means of maintaining order in the ranks, something that in the eyes of many fellow officers made him less than a soldier's soldier.

The Abri that Murdani presided over in the late 1980s was beginning to realize its own political shortcomings. After years of manipulation under Suharto's presidency, senior staff officers were finally beginning to realize they had no leverage over the president. After almost a quarter of a century of playing a dual political and military role, a growing number of younger military officers had also, as already indicated, begun to question Abri's role in politics. The coincidence of these changing attitudes with a period of political uncertainty over national leadership, put Abri in a tight spot. It was probably as a result of this that Murdani and others fashioned in late 1987 a new law on soldiership which, in its original draft stages, aimed to boost the power of Abri commander and define more sharply the technical separation of powers between the executive and the armed forces. As in the late 1970s, Abri moved to put a distance between itself and Suharto.

The move aimed to play Suharto at his own game; achieve political ends by constitutionial means. A close reading of a draft dated 27 November 1987 revealed an attempt to 'correct' the oath sworn by every soldier to ensure emphasis on allegiance to the flag and the Constitution, not to the head of state.[30] The military has never been happy with the vague constitutional notion of the president as 'supreme commander'. But here Abri miscalculated the extent to which, if he wished, Suharto could manipulate the parliamentary process to suit his own ends.

In the closing weeks of 1987, the draft law received a surprisingly rough ride before a parliamentary commission. When it was eventually passed in Febuary 1988, the offending ambiguities had been ironed out. Crowning

Abri's defeat, Murdani was summoned by Suharto the same month and told he was to hand over command of Abri to General Try Sutrisno, who as army commander, was Murdani's predictable successor. Murdani was visibly shocked by the news. He, along with everybody else, expected no changes to the armed forces before the presidential election. Although he was expected to remain in the cabinet, the period he spent in limbo before the new cabinet appointments in mid-March was a personal embarrassment for a man whose rise had been meteoric since the 1970s.

From then on Murdani was dubbed the man most likely to lead a *putsch* against Suharto. His embarrassing dismissal before the presidential election was seen as enough of a motive. Yet, while there can be no doubt about his disillusionment with Suharto, it would be wrong to assume Murdani is a rebel. One keen observer of the military scene in Jakarta recalled how during a minor coup attempt in 1956 involving the special forces – to which Murdani was then attached – the young lieutenant reported sick that day and thus avoided being arrested by the authorities. 'It shows', said the source, 'that Murdani is not the rebellious type, and is more concerned with suppressing rather than inciting insurrection'.[31] During the events of March 1988 and subsequently, Murdani's loyalty to the system was tested and proven. Oddly enough, this only enhanced his perceived role as chief mischief-maker and Suharto protagonist.

In the shadow of Suharto's assured re-election for a fifth consecutive term in March 1988, Abri's esteem and power were at a low ebb. An attempt to enhance its grip on power, though subtle in its approach, had been thwarted. The strong man behind the move had been unceremoniously ousted. Murdani's replacement, General Try Sutrisno, was Suharto's former adjutant and regarded as the President's lackey. But if Suharto believed this to be entirely the case, he miscalculated.

The MPR convened on 1 March 1988. As previously explained, under the New Order the main purpose of the MPR was to re-elect Suharto by unanimous acclamation. The election of the vice-president, and adoption of the state's 'Guidelines of Policy', are the body's only other duties in this 'queen bee'-like display of activity before it adjourns for another five years. The beauty of the system is that the MPR which elects Suharto and his policies is composed of different members from the MPR which elected him and his policies for the previous term. Thus the notion of accountability loses currency, as the President himself has a decisive say in the composition of the body which will then elect him.

In this case, however, Suharto was unusually less explicit about his choice of vice-president, saying only that the MPR's choice of candidate should fit certain criteria. These, he said, included the stipulation that the candidate be acceptable to people 'who express their support through the dominant political group'. Suharto was referring to Golkar, which received a hefty 73 per cent majority in general elections the previous April. Although it seemed obvious Suharto was referring in this case to his long-serving State Secretary, Sudharmono, who at the time was also chairman of Golkar, the President's ambiguity opened the way for alternatives to be thrown up. Sensing an opportunity to make a point, Abri jumped in.

No one doubted the assertion of Jailani's Naro's 'alternative' candidacy for the vice-presidency on 29 Febuary was at Abri's prompting. Naro, the head of the Muslim-backed United Development Party (PPP) was not considered a man of principle. The 59 year-old West Sumatran's career was marked by opportunism and ambition, and he was not popular with the majority of Muslims. He was also unpopular in the ranks of the party – all the more so for having presided over a miserable loss of votes in the April 1987 elections. But the PPP was anxious to regain respectability as a political force, and seeing Abri's encouragement of Naro, they stood behind him.

Naro's nomination, together with the PPP's sustained stand on amendments to the outlines of state policy, electrified the assembly and generated a sense that new ground was being broken. 'He [Naro] has become a symbolic figure for those who feel the need for political diversity and who are reluctant to accept what seem to be prearranged decisions,' declared the English-language *Jakarta Post* at the time. The prearranged decision Abri most objected too, was Sudharmono's nomination for the vice-presidency, and at this point they appeared ready to take something of a stand against the president over the issue.

Sudharmono is almost as enigmatic a figure as Suharto, the man he has served since, as a young military lawyer, he joined Suharto's special staff in 1966. Born in Gresik, East Java, in 1927, Sudharmono joined the army during the independence struggle, probably as an irregular militiaman, or *laskar*. He went on in the late 1950s to attend the military law academy, and has seen no active military service then. In 1966, he joined Suharto's staff as a cabinet secretary, rising to the position of State Secretary in 1973. Despite seeing no active military service after 1945, he attained the rank of lieutenant-general and at one point in 1977 served briefly as Suharto's military secretary.

If Abri agrees on anything it is on a ferverent dislike of Sudharmono. The reason for this is clear. A shadowy figure who at the height of his career as State Secretary acted as principal gatekeeper for the President, Sudharmono actively sought to reduce Abri's political influence by undermining their financial strength and pull over the bureaucracy. While popular and powerful generals like Mohammad Yusuf fell prey to Suharto's resentment of potential competition in the late 1970s, Sudharmono's more subtle organizational prowess enabled him to become a virtual prime minister, controlling access to Suharto and dispensing patronage through appointments to the bureaucracy and contracts to the business community.[32]

As chairman of Golkar in the period 1983–8, he weakened Abri's grasp over the organization by cultivating civilian politicians. Under a presidential order he engineered, all tenders and contracts over Rp 200 million in value had to pass through his office. Using 'Presidential Decree No.10', the State Secretariat was empowered to nullify the recommendations of government agencies which in the past threw contracts in the direction of businesses linked to the military. Under the laudable umbrella of promoting indigenous business and the use of domestic products, Sudharmono began to cultivate his own group of favoured business interests. In the process, the military began to lose out.[33]

Incensed by Suharto's move to place Sudharmono, theoretically at least, a heartbeat away from the presidency, Abri conducted a more or less open campaign to oppose his candidacy at the MPR. Murdani, arm in arm with Sutrisno and Mohammad Yusuf – now head of the largely ceremonial Supreme Advisory Council, but still popular – paraded on the steps of the MPR building, in a symbolic show of force. The gambit failed. Abri's impotency at the MPR was amply demonstrated when a disgruntled officer, Brigadier-General Ibrahim Salleh, strode up to the podium and began to denounce Sudharmono. He had not got very far when he was removed, and declared to be under stress. Senior Abri officers, including Murdani and Sutrisno, also tried persuading Suharto personally to change his mind. Suharto refused to budge on the issue, and Sudharmono was duly 'elected' vice-president. The Abri leadership elected to challenge Suharto openly employing constitutional means, and failed. The attempt, though, set a precedent for subsequent jousts with the President, and appeared to set Abri apart from the Executive – so long as its unity held firm.

In hindsight, it must be said that Suharto has never selected a vice-president who concurrently held an influential military position. Such a move would undoubtedly be risky, as it would place the army in a position from which they could constitutionally challenge Suharto. Sudharmono was a logical choice. What Suharto did not bank on, or underestimated, was the strength of Abri's feelings against the man, and the way in which this resentment could subsequently be wielded as a weapon against the president. Perhaps also, there was by this stage, a feeling in Abri circles that

Suharto should pave the way for the succession by appointing as vice-president the military's choice for the leadership. For there is no doubt that most of the Abri leadership still consider the presidency to be a military fiefdom.

The row between Abri leaders and Suharto over Sudharmono marked a turning point for the military. It jolted senior officers into realizing, dual function notwithstanding, that they were powerless to influence the course of political events on a grand scale anymore. Of course, this had been the real situation for some considerable time. More importantly, it persuaded many of them that the time had come to begin redressing the balance of power. Outwardly, of course, it was important for Abri to maintain impeccably loyal credentials with the presidential palace. There were good reasons for this. First Abri had to avoid alarming the President and prompting another embarrassing outburst like the 1980 Pekanbaru speech. More important, however, was the necessity of preserving unity in the ranks. For any moves against the executive almost certainly would divide the army into camps of varying degrees of loyalty to Suharto as well as those for and against any overtly interventionist move.

By now, the officer corps was dominated in the middle and upper ranks by men who graduated after 1965. Of the 450 officers who graduated in 1965, 300 remained in active service. They had spanned the New Order, and witnessed its fiery birth. Were they willing to sanction a repeat performance? The legacy was still very much alive. They had all been taught that threats to the state emnanated from within. Ideologically speaking, they were committed to the defence of the state. Yet while the doctrine clearly implied this loyalty fell short of the elected executive, Suharto's conception was that anything less than Abri's commitment to the government was tantamount to treason. Many officers were confused by what the doctrine imparted on the one hand and by the political reality of Abri's position on the other. As one colonel put it: 'the army is the centre of gravity in this country; everything eventually returns to the centre of gravity'.

Another way of looking at the situation by 1990 is to draw comparisons with the army's position in the mid-1960s. Declassified US embassy material from the period leave the impression of a military establishment confused and undecided about how to head off Sukarno's tilt towards the Communist fold. In March 1965, alarmed by the growing strength of the PKI in Indonesia, President Lyndon Johnson despatched a trusted senior diplomat, Ellsworth Bunker, to Jakarta to make an independent assessment for the White House. Bunker concluded, among other things, that Sukarno's sympathy for the PKI created a 'serious dilemma' for the army:

How to inhibit the further expansion of PKI power while remaining loyal to Sukarno when Sukarno himself was encouraging PKI expansion. So far the army's response has been to remain publicly aloof from the conflict between the PKI and its civilian rivals, to concentrate on strengthening its own imperfect internal unity, to give ground grudgingly when pressed, and to plan against the day when Sukarno's death releases it from its dilemna.[34]

Arguably, the army faces a similar dilemma today. Suharto is, if not a popular president, strong enough to command popular support. Over the last decade he has often favoured elements unsympathetic to the army's pre-eminent role in the establishment – Murtopo and Sudharmono, to name but two. In the 1993–98 cabinet, this role seems to have been conferred on the minister of research and technology, Professor B.J. Habibie. Grudgingly, Abri has been forced to give way on a number of occasions and seen its influence over state matters ebb further. Publicly the army espouses loyalty to the New Order, while at the same time its leaders encourage moves to work quietly towards a change of its leadership. Internal unity is as imperfect today as it was then – not so much overtly, but if the army were to take a stand, no one can be sure they would all stand together. Murdani tacitly admitted as much when he said in early 1991 that a similar 'atmosphere of confusion' to that prevailing in 1965, exists today.[35]

The period 1988–91 saw Abri grapple with its political dilemma. Behind the scenes the *Sospol* chiefs and Murdani's military intelligence network attempted one strategy after another to discredit Sudharmono. They went as far as reviving the Communist threat and linking Sudharmono to the left – an allegation he was forced to deny publicly. Abri spent vast sums on a campaign to dislodge Sudharmono from his position as Golkar chairman in the run-up to the party's quiennial congress in November 1988. To do so meant having to persuade many Abri officers to leave their active service careers and serve as party functionaries at the grass-roots level. Abri's efforts paid off. 120 military officers were elected as regional Golkar chairmen, securing 60–70 per cent of all regional delegates to the congress. With a comfortable majority of delegates at the Golkar congress, Abri cut the ground from under Sudharmono. He was replaced by Wahono, a some-what colourless but fastidious general who was a former East Java provincial commander and later became governor of the province.

To what extent Abri scored points at the 1988 Golkar assembly is another matter. At the time it seemed like a restoration of political balance, crediting a much depleted military account. But equally, Suharto's interests were served by the outcome of the congress. Sudharmono's appointment as vice-president in March 1988 made many feel uneasy about his continuing leadership of Golkar. Sudharmono needed to be reined in. By allowing Abri to do the job, Suharto split Golkar and intensified civilian-military antipathies within the establishment. Thus the affair may ultimately have worked to Suharto's, not Abri's advantage. Ironically, Golkar, without Sudharmono at the helm, looked less capable of action independent of Suharto – less the 'ruling' and more the ruler's party. In the wake of the Golkar congress, Abri's capacity to influence events became less evident.

Complicating their campaign to maintain a stake in the national leadership, Abri increasingly found itself drawn into the broader atmosphere of political catharsis gripping the upper levels of society. Another dilemma evolved. Was Abri to support or suppress these calls for more political openness in the country? Abri's doctrine preached that it stood with the people. But in practice the apparatus of control symbolized by the all-pervasive territorial system, required strict discipline and order – neither quality fitted the newfangled ideas of openness and democratization.

There appears to be no consensus within Abri on this issue. In December 1989, Army Commander General Edi Sudrajat, regarded by many as the epitome of a tough infantry officer, surprised everyone at a meeting of active commanding officers at the Magelang Military Academy. Indonesians were now better educated, he said, they want their differences discussed more openly. 'As such they want more active participation in the decsision making process'. Sudrajat went on to call for an end to the 'foot-stomping, father knows best style of leadership'. In this context, he warned, the military did not wish to be 'mere fire-extinguishers' for those in power.[36] Sudrajat was not the first or the last openly to put a distance between Abri and the New Order leadership, and he seemed to reflect a revival of this kind of thinking within the army.

The results of an army seminar presided over by Sudrajat in December 1990 lent credence to this view. Set against a background of intense debate in civilian intellectual circles about political openness, senior officers concluded that in the coming twenty-five year period, changes to the established political culture would have to be contemplated. Joined in their deliberations for the first time by civilians from all walks of life, the seminar concluded that Indonesians were becoming more educated, critical and wanted more of a stake in the system. They would therefore almost certainly want a bigger say in selecting the national leadership. Even more significant given the heated debate over succession, the army recommended that 'officials' must be given a clear set of guidlelines about the length of their tenure, and must be 'ready to be replaced if they are no longer capable of serving and endanger the interests of society'.[37]

A consensus was hard to discern. Abri Commander Try Sutrisno stuck valiantly to the old line. Abri remained the 'stabilizer' and 'dynamizer' of society; a sense of 'national discipline' was essential. The dual function was irreversible, and will never change, Sutrisno declared in August 1990. This despite earlier statements from his *Sospol* chief, General Harsudiono Hartas, and his own information officer, Brigadier-General Nurhadi Purwosaputro, which implied that a reassessement of the dual function was under way.[38] Meanwhile, the Minister of Home affairs, Rudini, announced in mid-1990 that the government was actively reducing the proportion of senior appointments to the bureaucracy allotted to Abri personnel.

Part of the problem was the difficulty reading the new Abri leadership. Sutrisno confused political analysts. His former role as presidential adjutant led many to assume he was in Suharto's pocket. The fresh-faced East Javanese had also been taken under Murdani's wing when he was Army Commander. Murdani placed some of his most trusted men on Sutrisno's general staff at Abri headquarters. Sutrisno was considered popular with Muslims because of a cultivated image of piety – and the more hesitant, compassionate role he played during the September 1984 Muslim riots in Tanjung Priok. He was popularly conceived as something Murdani could not be; when he became Abri Commander in 1988 Sutrisno moved to the forefront of those dubbed as likely presidential candidates.

Working against him in elite circles was his lack of intellectual clout, and a tendency to stick rigidly to established policy lines, policies which, in the charged political climate of the late 1980s, required a great deal more mental agility to defend or re-cast in more acceptable terms. Sudrajat was rigid too, in his own way. But his heart was deemed to be in the right place. The infantry is idealized as the wellspring of pure and uncorrupted defenders of the state, a mould Sudrajat appeared to be cast from. A former special forces officer with considerable field experience, Sudrajat was not associated with the politically inclined element of Abri. If anything, he was considered among those who advocated a more professional role for Abri. In late 1990 he underwent cancer surgery in Tokyo, a development which sparked off intense speculation about his replacement and fears that Suharto would move to replace independent-minded officers like Sudrajat with men closer to his own circle. Certainly it was beginning to look hard for promising younger officers who demonstrated too much intellectual curiosity about the political future to obtain promotion – even if they were favoured by their superiors.

Meanwhile, against a background of rising popular demands for political change on the campuses and in Jakarta intellectual circles, Abri found itself for the first time no longer in command of the national debate. A series of meetings with university lecturers from Gajah Mada University in Jogyakarta in 1989–90, saw Abri leaders ask the faculty members for advice on how to improve the intellectual standard of its officers. In an unprecedented move, university teachers were invited to give lectures at the Magelang Military Academy. This shocked the civilian faculty members involved. As members of the 1966 generation they saw the military spearhead the New Order's rise to power, learned to respect its leaders and fear the all-pervasive intel. Now they found Abri's leadership lacking in a sense of purpose and unable to match the civilian intellectuals who were calling for political change. This weakened their fear of military power, and ultimately their respect for those who wielded it.[39]

Amid the confusion about where Abri stood on social and political change, and the complex manoeuvring around the succession issue, Abri confronted two rather more serious problems. Early in 1990, it became evident that Suharto was pushing to have officers unambiguously loyal to him appointed to senior staff positions in Jakarta. All senior appointments were made on the recommendation of Abri HQ, but such recommendations remained subject to approval by Suharto. Some Abri leaders were astonished by Suharto's decision to ignore their advice and appoint a string of former adjutants to senior positions in the course of 1990. The new police chief and Jakarta garrison commander were both former presidential adjutants. In the case of the Jakarta garrison, Suharto's choice, Major-General Kentot Harseno, was not even on the army's list of candidates.

At the same time the intellectual crisis which had been brewing in the ranks over the reformulation of doctrine and redefinition of the dual function was intensifying in the wake of a round of seminars for each of the four branches of the armed forces. Clearly, as the results of the December 1990 army seminar indicate, there were those in Abri who saw the need to return to the people and adopt a platform of political reforms – echoing indeed, the rhetoric of the late 1970s. If not, Abri was in danger of being cast in an anachronistic and therefore unpopular mould. Equally, though, Abri was reluctant to cast off its role as the enforcer of unity and guardian against anti-national feelings. The army's tough action against so-called threats to the unity of the state in Aceh and East Timor presented a sharp contrast to the intellectual flirtation of senior officers with participatory democracy.

Thus by early 1991, Abri appeared to be losing its way. The image of the firm steady hand on the national tiller, with the president in command, had been dislodged by another image; that of a military establishment weakly led and intellectually deficient, relieved of its helmsman's job and, echoing Sudrajat's apt metaphor, reassigned to the fire-fighting squad below deck. When the military is as deeply involved in politics as it is in Indonesia, the assumption is that intervention is the only recipe for reaffirming that role. So far, Abri shows no sign of pursuing this option. Whether this is because the military leadership genuinely believes such a move would ultimately be counterproductive both for themselves and the nation, or whether it reflects the extent to which disunity pervades the ranks, is quite frankly, debateable.

That this scenario seems like the rerun of an old film, is of some concern. In 1965, Abri was undecided, and to some extent powerless to topple Sukarno. Stripped of all the mystery, the actual stimulus for his removal – the murder of six senior army generals on 30 September 1965 by a rogue officer claiming to usurp power – was perhaps more a symptom of the army's hesitancy than Sukarno's excesses. Sukarno was not the target, the army leadership was. Javanese tradition has it that to replace an unpopular but powerful village chief, the direct approach must be avoided. Instead, arrange a crime or scandal within his own household, and his power will naturally dissipate. Similarly today, any move to topple Suharto directly would run the risk of dispersing the small but noticeable accumulation of resentment and have to face an overwhelming mood of support for the 'father of development' at the national level. Rather than commit 'regicide', those in favour of abrupt change might opt, as someone or some group did in 1965, to commit 'fratricide' instead.

4

NEW ORDER SOCIETY

> The New Order is like a ship swinging at anchor. It may drift, but it always swings back to the same place.
>
> (Harry Tjan Silalahi, 1 March 1990)

Indonesians are fond of marvelling at the complexity of their own society. The very fact that it resists flying apart at the seams despite an almost impossible diversity, is something they are rightly proud of. The unity forged by the struggle for independence is hallowed with an intensity verging on fanaticism. So much so, the prominent Sumatran writer, Mochtar Lubis, goes to some length in his recent history of Indonesia to argue the case for an 'Indonesian' identity as far back as the archipelago's proto- and prehistory:

> Despite the appearance of great diversity, there is a strong underpinning of unifying force. In the languages and in the artistic expressions such as ornamentation, in the indigenous religions and traditions, very close relationships, linkages, interconnections, which go far back into pre-history, can be discerned.[1]

Indonesia rejected plans for a federal structure which the Dutch tried offering in the period shortly before independence, opting instead for a unitary state system. At the time, the move was motivated by a fear the Dutch might persuade components in any federal set up to secede from the union – as much of Eastern Indonesia might well have done. But ever since, this has meant that pronounced local autonomy is perceived as contrary to the principles of the state – except for honorary 'special area' status conferred on Jogyakarta and Aceh, which the government has plans to phase out. The unity of the state lies at the very heart of its being. This explains why external criticism of the harsh methods employed to suppress lingering irredentist movements in East Timor, Irian Jaya and Aceh raises nationalist hackles in Jakarta.

To make up for this intolerance of regionalism, on a broader cultural level the national motto, 'unity in diversity' (*Bhineka tunggal ika*) conveys a sense of active pluralism similar, though not the same as America's *E Pluribus Unum*. The difference is, that in contemporary Indonesia the means of giving expression to the country's diversity are rigidly circumscribed by what some regard as an excessive emphasis on unity.

The New Order sold itself to the people as the very instrument of harmony. The Sukarno period had left a legacy of chaos and betrayal. Neither the pre–1959 party-based parliamentary system, nor the more authoritarian era of 'Guided Democracy' which followed, offered stability. Even the harshest critics of the New Order today concede this point. Sukarno's elevation of the revolutionary struggle as the sole aim of politics instilled fear into those who chose not to toe the line and generated reactionary vindictiveness among those who did. *Politik adalah Panglima* (politics as commander) summed up the fiery brand of politics Sukarno kindled. It is hardly surprising, therefore, that many were ready by 1965 to accept order and authority in its starkest form. Yet this urgent wish to be rid of the accusatory, reactionary blend of politics Sukarno offered, paved the way for governance to become steadily more authoritarian.

Intellectuals embraced the military, with its proven discipline and ideals, because the only alternative, it seemed, was anarchy. The extent to which democracy, as enshrined in the country's Constitution, existed 'temporarily' became a secondary concern. It is important to understand the extent to which the country's intelligentsia in the mid-1960s willingly threw their weight behind the New Order. Their support enabled the ruling elite to develop an authoritarian social and political system with impunity. Reversing Sukarno's 'politics as commander' dogma, economic development took precedence over political development. The new slogan was: 'economics first, politics later'. Added to this, the constant need for vigilance against the Communist threat unleashed by Sukarno lent the military's heavy-handed security approach an almost religious sanctity.

The acquiesence of students and intellectuals who supported the New Order at its birth, paved the way for the erection of ornate democratic symbols instead of truly democratic mechanisms. Political parties became stylized and subordinate; their platforms provided only shades of difference for which the voter could express a symbolic preference at election time. Again, society's memory of the chaos generated by the multi-party system which held sway until the mid-1950s, helped dilute opposition to the New Order's emasculation of the parties. The government defended a stringent law on mass organizations by insisting that the three sanctioned and strictly controlled parties provided sufficient 'facilities for the channelling of opinions and ideas of members of society'.[2]

The government initially focused on fashioning a monolithic political organization out of a collection of groups set up by the military at the end of Sukarno's rule to combat the influence of the Communist Party. Among them was an obscure group called *Golongan Karya*, or Golkar, which was first set up in 1964 as an umbrella organization for anti-communist cadres. Golkar has never been styled a party, but is defined instead as a 'functional group', an ambiguous term supposedly referring to the basic functions of society it serves. Also functional in this respect was the later fusion of the three secular-nationalist political parties of the Sukarno era into the *Partai Demokrasi Indonesia* (PDI). The PDI, together with an amalgamation of Muslim parties under the purposely un-Islamic banner of the 'United Development Party' (PPP), were launched in 1973 in the wake of the Political Parties and Golkar Bill.

While these new groupings were offered as avenues for popular political expression, the reality was that the state wished to channel the people. Traditional values of collective discussion and decision-making, which the country's founding fathers had revived to foster nationalist sentiment, now became the only acceptable mechanism of decision-making. Following, ironically enough, the later thinking of Sukarno, the concept of voting whereby '50 plus 1' comprises a majority was dubbed alien. Indonesia's social and cultural diversity was thought too delicately balanced to allow majorities to impose their will. The success of the PKI in mobilizing mass support left a deep impression on the group of Catholic Chinese students who came to influence early New Order policy-making. Their other fear, probably instilled by the Jesuits who taught them, was that the Muslim majority could conceivably stir up the population against the Christian minority in the same way.

Remarkably enough, the Christian Chinese students close to Ali Murtopo and the Kostrad group surrounding Suharto in the early, formative period of the New Order, helped fashion a new concept of political action styled the 'floating mass'. Hence the interests of a Christian and mainly Chinese minority dovetailed neatly with a military establishment fearful of a Muslim political revival. The floating mass concept rested on the assumption that the vast majority of Indonesia's population was unsophisticated and prone to the ill-effects of politicking at the village level. Political parties were therefore banned from operating in the villages, and political activity was severely restricted except for brief periods close to elections.

The idea behind the 'floating mass' concept, as Leo Suryadinata aptly puts it, was to 'depoliticize the Indonesian population'.[3]

Meanwhile, the army and the bureaucracy were entrusted with the task of disseminating the national philosophy of *Pancasila*. *Pancasila* was another concept inherited from Sukarno's armoury of hypnotic slogans. Literally the 'five pillars', or principles, *Pancasila* comprises: belief in one God; just and civilized humanitarianism; a united Indonesia; democracy guided by wisdom, through consultation and representation; and social justice for all the Indonesian people. The beauty of *Pancasila*, as Sukarno conceived it in 1945, was as a device to express the unity of such a diverse people, and above all to ensure that national identity was not defined with any reference to Islam. The safest way to define *Pancasila* is as a vague philosophical rationalization of a plural society. It seeks to enhance togetherness among people of different races and creeds who find themelves rubbing shoulders with one another under one umbrella of state. In this respect, *Pancasila* is an admirable device, and few question its validity.

The New Order elevated *Pancasila* to the status of an ideology. It is commonly referred to as the state ideology, and several attempts have been made to deny Sukarno's authorship of the concept. By the mid-1980s, under the Law on Mass Organizations, all social organizations and political parties were legally required to make *Pancasila* their sole principle, or *asas tunggal*.

Pancasila is a great leveller; tolerant of diversity, but insisting on beliefs. Thus the Muslim must tolerate his Christian brother but never slacken the practice of his faith. Agnostics or atheists are branded Communists of the extreme left; religious extremists inhabit the extreme right. In the process, secular, moderate beliefs have been squeezed; hemmed in by strict definitions and rigid screening procedures. Socialists and nationalists – in effect the secular middle ground – became the chief victims of this 'Pancasilazation' of the nation.[4]

The old Sukarnoist Nationalist party (PNI) and its Socialist rival (PSI) were considered too 'socialistic'; their platforms laying too much stress on mobilizing the masses. Their loss erased the country's only broad-based secular grouping. The beneficiaries have been, ultimately, the polarizing forces of race and religion the state was so keen to suppress in the first place. That these forces have not come back to haunt Indonesia in a full-blown way is remarkable, and says much about the New Order's effective containment of society. This entailed neutering all political parties, chanelling Islam through state-controlled institutions, de-politicizing the campuses and squashing all thoughts of autonomy for the regions. By these and other means justified in the name of harmony, the New Order strengthened its grip on power. In the process it stifled expression and required uniformity of a society which is anything but that.

The hallmark of Suharto's New Order has been the totally successful extension of state power to all corners of society. Ride through any Indonesian town and the first thing that strikes the visitor is a profusion of official signboards. Typically, one sees a cluster of offices housing the local administration, then representative offices of all the major provincial departments, added to this there are state-level representative offices; information, agriculture, co-operatives, justice, forestry and so on. The state's largesse is not distributed solely by the provincial authorities. This might lead to dangerous levels of loyalty to the local authorities and ultimately threaten the unitary state. Instead, the central government ensures that a large portion of public spending is distributed directly to the provincial and village level via what are called 'Inpres' programmes. This direct aid is made at the president's discretion, for which a large portion of the government's development budget is set aside. For the financial year 1991–2, 16.3 per cent of the development budget, or Rp 3.27 trillion, was allocated for Inpres funding. In the process, Suharto guarantees himself direct responsibility for the welfare of his people, and guarantees grass-roots support for his mandate.

The welfare and economic progress fostered by this super-state is hard to argue with. The efficiency and quality of some of the infratsructure might be questioned, but the sheer fact that it extends to the most remote areas of such a vast country is an achievement few dare to challenge. In the largest province of Irian Jaya, where low densities of population and the cultural gulf between mainly Javanese bureaucrats and the native Melanesian population have posed difficulties for the government, a frequent complaint is that the pace of development is too relentless. Schemes to resettle landless Javanese in Irian Jaya's ample lowlands have aroused anger and resentment among the Irianese whose cultural traditions and agricultural systems depend on a footloose and sparse pattern of settlement.

At the other end of the spectrum, in Jakarta, the upper reaches of Indonesian society are growing weary of the state's paternalistic manner. This may have suited conditions where a largely rural and poorly educated population accepted the state's wisdom without question. But a quarter-century of more or less uninterrupted economic development has transformed Indonesia into more of an urban society. The 1990 census revealed that over fifty million people – almost one-third of the population – were living in urban areas. Since 1986, the industrial sector has grown by 13 per cent, and even portions of the rural labour force are now dependent on urban areas for employment.

Accompanying these structural changes, traditional patterns of inter-communal relations, labour relations and even family relations have altered. Prone to over-claiming traditional values, the government is having to come to terms with what it means to become an industrialized nation. The growth of an educated professional class in urban areas has unleashed demands for less ideological uniformity, more tolerance of dissent. 'Open-ness' – a popular byword for democratization – has become a recurrent theme in political debate. However, to equate the wishes of the vast majority with the liberal concerns of a rather limited circle of urban intellectuals would be misleading. The rise of middle-class social conscious-ness in the classical Weberian sense is discernible, but its wider impact is hampered by the comparatively small size of the nascent bourgeoisie – and their continued reliance on the patronage of the elite.

Even this traditional barrier to change was under stress. The elite was also growing concerned about their future. What if the monolithic edifice which had afforded them protection for so long really was going to change? Uncertain of where to find the next safe haven, many peers and leaders of larger social groups began to hop on the openness bandwagon by the early 1990s. What alarmed government officials about the Forum for Democ-racy, launched in March 1991, was that it was initiated by one of the country's most respected Muslim leaders, and head of the twenty million-strong *Nahdlatul Ulama*. The fact that the military did little to oppose the move, and may even have lent some tacit encouragement, completed the ring. There appeared to be a growing consensus on the need for political change.

Suharto either recognized himself, or was persuaded to recognize that these demands for social and political change were here to stay: In our hetergeneous and ever-changing society, new aspirations, new forces and new hopes will definitely emerge', he opined in a speech to parliament in January 1991.[5] Instead of offering the familiar menu of external threats and the need for constant vigilance, Suharto made attempts to add spice to the recipe:

> National Stability that offers room for dynamism and dynamism that refreshes national stability are the prerequisites we need in preparing to enter the take-off era.[6]

Many who listened doubted Suharto's commitment to thorough social and political change was sincere. His speeches had a defensive ring about them; little was offered in terms of concrete policy to satisfy the swelling chorus of popular demands for change. There was no evidence of any change in the style of Suharto's leadership to back up his rhetoric. If anything, the president was becoming more remote, more reliant on quasi-feudal symbols of power.

Yet the democratization debate, which dominated the close of the 1980s, seemed to pose as the agenda for the 1990s. The remarkable recovery of the economy from the oil shock in the early 1980s and evidence that 'take-off' was just around the corner, prompted people to ask why the government was reluctant to relax its hold over political and intellectual expression. Surely, they asked, the Communist threat had been stamped out; the state of vigilance which had prevailed over the past quarter-century was now redundant. This was, of course, primarily a middle-class intellectual's view, but the country's economic growth was quietly strengthening the middle class. The Australian academic Jamie Mackie, in a paper reflecting – albeit generously – on the New Order in December 1989, argued that it had become 'increasingly exclusionary rather than participatory'.[7] Along with others who watched Indonesia emerge as a new economic force in the region, Mackie was aware that more and more Indonesians were expressing concern at the actual concentration of power at the apex of the political system.

To make this kind of generalization, so tempting against the background of crumbling totalitarian states in Eastern Europe and elsewhere, runs the risk of ignoring the fundamentally stable character of societies in South-east Asia. They may heave and convulse periodically; but this is usually brought on by a power struggle at the top, rather than instigated from below. Political change in modern Indonesia has never been precipitated by a rush to the barricades. The only acceptable form of politicking is that conducted by the elite without resorting to seeking popular support. The natural state of these societies is an equilibrium in which order and authority tend to be the norm. Stability is craved and change resisted out of fear of the chaos it may bring in its wake. Lucien Pye describes 'the overriding Indonesian need for the psychological suppression of individuality and for the comforts of dependency and conformity'.[8] Only time will tell if these ungenerous observations will prove correct in the case of Indonesia.

There is a sense in which Indonesia has almost run the whole spectrum of political options in the course of its independent history. Beginning with constitutional democracy, followed by 'Guided Democracy', a brief flirtation with Communism, and now something resembling a throwback to the patrimonial rule of the Hindu-Bhuddist kings of the pre-colonial period. Before asking the question 'what next?' it is pertinent to ask what kind of society has the New Order fostered? Is it in transition and if so, towards what?

On a blistering hot day in October 1988, upwards of a million and a half people were drawn from all over Java and beyond to the town of Jogyakarta in Central Java to witness the final journey of Java's last feudal king. A week or so before, on 2 October, Sultan Hamengkubuwono IX died of a heart attack in a Washington hospital. News of his death stunned and saddened the nation. His staunch defence and generous financing of the infant republic had made him a national hero. The Dutch had tried to buy off the Javanese aristocracy in a bid to weaken the republic. They invited the Sultan to form a government in collaboration with them in 1949. The Sultan instead helped organize an Indonesian counter-attack. Hamengkubuwono's resistance helped convince the Dutch that if the aristocracy they had so carefully nurtured was against them, their traditional policy of *divide et impera* was not going to work.

Seldom has such pomp and ceremony been witnessed in post-war Java. President Suharto and almost the entire cabinet attended the funeral, which had all the trappings of a state occasion. As the late Sultan lay in the palace grounds, for over sixteen hours, 150,000 people entered the palace gates to honour him. The people of Jogyakarta, and to a considerable degree the entire country, revered the Sultan both for his symbolism of a dim and distant sovereign past and his stout defence of democratic principles. Remarkably in a republic, people referred – and still refer to him – as *raja kita*, 'our King'. The Sultan himself posessed a talent for preserving the sacred image of the wise king with all the feudal trappings, using the modern language of Indonesia and espousing western principles of democracy. He served as Defence Minister in the country's first government from 1948 to 1953, and later as Vice-President under Suharto from 1973 to 1978.

In the upper reaches of society, people were also aware of the Sultan's unexpressed distaste for Suharto and his methods, which he considered rough and prone to corruption. The masses saw in the Sultan the values of the good and just king, or *ratu adil*. He was a rich man, owning a bank and several companies, but lived in comparative modesty and gave generously. By contrast, members of Suharto's family and inner circle were considered shamelessly greedy. The contrast is not entirely fair; the Suhartos are also modest about their wealth in typical Javanese fashion, and have been conspicuosly generous to social causes. None the less, many wondered why to the very end the Sultan never once played on his popularity to influence political events. He took his views, and the knowledge he posessed to back them up, to the grave.

Indonesians were at something of a loss to explain the grief they felt for this anachronistic figurehead. The Jogyakarta daily, *Kedaulatan Rakyat*, soberly reported the succession of supernatural acts which were said to accompany the Sultan's death – objects belonging to the Sultan mysteriously disappeared; an old banyan tree in the palace grounds was struck by lightning the night the Sultan died. In an apologetic editorial the paper opined that the despite years of education and development, the Javanese were clearly still steeped in superstition and mysticism.[9]

The Sultan's death offered a startling perspective on modern Indonesian society. It showed the strength of tradition – specifically Javanese tradition – and the extent to which it has become closely identified with the state. Yet if society clings to – even appears to be reinforcing – its primordial roots, does this not suggest a collective insecurity, or lack of direction? Given the clichéd explanations to which Javanese culture and its impact on society have become prone, the question is hard to answer. All the more so since one important focus of calls for change in the 1980s has been on the extent to which the national leadership has employed Javanese culture to reinforce 'feudalism' and deny freedom of expression and popular participation in government:

> The mentality of the 'priyayi' (Javanese aristocracy) which attaches importance to position, power and the physical symbols, and which is not achievement oriented, only vertical oriented.[10]

Sociologist Aswab Mahasin points out that Indonesian society since independence has swung between two cultural extremes; a sense of being 'modernized' in the western sense, and the search for values of the 'idealized East'.[11] In such a state of flux, Mahasin says: 'Many feel the need to cling to something more solid, the cherished traditions of one's ancestors.'

The death of Sultan Hamengkubuwono – and the indirect contrast of his leadership with that of Suharto's – presented the sort of paradox commonly encountered in Indonesia. Here was a traditional feudal king being compared favourably with the modern republican president – because the latter's kingly qualities seemed wanting. Suharto, for all his traditional ways, must have felt ill at ease with the atmosphere that day in Jogyakarta. For the masses who turned out to see the Sultan's coffin wend its way to the royal graves at Imogiri, to rub their sarongs against the carriage carrying the coffin, or collect shrubbage from the hill on which the cemetry is perched for its sacred powers, Suharto's presence was, for once, secondary. The Sultan's sanctity and popularity drew vast crowds, but Suharto has done more to shape Indonesian society than any other figure in the country's history. Yet in subduing the centrifugal forces which threatened to destroy the nation in the mid-1960s, many now feel he has muzzled society so effectively it is incapable of adapting to new stresses and strains imposed by development and growth.

Indonesian society is caught somewhere between tradition and renewal. The Suharto regime has drawn, like the Sukarno government before it, on tradition to maintain control. Yet to foster development it has embraced modernization and triggered a surge towards social change. In a sense, this disjuncture has been accommodated surprisingly well. Indonesians are masters at managing the contradictions in their society. Also by qualifying 'modern' concepts such as democracy and capitalism in their own specific terms, they have persuaded themselves – as well as the outside world – that the spirit of these principles is being upheld.

Three aspects of modern Indonesian society as it has developed under the New Order stand out. None of them seem to mesh, however. Modern Indonesia is the largest Muslim country in the world and lately has shown signs of becoming more Islamic. Yet the growth of its economy is rapidly developing a consumer-oriented, western-educated, middle-class culture, prone to liberal political views. At the same time there appears to be no hint of change to the way society is regulated by the state. Indonesia continues to host one of the more restrictive political systems in the region.

The fault lines along which Indonesian society divides in ethnic and socio-economic as well as religious terms are, like the San Andreas geological fault in California, easy to discern, potentially unstable, yet somehow maintain an equilibrium which permits a normal organized existence. Sumatrans and Eastern islanders resisted domination by a Java-nese-centric government in the early years after independence, and there were revolts in the Moluccas (1950), Sulawesi (1957) and West Sumatra (1958), which had to be put down, often harshly, by the military. In each case, long periods of mistrust between the centre and the outlying regions where these revolts occurred have ensued.

The country's estimated six million people of Chinese origin, as elsewhere in the region, dominate commerce and have historically been the target of popular unrest in urban areas. Unlike their ethnic cousins in Malaysia, the small proportion of the total population the Chinese in Indonesia represents, guarantees that they are tolerated under stable socio-economic conditions. In rural areas the Chinese dominate the petty trading occupations, in urban areas they are pre-eminent in retail and wholesale trade. Higher up the social scale, successful Chinese entrepreneurs are among the richest overseas Chinese in South-east Asia. The tax burden is light, and their links to the political establishment are impeccable. Relative invisibility and their complete withdrawal from politics has helped preserve their position.

> The Chinese became like minor wives. They are enjoyed, but never taken to official receptions. The more enjoyable they are the less they can be shown in public.[12]

Around 90 per cent of Indonesia's population professes the Muslim faith. Yet Indonesia has consistently confounded those who expected the wave of fundamentalist Islam which blanketed the Middle East in the late 1970s to settle here too and have similar revolutionary repurcussions. They were disappointed partly because of the uniquely syncretic nature of Indonesian Islam, which has accommodated the pluralistic nature of Indonesian society and ensures that devout Muslims and their nominal co-religionists can coexist. Partly too, because the state has always worked assiduously to undermine the basis for any politically motivated Islamic movement. It is also important to remember that Indonesia is home to at least fifteen million Christians who, despite frequent allegations from the Muslim camp of aggressive proselytization, have enjoyed tolerance and even an elite status under Indonesia's secular constitution.

A common interest in maintaining harmony is the most logical explanation of why violent reactions between the elements have not occurred for so long. Why is it that the hundreds of thousands of political killings – over Islam in the 1940s and 1950s, over Communism in the 1960s and 1970s – left no apparent trace of bitterness or latent urge for revenge in society? Anyone who has witnessed a mass gathering in Indonesia is full of praise for the way Suharto's New Order has balanced the centrifugal forces in society. They may also wonder how much longer they can be kept in check. The collective restraint preventing a sanctioned political rally at election time, or New Year or Idul Fitri celebrations becoming a violent riot, appears eggshell-thin. Tension is palpable at any of these occasions. That order is generally maintained, needs explaining.

Outwardly, the peaceful passage of the past twenty-five years appears to have helped erase antagonistic emotions from the collective memory. More accurately the process has been aided by the New Order's own rigid ordering of society. Sukarno cultivated synthetic emotions and fanned the flames of nationalism for his own ends. In 1965, an American observer wrote in the journal *Encounter*:

> In so far as a collective psychosis controlled by a charismatic leader is accessible to reason, the case of Indonesia deserves analysis.[13]

Suharto and his men needed to bring these emotions under control. All the forces unleashed by Sukarno had to be put back in the bottle and sealed for good.

Nothing was left to chance. Not content with banning the Communist Party only, all the political organizations of the 'Old Order' were dismembered. Rather cleverly in 1973 they were distilled into three government-controlled 'functional groups': Golkar, representing the civilian/military bureaucracy, 'Partai Persatuan Pembangunan' (PPP), representing a coalition of Muslim interests, and the 'Partai Demokrasi Indonesia' (PDI), condensing the remnants of nine Christian and nationalist parties. The New Order's resistance to endowing Golkar with all the functions of a political party ensured that it always remained institutionally weak and firmly under Suharto's thumb. In the case of PDI and PPP, the fusion of rival parties guaranteed their endemic weakness. Rather than play an antagonistic role, the new parties were asked to be 'complimentary' to one another. This vague notion had its roots in the integralistic ideas of the country's founding fathers who sought to find ways of proving to the world that a society as diverse as Indonesia could rise above competition and strife by espousing 'family' values – the concept of *kekeluargaan*.

To ensure that nothing distracted Indonesians from feeling part of one large family, New Order ideologues developed the concept of the 'floating mass', whereby people at the grass-roots level were to be excluded from active participation in politics, except during the brief quiennial election campaigns. Those bent on cultural explanations see this as an imposition of Javanese patterns of hegemony; ignorant and obedient servants *kawula* beneath their powerful lords, or *gusti*. Perhaps more realistically, the new rulers feared the strength of society's natural political urges. The results of the 1955 general elections are considered the last to reflect those urges, when Muslim parties accounted for almost 40 per cent of the vote. In the 1987 election, Muslim political interests under the banner of the PPP could only muster 15 per cent of the vote.

Despite the marginalization of potential alternatives, official unease heightens around election time. The government's refusal to hold general elections on a public holiday suggested considerable insecurity about how people would vote if allowed to do so away from government offices where the voters can be safely persuaded to vote for Golkar. On a visit to rural Ambon in October 1990, Minister of Home Affairs, Rudini, was met by a village chief who informed his boss that all but 10 per cent of the villagers under his authority had already agreed to vote for Golkar. As for the dissenters, the loyal headman informed an embarrassed Rudini that 'I have written down their names and I will punish them by all means.'[14] Rudini chided the overzealous headman on the spot, but later announced that provincial governors whose areas turned out a low Golkar vote, might be punished in their capacity as Golkar cadres.[15]

The process of muzzling political alternatives culminated in the 1985 Law on Mass Organizations. The law decreed that all mass organizations had to suscribe to the state ideology of *Pancasila*, and the executive board of each organization with all its members must be registered with the government. The government was given the right to freeze any mass organization if it disturbed public order, or received aid from foreign parties without government approval. The new law deprived Islamic political parties of the right to promote Islam as the central platform of their manifesto. Anyone who publicly preached against the law was tried for subversion. In General Nasution's view, the Law on Mass Organizations contravened the spirit of the 1945 Constitution and *Pancasila*:

> Pancasila stresses harmony between diversity and unity. One cannot exist without the other. To emphasize diversity alone will destroy unity. On the other hand, to centralise unity through losing diversity will lead us to regimentation of our lives as a nation, as citizens and as ordinary people, closing out the space for initiative, creativity and dynamism.[16]

Significantly, by the end of the 1980s, regimentation and the lack of creative energy induced by the Ormas Law was seized on by critics and those within the establishment who counselled gradual political change. In one of his speeches, Murdani warned of the 'robots' Indonesian youth were in danger of becoming:

> Discipline must not cause initaitives and creativity to disappear.... the obligation to full obedience and loyalty might produce humans who are like robots that move only when commanded.[17]

The New Order was interested as much in the preservation as the concentration of power. If Suharto had pressed ahead too quickly with these levelling measures, he might have faced opposition – even outright insurrection. Instead, his approach has been cautious and always well prepared. Since the source of his government's legitimacy lay in the 1945 Constitution, liberal interpretations of what was after all a broadly inter-pretable document had to be limited to prevent the Constitution's being employed against them. Thus the highest sovereign body, the MPR, which was theoretically capable of changing the Constitution by two-thirds majority vote, became instead capable of very little because two-thirds of its members were effectively appointed by the government.

Employing regulations enacted by the MPR to govern itself, Suharto ensured it was packed with pliant clients and excluded independent politicians. By conferring membership of the MPR on key intellectuals and influential media editors, he bound them tightly to the system and guaranteed that their criticism of the system would be construed as hypocritical. Even elected members of the supreme body could not take up their seats until 'screened' by the government. This ensured that the whole process of electing the president became little more than a well-choreographed show, the final act being a foregone conclusion.

The country's lower house, or *Dewan Perwakilan Rakyat* (DPR) has been similarly filleted to strip it of consequential powers. The body's 500 members are organized into four factions; Golkar, Abri, PDI and PPP. Although divided into various committees charged with overseeing the work of government, the DPR is not empowered to legislate. Laws are debated in the DPR only after their final drafting, and are usually – but not always – passed without amendment.

Suharto was aided by the 1945 Constitution, which vaguely recognizes democratic freedoms, but more explicitly sanctions a strong executive. The Constitution vests 'All power and responsibility [for the conduct of state government] in the hands of the president.' The right of political parties to exist is recognized, but the duty of organizing them is expressly devolved to the state. This inexorable limiting of the freedom of expression by institutional means has proceeded virtually unhindered under the New Order. In the first place the regime effectively ensured that all possible avenues for protest were blocked. Second, it imposed rigid ideological uniformity on society.

After the student protests of the 1970s, the government announced a 'normalization' of campus life, which banned demonstrations, muzzled the campus press and effectively extinguished academic freedom. Powers conferred on the attorney-general's office have been widely used to ban books regarded as critical of the regime. Several books by the prominent author Pramoedya Ananta Toer have been banned, and their sale or possession is regarded as a subversive act. In September 1989, Bambang Isti Nugroho, a 29 year-old laboratory assistant from Jogyakarta's Gajah Mada University was sentenced to eight years' imprisonment for allegedly selling books by Pramoedya.

The Communist threat has been skilfully drawn out to maintain an extra-judicial hold over individual action. Human rights organizations have highlighted the manner in which compulsory screening of former political detainees and prisoners can effectively bar them and members of their extended families from actively participating in political, commercial and intellectual life. A recent update of screening procedures issued by the government in 1988 states that 'mental ideological screening' is essential for those entering any of the following professions; the military, civil service, teachers, political parties, the press, shadow puppeteers, mayors, legal aid societies, the church.[18] Those with a history of detention for political reasons have the fact denoted on their identity cards.

The fear of a Communist comeback is puzzling twenty years after the Communist Party was so effectively wiped out. The government only waived screening for those from the extended families of those implicated in 1965 in April 1990. Can they really believe that Communists lurk in every village ready to subvert when the government's attention is relaxed? There were stories in the late 1980s about Indonesian party cadres still being trained in China and Eastern Europe. Army ideologues insisted the Communist threat was a real one. Not even the collapse of the Berlin Wall and Stalin's legacy in Eastern Europe persuaded the army leadership. Their response was that Communism would now go even further underground to achieve its ends. Armed Forces Commander General Try Sutrisno argued in a January 1991 interview that Communist and 'neo-Communist' forces were simply 'lying low'.[19] Naturally, even more intense vigilance was prescribed.

The normalization of relations with China in August 1990 was resisted by a hard core in the military on the grounds that China was still committed to exporting revolution and that Chinese diplomats would pose a security risk. 'Communism as an ideology is still a danger to the Indonesian people,' said former intelligence chief General Yoga Sugama in July 1990, 'because if tolerated, communism could diffuse the people's belief in Pancasila'.[20] Perhaps a better explanation in this country of symbols and symbolism, is that the Communist threat established a useful atmosphere of fear and vigilance which enabled the government to justify its levelling of society, and thus, in their eyes, safeguard stability.

Rigid adherence to the state philosophy of *Pancasila* is enforced by attendance of *Pancasila* Guidance courses, known as P4 (*Pedoman Peng-hayatan dan Pengalaman*). The courses themselves are not officially compulsory. But since 1978, all civil servants who wish to gain promotion or even travel overseas have to prove attendance of the two-week course. P4 courses are even conducted overseas to maintain a hold over Indonesian students studying abroad. The fact that *Pancasila* defies any deeper analysis as a philosophy, beyond its laudable principles of collective harmony, means that at every level from school to university and beyond, the content of these courses remains virtually the same. There is little discussion of *Pancasila* itself; no deep introspection on its meaning, for it is chiefly designed as a principle about which there can be no argument. Although hard for outsiders to understand, *Pancasila* is not questioned by opposition figures and critics of the New Order as a basis for the organization of state. *Pancasila* is designed to encompass all aspects of social, spiritual and political life – and rules out alternatives. Even those intellectuals seeking to articulate alternative and more pluralistic expressions of political activity never questioned the relevance of *Pancasila*. Instead they argued that the New Order's definition of *Pancasila* was too narrow.

The press, which had been nurtured by the military to rail so effectively against Sukarno in the 1960s, became subject in the 1970s to progressively severe censorship. On occasions, the government has resorted to banning or closing publications – most recently with the closure of the Jakarta daily *Prioritas* in July 1987 and the *Monitor* tabloid in October 1990. Yet in contrast to some neighbouring countries, Indonesia allows its press to retain a measure of independence. It has not been forced under state-controlled holding companies, as in Singapore or Malaysia. The government may not own the press, but the Indonesian ministry of information has a vast and varied portfolio of shareholdings in media companies, none of them majority shares, however. Unlike the Malaysian press also, Indonesian newspapers and magazines are not forced to renew their publishing licences on an annual basis.

The state prefers to exercise its control over the press more indirectly – by employing patronage and co-option. An amendment to the 1966 Press Law in 1982 stipulated that the press should conduct itself in a 'free and responsible' manner. The US-based Human rights organization, Asia Watch, in a comprehensive report on Indonesia published in 1989, interpreted this to mean that the press 'is very much a partner of the government, and not an independent or autonomous institution'.[21] If this is the case, the partnership works. Rather than face interminable closure, the press has adapted to the restrictions largely by censoring itself. A style of writing has developed which accomodates the establishment's rejection of direct criticism of its policies and practices. Thus a report on the problems of development in a certain province is more likely to lead off with the line '.... has yet to realize its full potential', rather than state bluntly the shortcomings of local officials or a lack of funds.

In a startling reification of Javanese cultural values of respect and politeness towards those in authority, the New Order insists on the positive being stressed and the negative being suppressed. Editors receive regular briefings or telephone calls with 'advice' on how to report sensitive issues. Styled 'telephone culture', the system can suggest a story idea as well as suppress them. More often than not something can be said, but the real story is buried in an oblique and, to the untrained eye, meaningless stream of stodgy prose. Yet in the absence of freedom of thought on the campuses, the press has assumed the role of national repository of intellectual opinion. A legacy of influence inherited from the nationalist period has maintained the strength of Indonesia's press despite the difficulties it has faced under the New Order. But this also means it is subject to manipulation in times of political stress.

In the course of 1990, the government made noises about easing restrictions on the press in the name of 'openness'. There would be no more banning of newspapers, the Co-ordinating Minister for Security and Political Affairs, Admiral Sudomo, said. Embarrassed, the Minister of Information was forced to concur, adding only that the government retained the right to revoke publishing permits. This kind of double-speak began to annoy local journalists, who were aware that some areas of the government were in favour of a genuinely freer press. In fact, key political players were making efforts to patronize the press in order to have their views – and profiles – projected. The military, for example, had become less hostile towards the press, and actively encouraged journalists to write about selective social and economic issues. Few senior editors ascribed this to a change of fundamental attitude. Rather, a freer press was regarded as a necessary component of Abri's strategy to regain political influence. Suharto himself left it to his ministers to castigate the press, leaving himself in a position to adopt a more flexible attitude.

At the same time, the growing financial power of the press was grafting commercial and political pretensions onto a generation of senior editors who were fast becoming intellectualy disillusioned with the New Order. Cowed by the authorities they may be, but other than watching their standing with the palace and the armed forces, media editors could be very much their own bosses in financial terms. As the political situation became more fluid, this commercial security allowed some editorial comments to become more lucid. In fact, one way in which Suharto appeared to be trying to curb the press by early 1990 was by having members of his own family buy into the media. All three of the commercial television stations, and a major publishing group, 'Media Indonesia', were controlled by family members. Suharto's eldest daughter, Siti Hardijanti Hastuti Rukmana, was chairman of the Association of Private Radio Stations.

The ambiguous nature of press freedom in Indonesia raises an interesting question. One of the most intriguing – and perplexing – features of the New Order has been the ease with which it has imposed its will on society. What explains the acquiescence of the civilian and military elite – and in a broader sense of the middle class? The New Order rode to power on a tide of demands for change, mainly articulated by urban middle-class professionals. They were frustrated by the Old Order's rejection of their professional ability in favour of demands for ideological purity. These student leaders and professionals were full of hope after 1966. Amid the euphoria of Sukarno's downfall, they initiated debate about the future. By the early 1970s, though, such brainstorming was quite likely to land those who participated in jail. Yet a feeling of security made people more complacent towards the regime. One way of interpreting this is to argue that the power of the state to provide overcame efforts to question its form.

As the bureaucracy expanded and the power of the state grew, two things occurred. The well-being of the people improved so that the numbers of those living in intolerably poor conditions declined from well over half the population to around 20 per cent by the end of the 1980s. The state became the great provider. Everything, from patronage to rice, emanates from the state. For most people it represents a means of plugging in to a secure well-being. Young Indonesian graduates strive very hard to obtain their NIP, or civil service registration number, even though salaries are abysmally low. A junior civil servant in Jakarta makes the equivalent of less than US$ 45 per month. There is something more than an income at stake here.

As well as a regular salary, the bureaucracy provides its four million employees with rice, housing, transport to and from work, and comprehensive medical care. In return, rigid conformity and total commitment to the government's policies are demanded. The values fit more or less exactly those expected of the good Javanese, prompting Koentjaraningrat, the great Javanese cultural anthropologist to remark that classical Javanese cultural behaviour 'fits the civil servants' mentality' with an emphasis on self-control and a lack of initiative-seeking. In so far as debate is tolerated, observed the journalist Susumu Awanohara:

> The regime seems not only to tolerate debate, but also to welcome controlled debate, which lends it an air of enlightenment, diffuses tensions and serves as an early warning system.[22]

Controlled debate meant that academic discourse was severly restricted. The campuses became intellectual ghost towns, where university lecturers eked out a bare existence on meagre government salaries unless they neglected their students and spent all their time working off-campus. The more talented among them longed for overseas sabbatical, only to find that whatever they learnt overseas could not be fully imparted to their students without disturbing the authorities. One of the saddest aspects of the New Order's impact on society has been its stultifying numbing of intellectual institutions.

As government employees, university teachers were hardly in a position to argue about academic freedom. The tight-knit web of social organizations woven around all civil servants is designed to embrace all aspects of their lives. All civil servants are compulsorily members of *Korpi*, the civil servant's organization, and as such are expected to vote for *Golkar*. As Don Emmerson notes: 'Of Korpi's five objectives, only the last one mentions welfare of the civil servant and his or her family; the others stress patriotism, discipline, and devotion to duty.'[23] New Order Society lays great stress on collective participation. Fun walks, calisthenics, outings to recreation spots are all imposed on employees regularly. Non-participation invites suspicion. Even the suspicion of non-conformity brings sanction. Those whose mental and ideological 'environment' are considered 'unclean', must attend 'refresher courses' in '*Pancasila* ethics'. On such courses, civil and military intelligence officers drum home the key themes underpinning New Order ideology; the ever-present Communist threat, and the need for military guardianship of the state. Naturally, ideological conformity fosters a rejection of criticism. Initiative and creativity are stifled by official attitudes towards criticism from below which is regarded as 'impolite'.

On a broader scale, an attempt was made to mould Indonesian society into a more uniform shape employing Javanese cultural norms. Law No.5 (1979) tried to model village adminstration throughout the archipelago on the Javanese *desa*. Traditional Javanese villages are self-contained units led by an appointed headman with wide-ranging powers. High population densities and a hierachically ordered society are the norm on Java, but conditions vary elsewhere in the archipelago. In parts of Irian Jaya, for example, population densities are as low as two persons per square kilometre.

In 1988, the sociologist Taufik Abdullah was commissioned by the interior ministry to study the impact of Law No.5 in ten provinces outside Java. Abdullah found that traditional non-Javanese patterns of village organization persisted. In Aceh, for instance, villages are subject to a supra-authority grouping several settlements under one local leader. In North Sumatra, clans are more influential than village ties. He also noted that in many cases the Javanese-style village chiefs had lost the respect of villages, they and the system imposed on the villagers were regarded as alien. He concluded that the law had no respect for the organic communities on which it was imposed, and in practice was operating below par.[24]

In true corporatist tradition, the state has worked assiduously to ensure that all social activity is co-opted. This is usually done either by providing patrons – in the form of a minister or senior government official – or by granting an association a representational monopoly and enforcing compulsory membership for all those engaged in the activity concerned. Trade unions are a case in point. In 1985 the federation of Indonesian trade unions became a unitary organization, the *Serikat Pekerja Seluruh Indonesia* (SPSI). This, in effect, made illegal the formation of independent trade unions because, according to the government, which placed the manpower minister as head of the new union's advisory board, the consensus was for unity under one body.

Such a process of social coagulation in an intrinsically pluralistic context is conducted in the private sector too. Manufacturing monopolies in Indonesia have lately been effectively revived through overarching trade associations, of which Bob Hasan's wood manufacturing group, Apkindo, is a good example. All those engaged in the wood industry must be members of Apkindo. On their behalf, Apkindo fixes prices for exports of the finished products, organizes their marketing and in the process rakes off an astonishingly large profit for itself. Here the political and commercial interests of the elite cleave neatly.

The rigid ordering of a society as intrinsically heterogeneous as Indonesia's could only have succeeded with the acquiescence of its peers. Suharto has demonstrated consummate skill in manipulating Javanese society's innate respect for mandated authority. More importantly, the New Order has ensured that this and other aspects of Javanese society become pervasive norms in the wider Indonesian social context. Intellectuals of the generation that fought for independence recall the atmosphere of equality that pervaded society after the Dutch left. The journalist Rosihan Anwar recalled once how in Jakarta during the war against the Dutch, telephone operators refused to connect callers who failed to begin with the word *Merdeka*, meaning 'Freedom'. While the Dutch strove to divide society by fostering its natural hierarchical tendencies, after independence all citizens belonged to a unitary state with a new common language, *Bahasa Indonesia*. The honeymoon was short-lived. By the end of the 1950s, Sukarno had circumscribed the multi-party system by imposing executive rule and the military was growing impatient with the actual practice of the freedom they had fought for. Once Suharto was securely in power, he continued the authoritative trend.

Javanese culture has been a primary resource for New Order ideologues. The conjunction of politics and culture has virtually been institutionalized. Like the Dutch colonial administrators, the New Order has found the natural hierachical tendencies of Javanese society extraordinarily useful. Traditionally, a Javanese official in high position demands respect and unquestioning loyalty. In equal measure there is Javanese society's

111

unquestioning acceptance of authority. The principle of *sapto pandhito ratu*, an expression for the sanctity of the ruler's utterances, ensures compliance even in situations where it is clear that the rulers are riding roughshod over the interests of the ruled.

At the court of Sultan Agung of the great Martaram dynasty, which held sway over Central Java in the early seventeenth century, government office conferred prestige and status, allowing the king – who controlled all appointments – to keep the aristocracy in check to an astonishingly effective degree. As the historian Anthony Reid generalizes so aptly:

> In this part of the world where land was abundant, buildings impermanent, and property insecure, it was in followers that power and wealth were primarily expressed. [25]

Suharto has evolved a strikingly similar system whereby, in the absence of a truly democratic exercise of power at the ballot box, much of his actual support rests on his powers of patronage. The allegience of officials is ensured not only by his sole power of appointment, but also by additional payments out of his own purse. All first-echelon officials (ranked below minister) in the bureaucracy receive small, but not insubstantial monthly or annual alowances directly from the president. Such pecuniary incentives come with the added advantage of diluting their allegience to the ministers above them, thus precluding the formation of competing power bases. The emphasis placed on the power and prestige of office since independence has had a transformational effect on society and to a much greater degree hindered the evolution of a modern bureaucratic polity. The Indonesian scholar Ignas Kleden argues:

> The wide use of Sanskrit words and the words of the old Javanese Language to name buildings, hotels or in state protocol, the use of feudalistic words like 'Bapak', 'berkenan' and 'memohon' to replace more democratic words like 'anda', 'saudara', 'bersedia' and 'meminta', the greater emphasis on politeness in political and formal relationships, the use of Javanese language among Javanese during office hours, the fact that social prowess is given preference over technical skills – all these things are quite characterstic of a culture which is basically aesthetic in nature.[26]

Hard though it is to quantify cultural contributions to political systems, culture clearly plays an important role. More so in Indonesia where the official political creed is identified frequently with *budaya kita*, 'our culture'. Without actually making it explicit, under the New Order this has strictly meant Javanese culture with all its accompanying paternalistic and hierarchical baggage. South-east Asian nations tend to place their cultures high on the altar of state. Thailand has shielded itself, though somewhat unsuccessfully, from foreign influence with the 'Thai way' of doing things. Malaysia deploys Malay culture as a tool of political dominance. Singapore is trying to employ Confucianism and the Mandarin Chinese language to define itself. All this is understandable given the ravaging effects of colonialism in the region. Culture proved useful as a tool of nationalism and subsequently armed the state to deal with demands for democracy and human rights.

Lately in Indonesia, progressive circles have begun to regard Javanese cultural hegemony more and more as a regressive phenomenon. Critics of the New Order in the 1980s were fond of using terms like 'neo-feudal' or 'aristocratic' to describe the attitudes of officials towards the people. 'On paper, our bureaucracy emulates a modern, rational bureaucracy. In practice, everything is subject to a small elite who can take whatever they want', said Umar Kayam of Jogyakarta's Gajah Mada University on the occasion of his appointment as professor of culture.[27] Kayam interprets these attitudes as anachronistic and more importantly as a departure from the 'free and democratic' spirit kindled at the birth of the nation. Instead, he asserts, 'we have gone back to the period of kingship and colonialism.'

To lay the blame entirely on the New Order is not fair. Indonesia's founding fathers were themselves close to or members of the Javanese aristocratic elite. Their Dutch educations filled their heads with the jargon of modern liberal concepts. However custom dictated an ambiguous approach to the rights of the individual which left plenty of scope for state interference with those rights. Article 28 of the 1945 Constitution states that freedom of association, thought, expression and so on, should be laid down by law. The government's interpretation of Article 28 is that these rights must be 'guided' by law. In other words, laws subsequently legislated will determine the extent to which such freedoms can be practised. Any expression of such freedoms outside the law is regarded as illegal.

The chief framer of Indonesia's 1945 Constitution, Professor Supomo, was a scholar of Indonesian customary, or *adat*, law. Under the Japanese occupation he held an important post at the Ministry of Justice. With only thirty-seven articles, the constitution he drafted, has been described as 'one of the shortest written constitutions in the world'.[28] The late scholar and humanist Soedjatmoko believed that Supomo's commitment to the liberal democratic values of the west was only skin-deep. As a member of the Javanese petty aristocracy who had received a Dutch liberal education, he envisaged a compromise between basic human rights and the right of the government to suppress them when necessary.

On the positive side, the influence of Javanese culture has encouraged a passion for tolerance, and distaste for extremes. This has to some extent enabled the country's Muslim majority to subjugate the theocratic excesses of Islam to the practical realities of life in a plural society, and help absorb useful modernistic elements. If Indonesian Islam remains a model of tolerance it is because of the cultural bedrock on which it sits in Indonesia. Innate tolerance also ensures that ethnic friction is for the most part contained, and limitations on personal and political freedoms are patiently accepted.

To what extent the New Order's longevity hinges on its symbiosis with the prevailing culture is debatable. Suharto has certainly benefitted from indigenous respect for authority and a reluctance to question its dictates. Some of Suharto's most potent political enemies have simply faded into obscurity because of their refusal, on the grounds of cultural piety, to confront the man they opposed. Yet on a broader level, the restrictions imposed on society by the New Order have alienated many educated Indonesians. Ironically, among those who were now criticizing the system were some of the very same middle-class professionals who had clamoured for Suharto to lead them in the mid-1960s.

By the end of the 1980s Indonesian society was pregnant with tensions. Institutions and practices fashioned to stabilize the country were fast becoming anachronistic. The development programmes promoted with such vigour and admirable commitment were bearing fruit. Better standards of education and welfare had been achieved for most of the population. As a result people's aspirations were becoming more sophisticated. Economic growth increased absolute incomes, but at the same time widened income disparities and created pockets of oppulence and wealth juxtaposed with lacunae of neglect and poverty. An independent survey determined that 50 per cent of the population in urban areas subsisted below the poverty line. The figure for Jakarta was 27.7 per cent.[29]

Better educated and with far greater access to the mass media than ever before, people living in poor conditions were less fatalistic about their social and economic difficulties. Slum-dwellers in Jakarta's Tanjung Priok port area spent most of their meagre income buying fresh water, but just across the street from their perennially inundated hovels, better-off Jakartans were paying more than the slum-dwellers could dream of in a month on one hour with a night-club hostess. Villagers in Lombok, some of the poorest in Indonesia with daily incomes as low as Rp 500 per day, knew that their land was being appropriated by the rich and powerful from Jakarta. Labourers in Java were no longer the 'ignorants' in need of 'enlightenment' that officials were fond of painting them as.

Demands for better wages and better work conditions, though inter-mittently reported, prompted regular strikes and walk-outs at factories in the industrial areas to the south and west of Jakarta. In mid-1989, several hundred villagers in the Boyolali district of Central Java refused to leave land about to be flooded by a government dam project. They were not satisfied with the meagre compensation for their land, nor were they eager to leave Java for transmigration camps in the outer islands. The *Kedung Ombo* dam dispute captured headlines and drew widespread support from students and environmental groups. The military, aware of its need to stand with the people, tacitly sided with the villagers. The World Bank, which funded the dam, was put in an embarrassing position. Remarkably for a local land dispute, the government was forced to cave in and provide an alternative site for the villagers nearby. Suharto himself intervened to deliver an anachronistic blast, saying the area was one he knew well for its Communist sympathies. But no one seemed to be listening to the old tunes anymore.

From the beginning of 1989 student protests erupted more frequently, and were boldly reported in the press. Rather than criticize the government directly, the students adopted land disputes and the welfare of the people as their cause. So-called committees for land disputes in East, Central and West Java sprang up, and thick photocopied documents giving details of the disputes were circulated to the press. For the first time since the 1970s, demonstrations grew in size – though they remained smaller than the mass protests which occurred in the mid- and late 1970s. Significantly, the military was reluctant to use force to disperse them. They were content instead to round up a few ringleaders in a show of concern. The demon-strations themselves were almost always peaceful, and siginificantly, went ahead with the tacit approval of the local military authorities. Much like the situation in 1966, it seemed as if the army was trying to forge a link with the campuses, albeit on a very limited scale, and always heavily camouflaged by attempts to restore discipline and order.

Intermittent student unrest occurred against a less voluble, but none the less detectable unhappiness in elite circles. Calls for political change began to be expressed more stridently shortly after Suharto's re-election for a fifth term in March 1988. Key figures in the military and civilian leaders of Golkar began to lend tacit support to calls for openness. Senior officials, anxious to keep up with the trend towards openness, began describing *Pancasila* as an 'open ideology'. Key presidential advisers like State Secretary Murdiono were made all too aware of the lopsided image the New Order was acquiring overseas:

Deregulation in economics calls for its counterpart in politics. However, I will not invent the term 'political deregulation'. I would prefer to call it self-reliance of political organizations. On many occasions the government has urged socio-political organizations to build up their self-reliance, and there are indications of this development.[30]

Perhaps aiming to fill the breach opening up in the New Order edifice, the military loosened its grip over press censorship and themselves became more open to the media. Implicit criticism of the government's tight control over campus life emanated from security quarters. Defence Minister Benny Murdani's May 1987 warning that that too much control over the younger generation would produce a generation of robots, was echoed by Army Commander General Edi Sudrajat, who deplored the 'foot-stomping, father-knows-best' methods of those in power. Indonesian society would sooner or later demand more participation in government, reasoned Murdani, so there was a need to address the issue before matters got out of hand. In a resounding call for change – unspecified but clearly encompassing the current structure of the New Order and its leadership – Murdani said at the end of May 1990:

> In the decade that lies before us, the Indonesian nation will be confronting the challenge of change occurring at a fast pace, at home as well as abroad. Therefore a proper strategy is in order so we can meet such a future.[31]

As will become clearer in Chapter 6, the army had its own reasons to appear in a more democratic light. Politics aside, however, there were people at the top who saw the need for a change of approach, and these included many of the technocrats in whom Suharto placed so much faith. With their tacit encouragement the IGGI forum at the Hague in June 1990 took as its theme the question of participation in development. The central thrust of the participation argument was that pure economic growth was insufficient as a basis for development in the longer term. Sooner or later the complexities of the economy would demand more decentralization, more delegation of authority. US AID officials began talking about the need for 'public dialogues on development issues; opinion makers, advocacy groups, parliamentary committees and increasing interest and attention paid to what they say'.[32]

Those guiding the liberal economic reforms knew that the strict uniformity imposed on society was not conducive to sustainable economic development in the long term. How could they possibly entertain the notion of market forces being given a free rein when official ideology demanded a role for 'economic democracy' and 'co-operatives'? The restrictive effects of state control had already made themselves felt. No sooner had the private sector begun surging ahead, powered by the economic reform programme, than the state descended on it and demanded a share. A senior Japanese diplomat in Jakarta, when pressed to identify Tokyo's major concern about investment prospects in Indonesia, indicated their one real fear to be the ever-present threat of state intervention. Even more remarkably for the pragmatic and politically allergic Japanese, human rights issues and concern about the succession were raised with officials during a visit by Japanese Prime Minister Toshiko Kaifu in 1990. By late 1990, dissident circles, which had hitherto been given a wide berth by the Japanese, were being visited and invited by Japanese diplomats. It was not just that there was concern in the air, the Japanese were under considerable pressure to present a more concerned and responsible face to the world. A Japanese embassy official admitted that should things go wrong in Indonesia, and human rights issues were at stake, Tokyo would be forced to bring its considerable financial influence to bear. To some extent this happened when, after the army fired on a group of mourners in East Timor in mid-November 1991, the Japanese ambassador informed the defence minister that he could not promise the incident would not affect Japanese overseas aid to Indonesia.

Looking around them, Indonesian leaders were witnessing the turmoil generated in China and South Korea by rapid economic growth without accompanying political change. Yet the established methods prevailed. The familiar exhortations of development ideology continued. Like the grey-suited bureaucrats of Communist super-states, officials were always expressing progress in terms of figures – exports up, imports and inflation always down – and never alluding to difficulties or bottlenecks except to exhort the people to strive harder to achieve the country's development goals. Statements of policy always concentrated on what still needed to be done. Hard work, sacrifice, and of course vigilance, were always demanded. Criticism and protest beyond the tolerable levels continued to be met with sanction.

The crucial difference between this and earlier periods of when rumbles of discontent were heard, was that the regime's attempts to defuse the situation were apparently having less effect. Yet similarities with the period 1978–80 abounded. At the close of the 1970s, the army was fractious, student unrest was far worse than the present, and economic prosperity fuelled by the oil boom was generating social tensions. The difference between the two periods was clear enough: social and political aspirations were more articulately expressed and were becoming entangled with tacit moves towards a change of leadership. Suharto was powerful in political terms, but cracks were appearing in the edifice. Too many of his close advisers had either died or become alienated. He was becoming increasingly isolated, living on his wits and an unsurpassed ability to surprise. All that remained was for external support of the regime to be withdrawn, and the wolves circling at a safe distance would move in for the kill.

However, so long as public spending was maintained, and prices of staple foods and fuel were kept down by means of subsidies, the critics were deprived of the necessary fuel to promote social discontent. This made it difficult to decide to what extent demands for change had deeper roots in society. Most clearly discernible was the changing mood among the more liberally educated middle-class beneficiaries of New Order patronage in business and politics. Typically, an ambitious civilian politician, a young military officer, a foreign-educated economist or a young entrepreneur, their numbers were not great but their voice was magnified by their access to the media. It was in the military's power to muffle that voice, as they had done so before. But their patience was wearing thin, and their tolerance of dissent grew accordingly.

When the New Order is laid to rest and, like its predecessor, becomes known as the 'Old Order', many will say society was stunted by the regime's excessive concern for order and stability. Others will conclude that this 'security approach' none the less cushioned the country against the worst excesses of development. From the brief observations made above, both these arguments are to some extent borne out. Concerning society in the strictest sense, the New Order has had a fossilizing effect. Society has been shaped, levelled and co-opted; those innate qualities useful to the regime have been promoted. This has preserved – even intensified – society's primordial components: Islam, Javanese cultural dominance and the baggage of patron–client ties.

Whether or not this changes when the leadership changes is of course what many earnestly hope for. They may be disappointed. Drawing on lessons from the past, it would seem logical to suppose that the military's support for democratic forums and student movements is driven by the need to fuel its own campaign to persuade Suharto to step down, rather than any urge to reform a system of which it sees itself the natural inheritor.

As with the birth of the New Order in 1966, its passing may justify the need for a period of intense vigilance; perhaps a decree of martial law, and in the final analysis the rule of a strongman to maintain this vast and complex nation on a steady course. Few Indonesians, at the bottom of their hearts, believe the country can be run in any other way.

5

TOWARDS AN ISLAMIC
IDENTITY?

The dilemma for Muslims is that they always want to play politics,
but they are always in a position to be co-opted.
(Mohtar Mas'oed, Krapyak, 29 November 1989)

In popular Indonesian films the hero of the pre-independence struggle is
virtuous and kind-hearted to the weak and oppressed living under the
arrogance and excesses of the the Dutch *Kompanie*. The hero is also usually
a devout Muslim, embodying the ideal qualities of a just and virtuous being.
A newcomer to rural Java today would find it hard, though, to believe he
was among a mainly Muslim people – in fact, the largest Muslim population
in the world. The contrast between ideal and reality is great. For although
as many as 90 per cent of Indonesia's 180 million people profess Islam as
their faith, there is no easy way to describe the extent to which Indonesia
actually is a Muslim country.

Rigid adherence to Islamic *shariah* law is not found, and certainly not
officially encouraged. Religious courts exist specifically for the determina-
tion of marital and inheritance disputes. Strict observance of Islamic ritual
is in some communities the exception rather than the norm. In almost all
parts of Indonesia, traditional, culturally based law, or *adat*, takes precedence over strict Islamic custom. In Java, many aspects of the preceding
Hindu-Buddhist era have become entangled with Islam, such as a belief in
saints whose holiness in the Islamic sense bears no relation to their origin
in the pre-Islamic past. Tolerance and syncretism seem to be innate to
Indonesian society. During the religious fasting month of Ramadan, it is
as common to find non-Muslim Javanese fasting in spiritual companionship
with their Muslim brothers as it is to find Muslim Javanese claiming the
smallest excuse not to fast. The New Order's impact on Muslim society
has further muddied the waters because of its suppression of religious
politics in the interests of social and political harmony.

By the mid-1980s all traces of formerly influential Muslim parties like *Masyumi* and *Parmusi* had been effectively obliterated. In army circles, Muslim extremism continued to be regarded as a latent threat, and there were frequent trials of alleged Muslim extremists. Yet the government cannot be accused of neglecting the Muslim faith. Annual pilgrimages to the holy sites of Mecca and Medina are arranged under government sponsorship. Each month, a small proportion of each civil servant's pay is docked as a contribution towards a national mosque-building programme. More recently, the government promoted the establishment of an Islamic Bank.

All this and more, short of encouraging Indonesia's Muslims to feel that Islam is the basis of the state. The Suharto government seemed to be emulating the old Dutch policy of emasculating political Islam while outwardly promoting its spiritual health. The Dutch regarded Islam as a potential rallying symbol of anti-colonial feelings, and political expression of Islam was strictly circumscribed. The Dutch Islamic scholar, Snouck Hurgronje, fashioned a policy which promoted Islam as a religion, confined it to the mosque and precluded it from any affairs of state. This conscious separation of theology from the state helped Indonesia's Muslim majority develop what the Dutch sociologist, W. F. Wertheim, aptly described as a 'minority mentality'.

Like the Dutch, the Japanese occupation authorities feared the political impact of Pan-Islamic influences. But the Japanese also saw the advantage of mobilizing Islam to tap support for their war effort. Islam was therefore given it first official recognition under the Japanese, who allowed the appointment of a Muslim to a newly created office of religious affairs, and permitted the establishment of two Muslim political parties, *Masjumi* and *Hizbullah*. The move ensured that independence would be accompanied by pressure on the country's new rulers to accomodate Islamic political aspirations.

Early on in the deliberations over what form the new Indonesian state should take, those advocating an Islamic state were marginalized. Article 29 of the 1945 Constitution insists only that 'the state shall be based upon belief in One, Supreme God'. The substitution of syncretism for the majority creed as the basis of the state set the stage for Muslim political disaffection. Tension between the Muslim community and the new independent government it helped install was therefore running high in the late 1940s and early 1950s. Disagreement among them over the eventual wording of the 1945 Constitution laid the basis of later divisions in the Muslim political establishment, which the government has been in no hurry to repair. Numerically at least, the basis of Muslim support was

121

broad, and the government had every reason to be concerned. The 1955 general elections, considered by some to be the most representative ever held in Indonesia, gave the two main Muslim parties almost 40 per cent of the vote. For this reason, early governments in the Sukarno period sought to bring the more modernist Islamic parties into their short-lived coalitions. They did so against a background of regional rebellions which sought popular support by articulating Islamic aims.

The size of the Indonesian Communist Party in the early 1960s suggests that large sections of the population found secular ideological belief more comforting than any spiritual alternative. The Communists offered bold plans for land reform at a time when Islam was perceived as the driving force behind regional insurrection against the state. Many of the land-owners targeted by the reforms were also pillars of the Muslim establishment. Once again, Islam suffered from minority perceptions, and the stigma of being somehow less committed to nationalist ideals. Not surprisingly, the demise of the PKI in 1965 allowed Muslims to wreak a bloody revenge in rural Java.

The New Order acted promptly to disabuse the Muslim political camp of notions that Communism's defeat would be to their advantage. The Muslim parties of the Sukarno era were never fully restored. The decorative coalition of Muslim interests eventually set up under the banner of the United Development Party (PPP) was perceived as a wholly unsatisfactory vehicle for Islamic interests. It was designed to be just that. Suharto set about undermining what little potential the PPP had by forcing it in 1984 to replace Islam with *Pancasila* as the party's sole ideology. No longer able to campaign using the *ka'ba*, or holy shrine of Mecca, as its symbol, the PPP lost all significance to the Muslim community. In the same year the country's largest Muslim organization, *Nahdlathul Ulama* (NU), withdrew from the PPP and politics altogether. In the 1987 election, the PPP's share of the vote declined drastically from 27 per cent in the 1982 elections to a little over 15 per cent.

Islam has declined as a political force, but not as a potent influence on society. Indeed, there are those who argue that Indonesia has become more Islamic under Suharto's rule, despite the regime's secular leanings.[1] Proponents of this view cite the decline in nominal adherence to the religion, the spread of Islam on campuses and growing Islamic intellectual influence on attitudes towards national social and economic development. Accepting these conclusions at face value, and assuming that Indonesia is under pressure to incorporate these spiritual urges into the framework of the state is fraught with risk, and demands closer examination.

Traditionally Indonesian society – more explicitly Javanese society –

was regarded as perpetually in a state of dynamic tension between devout followers of Islam, termed *santri*, and more syncretic elements concentrated in the ruling class, termed *abangan*. The series of Islamic revolts which plagued Indonesia's early independent history provided some – but by no means conclusive – evidence that this was the case. As is commonly the case in Indonesia, classifications of this kind are useful, but should never be taken as absolute.

Among the *santri*, a distinction can also be drawn between modernist and traditional approaches to Islam. Islamic modernism sprang from the Muslim merchant community at the turn of the century and was an important component of the early nationalist movement. The modernists found it easy to achieve influence in a society which was looking for ways to throw off the colonial yoke and which, at the same time, saw its links to the traditional centres of Islamic scholarship in the Middle East decline due to that region's own upheavals. The First World War curtailed all visits to Mecca and the Middle East, as did the Pacific War.

More conservative trends in Islam have always been fostered in the country's traditional Islamic schools – *pesantren* and *madrasahs*. The teaching in these schools draws predominantly on Sunni thought. Until their supervision by the state, followed by the spread of the state schooling system to more areas of the country, these institutions provided the only source of education in many areas. A small Sufi mystic tradition also exists, mainly attracting the more superstitious Javanese – especially those who feel in great need of spiritual refuge. Most of the traditionalists belong to what is today Indonesia's largest and most effective Muslim organization, the *Nahdlatul Ulama* (literally 'Awakening of the Ulama'), an ulama-led movement founded in 1926.

NU's strength is concentrated in rural East and Central Java, where the *pesantren* are numerous and the practice of educating children in religious schools is maintained. In these areas, the stature of the religious teachers, or *kiayi*, is that of leaders of society, and though much weakened by the spread of state education and migration to the cities, their influence remains strong. Though less well defined, these rural religious scholars play an important role as an interface between rural ignorance and urban modernity. Today, NU claims a membership of over twenty million, concentrated mainly in East Java.

With the declining importance of the Muslim vote at elections, NU's effectiveness as an organization was preserved by detaching itself from the formal political system and becoming instead a pressure group, trading electoral contest for the complex inter-group rivalries of Jakarta politics.

INDONESIAN POLITICS UNDER SUHARTO

The chief architect of this new approach was NU's long-standing executive chairman, Abdurrahman Wahid.

Wahid is considered a wily politician, who has parlayed his status as grandson of one of NU's founders, Kyai Wahid Hashim, into an unassailable grip over the leadership. It was Abdurrahman Wahid who persuaded the ulama of the wisdom of withdrawing from formal politics in 1984. He argued that NU's status as a political player limited its acceptability to the military and the bureaucracy. He saw instead the possibilities of NU acting as a pressure group; plying the choppy waters between interest groups, and touting the organization's vast rural membership as a valuable barometer of social opinion. Wahid's vision, in effect, amounted to a reassertion of Islamic political influence using the guise of a non-governmental organization. The ruse seemed to be working. Shortly before the quiennial NU congress in November 1989, Wahid claimed:

> We are free to pursue our activities without government interference. NU has publications, internal newspapers, and disseminates ideas through public meetings and oral instruction. Before we had to secure permits for all these activities. With the permits, there were limitations on what we could do.[2]

The 1989 congress itself was a disappointment for Wahid in some ways. For although it confirmed his chairmanship and ensured him an influential perch in the run up to the national and presidential elections in 1992–3, it also demonstrated the political immaturity of the Muslim community. Meetings in the course of the congress dwelt more on simple issues such as whether it was *halal* or *haram* (permitted or forbidden under Islamic law) to earn wages working in a beer factory. More complex issues of social and political change seemed beyond the grasp of many rural religious followers. Wahid argued that the more educated membership recognized the need to adjust to new situations; that Islam must respond to these complex issues:

> I would say in five years time, we will be able to formulate a more socially-orientated approach; not just talk about 'halal' and 'haram'.[3]

This conscious articulation of Islam as a social rather than religious force highlights the dangers of interpreting Indonesian Islam in strict terms. Traditionalist Islam is often confused with a nominal adherence to the religion, and affiliation with the *abangan* stream.[4] Instead, Tamara argues that the traditionalists, who constitute the majority of Muslim scholars, have played a far more dynamic role than is often ascribed to them. As important pillars in society, the *kiayi* have acted as mediators between the expanding state and the people; they have helped society accustom itself to the influx of new ways and ideas which followed independence. It is a role which the traditionalists are being called in to play again, and perhaps with more striking effect, as Indonesian society begins to feel the strain of recent economic growth. The contemporary role of Muslims in the Indonesian polity is considerably more complex and therefore more difficult to define than ever before.

Historians are likely to conclude that one of the New Order's primary social achievements has been the suppression of the primordial *santri/abangan* conflict, thus saving Indonesia from becoming caught up in the tide of Islamic fundamentalism which swept the world from the late 1970s onward. While neighbouring Malaysia has swung close to taking that route, and Brunei teeters on the brink of Islamic conservative hegemony, Indonesian Muslims have shown no sign of embracing fundamentalist notions of Islamic statehood. As generalizations go, this is a fair conclusion. But it assumes the only politically volatile brand of Islam is 'fundamentalism'. Recent events have demonstrated how conservative mainstream Sunni Islam in the hands of western-trained modernist intellectuals can also act as a potent force in Indonesia.

There is a tradition of Islamic extremism in Indonesia, but it tends to be isolated, rural-based, short-lived and is commonly stimulated by localized socio-economic discontent. Historically, when rural discontent reached breaking point, villagers frequently turned to charismatic religious leaders or prophecies of a just and divinely blessed prince (*ratu adhil*) who would set right all that has gone wrong. At this point indigenous Buddhist notions of just leaders emerging out of chaos blended with messianic aspects of Islam associated with Day of Judgement.

More recent Islamic radicalism appears to have been rooted in disaffection with the authorities. Leaders of the so-called *jemaah usroh*, a network of Islamic studies groups which urged strict implementation of Islamic law, were all arrested or imprisoned previously on suspicion of subversive activities. Radical influences from Malaysia also percolated down the peninsula and across the Malacca straits. These *dakwa*, or missionary groups, specifically a deeply conservative sect known as *Darul Arqam*, have had some impact as well as offering a place of refuge in Malaysia for fleeing radicals. *Darul Arqam* claims some thirteen branches in Indonesia. However, there is no evidence anywhere of a growing mass-based radical Islamic organization, which remains a fringe phenomenon in Indonesia.

The majority of Indonesia's Muslims are Javanese. But unlike the Malays in Malaysia, there is no sense in which being Muslim is an inseparable part of being Javanese. The Javanese are too tolerant or respectful of other people's beliefs, and ultimately reduce religion of any kind to a common

125

spiritual denominator, namely belief in one God. Thus any resurgence of specifically Islamic belief is more likely to reflect social, political or economic frustrations. The specific aspect of Islam having popular appeal is the messianic phenomenon of a just leader appearing at a time of crisis. This may be true of all fundamentalist movements in one way or another, but being a primary factor in Indonesia, the staying power of religion as a political force must be questioned.

It was fear of a Communist resurgence after 1966 which prompted the military to declare atheism illegal. This forced many nominally Islamic *abangan* Javanese to declare themselves Muslims in name, if not in deed. Many, especially in Central Java, adopted Catholicism instead. The need was for refuge in a religious identity, not necessarily an Islamic identity. It should also be remembered that the country is home to ten million or more Christians (about half of them Catholics) and that the Indonesian constitution is careful not to give Islam pre-eminence as the state religion. With characteristic ambiguity, Suharto likes to describe Indonesia as 'neither a secular, nor a theocratic state'. Christians are freely allowed to worship their faith, and have their children receive Christian instruction in state schools. Neither are Christians denied high position in the state. In fact, they have been favoured by the military establishment, whose experience of Muslim revolts in the early years after independence embedded a deep mistrust of Muslims in high places.

As a minority, Christians have kept a low profile, choosing, rather like the Jews in the US, to work assiduously to accumulate influence beyond their numbers. They hold the key economic positions in the cabinet, are prominent in the armed forces leadership, and dominate the mass-circulation national press. Two of the most widely read dailies in Jakarta – *Kompas*, with 19 per cent of the readership, and *Suara Pembaruan*, with 8 per cent of the readership – are controlled respectively by Catholic and Protestant shareholders.[5]

Relations between the religions are usually considered excellent. So much so, that Indonesia's former Religious Affairs minister, Munawir Sjadzali, has often boasted that the Islamic world has a lot to learn from Indonesia's pragmatic approach to religious tolerance. Indonesians, he said, 'cling to Islamic tradition but at the same time behave differently'.[6] Munawir, combining his former career as a diplomat with that of religious scholar, even proposed a controversial rationalization of Islamic *shariah* law which would allow jurists to interpret the law concerning 'wordly affairs' more flexibly. His 'reactualization' of the *shariah* represents a typically Indonesian urge to embed all aspects of behaviour in the indigenous cultural context.

126

Such an approach not only neatly solves the problem of permitting *shariah* law to exist within the body of secular national law, but also reduces the chance of friction between the religions. How else could the head of the Roman Catholic Church visit Indonesia in 1989 without a murmur of protest from the country's Muslim majority? The 1989 Papal tour was conducted as a state visit, with President Suharto as host. The government was even willing to have the Pope visit the disputed territory of East Timor, where a predominantly Catholic population of some 600,000 people live under sometimes harsh rule. If the government harboured fears that the Papal visit could bring barely concealéd irredentist emotions to the surface, these fears were justified. Following the Papal mass on the outskirts of the capital, Dili, a group of young Timorese unfurled banners and demanded self-determination, after which scuffles with the security forces led to dozens of arrests, and a prolonged period of tension. Yet for all this, Pope John Paul II was said to have been greatly impressed by the religious tolerance implicit in Indonesia's *Pancasila* national ideology.[7]

The key to this tolerance has been the state's careful separation of religion from politics. The most important tool used to achieve this end has been the government's successful management of religious education. Secular-orientated policies favoured by Suharto drew on Muslim intellectuals with a western education and close ties to the Javanese establishment. All religious preachers licensed to preach in mosques pass through a government Institute of Islamic Studies (IAIN). At the tertiary level, 95 per cent of Islamic institutions are government-run. Religious leaders mistrusted by the government are banned from preaching in mosques beyond their own domicile. The government has more recently adopted a programme of sending religious teachers overseas to western centres of Islamic study in Canada, the US and UK, steering them away from traditional centres of Islamic teaching in the Middle East. In 1990, seventy-five students from IAIN, the State Islamic Education Institute were studying at Canada's McGill University, a further forty-five were destined for Leiden in Holland.[8]

Outside its official patronage of Islamic institutions, for most of its twenty-five year rule the New Order government has demonstrated more suspicion than trust towards Islam. The military has always been fearful of Islamic extremism. Religious extremists and their views were stamped on hard. Ever since the military was called upon to suppress a series of Muslim revolts which began in 1948 and dragged on till 1962, the threat of extremist Islam has been written into military history and is integral to officer training.

Contemporary military officers are not convinced that Islamic radicalism has been extinguished. The army's ruthless suppression of the Muslim riot at Tanjung Priok in September 1984, in which up to 200 people may have died, is an event yet to be erased from the minds of many Indonesian Muslims. Senior military sources now admit that the uncompromising suppression of this popular outburst was something of a blot on the country's record of religious tolerance. It was not to be the last. When a small group of Islamic extremists murdered a young infantry captain in the southern Sumatran province of Lampung in March 1989, the army also responded in a heavy-handed fashion. The official death toll after a three-day military operation was forty-one. However, informed sources now believe as many as 200 people may have died in the course of the subsequent military operation. As with the army's operations against Communist suspects in the mid-1960s, once poorly educated infantry-men have been told to root out a threat to the unity of the nation, it becomes difficult to control their enthusiasm. Tragically, in this case, it seems certain that social discontent over land tenure, not religious fanaticism, was the root cause of the problem. The army chose to blame the incident on a Muslim extremist movement linked to other extremists seeking to establish an Islamic state in Indonesia.[9]

As if to drive the point home, arrests and trials of people accused of belonging to extremist Muslim groups continued throughout the latter part of the 1980s. Since the beginning of 1990, at least half a dozen men have been charged with subverting the state with a view to establishing an Islamic state. Most were sent to prison on sentences ranging from eight to ten years. The US-based human rights organization, 'Asia Watch', argues that in many of the cases recently brought to trial, 'There are strong indications that the government either instigated or encouraged actions that it later prosecuted.'[10]

Why it should be that despite the battery of sanctions imposed on Muslim political activity, the New Order remained fearful of the Islamic radical fringe, is hard to explain. One view is that the threat of religious extremism was deployed as a device to justify tough security measures as the Communist threat receded. The military always talks about threats either from the extreme left, meaning the Communists, or from the extreme right, a euphemism for Islamic radicalism. There is also partial evidence that radical Islamic movements may have been instigated in the 1970s and 1980s by the state for the purpose of cementing political support. It is believed, for example, that the Ali Murtopo brought together former leaders of the West Java-based *Darul Islam* revolt, which had been crushed by the army in the 1960s, and actually asked them to reactivate the movement. He is said to have told them they would be helping to stamp out Communism. The real reason is thought to be Murtopo's desire to discredit Islamic political forces before the elections. In the next two years, hundreds of people were arrested and accused of belonging to an extremist sect known as *Kommando Jihad*.[11] Implausible as this sounds – audacious even – the habit of some New Order followers to believe the best way to shore up their power is to 'engineer' political threats is well attested. Most often such threats were conceived as either from the Communist 'left', or Islamic 'right'.

Given the state's uncompromising attitude towards Islamic political expression, the only safe avenue open to Muslim thinkers has been to adopt a pragmatic, flexible approach, weaving a difficult course between official suspicion of Islam, and the conservative tendencies of the ulama. Many have been forced, as a result, to compromise their own independent values to obtain government support or acceptance. On the other hand, their forced co-option does not seem to have diminished the popular appeal of many Muslim intellectuals.

Unable to promote fundamentalist or political religious dogma, these scholars cloaked their ideas in notions of social justice and welfare. Government-sponsored training in the West taught them western theories of social and economic development, which they dressed up in Islamic packaging. The 1980s saw debate about the social impact of development become a characteristic feature of Indonesian Muslim thought; offering religious faith as a means of coping with economic hardship, or striving to weave religious principles into the technological era. While this movement stemmed from the need for Islamic intellectuals to find a niche acceptable to the state, coincidentally, pressures welling to the surface in Indonesian society were forging new interest in religious belief.

Perhaps no better example of this is the development of Islamic studies and activities centred on Salman Mosque, attached to Bandung's prestigious Institute of Technology. Situated off ITB's frangipani-wreathed campus, on a broad lane shaded by majestic trees, the mosque itself looks at first glance like a technical faculty, shunning as it does any pretext of Islamic architecture. The building was designed and erected in the 1960s – a gift from Sukarno, who himself was an ITB student. After the student upheavals of the late 1970s and the subsequent banning of student political activity, Salman Mosque became a magnet for the university's talented youth. Barred from organizing secular study groups, they turned to religion. The mosque became, in the words of one Muslim intellectual, 'a sanctuary for the expression of political disatisfaction and frustration'.[12]

In the 1980s, students at Salman Mosque were inspired by the preaching of Immaddudin Abdul Rahim, a fiery Muslim intellectual with distinct

129

leanings towards the Shi'ite thought of Iran's revolutionary mullahs. Immaddudin no longer preaches at Salman, and has abandoned his radical dogma in favour of acceptance by the establishment. But his students cultivate a spirit of subdued militancy. Militancy directed towards what or whom? This is unclear.

Most of the youngsters who attend classes at Salman Mosque come from middle-class families – not all of them religiously-inclined. What motivated them most was the opportunity to be involved in an extracurricular activity, to belong to a group with ideals. Often their ends were purely career-oriented: the enhancement of skills. Some of the students also felt that with increasing pressures on the job market, and society's headlong rush into the technological age in the latter part of the 1980s, life was moving too fast for them. They sought refuge in religion as a form of escapism. Religion was perceived as a respite from, if not a cure for, social and economic ills.

While the hotheads and firebrands preached Islam as a way of life, the youthful congregation craved relevancy to the problems they faced in society and the chance to learn an extra skill in order to compete for scarcer jobs. The mosque provided for them what the campus could not, and became a hive of activity, not all of it religiously connected. The programme of religious instruction offered by Salman Mosque's youth wing, *Karisma*, is accompanied by courses in English, computer programming and other vocational skills.

Islam in this context acted as a shelter rather than an ideal. The state's uncompromising treatment of religious fringe groups and extremists ruled out their role as idealists. But the social and economic fabric of the country was altering, especially in urban areas. The pace of this change increased noticeably in the latter part of the 1980s, driven by the government's liberal economic reform programme. In Jakarta and other large cities on Java, the physical infrastructure of a booming private sector mushroomed for all to see. Banks and offices, brashly clad in reflective glass, shiny ceramic tiles and marble, reflected a new wealth and symbolized the thrusting dynamism of the country's new rich. The change was also reflected in consumer tastes: credit cards, expensive European cars, idyllic homes and money to spend. Confronted by so many physical manifestations of wealth, but not yet in possession of its material benefits, elements of the mainstream Muslim community grew restless. They perceived the reforms to be favouring non-Muslim minorities. More specifically, economic growth was seen by Muslim intellectuals as favouring the Chinese. The policies promoting this growth were, they said, being directed by a mainly Christian economic elite.

At the same time the Muslim community was finding issues to raise, it also found it had a voice. The extent to which the Muslim intellectual community had adjusted to conditions under the New Order, allowed debate to be conducted more openly. By this time all those unacceptable to the regime had been 'screened out'. Those Muslim intellectuals considered acceptable began forming study and discussion groups to try and forge a Muslim consensus. The late 1980s saw a proliferation of avowedly Muslim publications; mosque attendance increased. Friday prayers in the mosque were, by New Order standards, a relatively uncensored source of views. Preachers like Zainuddin MZ drew crowds of thousands to large stadiums – and found the licensing of such events a relatively easy process.

There was broad agreement in intellectual circles on the need to employ Islam to narrow the incipient social gap, but differences of opinion emerged between those who believed Indonesia required a more Islamic Muslim community, and those who wanted Islam to become more Indonesianized. Religious and doctrinal issues were therefore marginalized in the quest for tolerance by the state on the one hand, and relevancy to the problems confronting society on the other. There was a consensus, though, on the need to assert a Muslim view.

In the late nineteenth century, Muslim merchants in Javanese towns provided the initial impetus to the nationalist movement in its early years. As an aspiring bourgeoisie they felt the brunt of the Dutch colonial practice of favouring the Chinese traders to keep the native population weak and divided. Similarly, in the late 1980s, the rapid growth of the urban private sector, stimulated by the economic reform programme, was raising the profile of its mainly Chinese beneficiaries, and highlighting their access to state patronage.

Rapid urbanization and access to education had swollen the number of practising Muslims who now belonged to the country's small, upwardly mobile, indigenous middle class. They brought Islamic religious belief into bureaucratic and business circles close to the ruling elite. At the same time, the government's rejection of secular political ideologies and sensitivity towards currying too much favour with the Christians, created opportunities for Muslims to advance. The cabinet formed in 1988 contained at least eight past members of the Muslim student association (*Himpunan Mahasiswa Islam*, or HMI).

This brief outline of Muslim intellectual development in the 1980s suggests that by the end of the decade, contrary to popular perceptions, Islam in Indonesia had survived and successfully adapted to the generally harsh environment in which the New Order expected it to thrive. Indeed, it seemed that Islam was poised to reap the benefits from the New Order's emasculation of secular political alternatives. Quite simply, all other avenues of political expression had been sealed off. Golkar and the other parties were perceived as state-controlled arenas where only sycophantic support of government policies was tolerated. Fringe groups with socialist leanings were rigidly proscribed by the state. Labour unions had no teeth, and legal rights and welfare groups no influence over policy. Thus there was a distinct niche which Islam was edging close to filling: the need of any society experiencing relatively rapid change for a stable source of faith and succour.

It was at this point that Suharto himself appeared to move closer to the Muslim community than at any other time during his presidency. From mid-1989, his actions and off-stage manoeuvres indicated a distinct softening of the regime's attitude towards Islam. A new Education Law, tabled after exhaustive drafting in early 1989, enshrined with more certainty the role of religious education, and appeared to grant more security to private religious schools. In June 1989, a draft bill proposing beefed up Islamic courts went before parliament. In March 1990, Suharto called together some of his closest Chinese business cronies and demanded they share their wealth more equitably. Meanwhile, it emerged that a former Religious Affairs Minister, Alamsjah Ratu Perwiranegara, was busy collecting the signatures of ulama in East Java to compile a petition calling for Suharto to be elected as president for another five years in 1993. Most surprising of all, in December 1990, Suharto lent his imprimatur to the first broad-based organization of Muslim intellectuals to be sanctioned under the New Order. Capping this, Suharto took his family and a caravan of loyal retainers on the pilgrimage to Mecca in June 1991.

To many observers, these moves amounted to what seemed an obvious gambit. The scenario-makers spun out a logical sub-plot: Suharto needed to enlist Muslim political support in the run-up to elections. With opposition to his re-election to a sixth term in 1993 under threat from an increasingly disillusioned military camp, Suharto appeared to be clutching at the only card left in his much diminished hand; he let it be known that when he died, he would like the Muslims to pray for him.

Certainly the evidence to support this theory was plentiful. 'I was born a Muslim; I will struggle for the Muslim cause' Professor B. J. Habibie claims Suharto told him one day over lunch. Habibie deployed this alleged confidence with brilliant effect at an inaugural meeting of Muslim intellectuals in December 1990. By imparting Suharto's wishes, the message was clear; the president was for the first time in his long rule expressing partiality towards Islam. For the Javanese present, many of them reluctant to join an organization with such transparent connections to Suharto, the

132

remark was also interpreted as a command – *sapto pandhito raja*: the words of the wise king, which must be obeyed.

By reasserting his faith, Suharto seemed to be marking a fundamental break with the New Order's disdain for mixing religion with politics. Totally reversing his earlier policy of regarding Islamic political tendencies as an enemy of the state – in step with the military – Suharto offered his considerable powers of political patronage to the Muslim community. Many were convinced the move was an attempt to compensate for the alienation of the military. Some even compared it with Sukarno's embracing of the Communists to counterbalance a hostile military leadership.[13] But in so doing, many believed he was gambling with the country's stability.

In December 1990, with Suharto's blessing, the largest group of Muslim intellectuals to gather under one roof since the mid-1960s, gathered in the East Java town of Malang to form an organization with the innocuous name of *Ikatan Cendekiawan Muslim Indonesia* (Organization of Indonesian Muslim Intellectuals, or ICMI). The move surprised those who doubted Islam could ever find shelter under Suharto. It outraged military leaders who saw it as a bid to circumvent their claim to have the support of the people. One senior general (himself a Christian) described the move as the 'biggest disaster to hit the New Order'.[14] But was Suharto really playing the Muslim card in so crude and risky a manner, or was he simply reading the signs right?

Recent incidents demonstrated the alarming extent to which Muslim opinion could be asserted independent of state backing. In mid-1989, rumours that pork fat was being used in the manufacture of several popular food items generated considerable social tension. There were isolated killings of people suspected of tampering with food. The government was forced to televise remarkable scenes of cabinet members and senior ulama publicly eating the so-called 'tainted' products, some of which were manufactured by close business associates of President Suharto. In October 1990 the government closed down a popular tabloid after it published a readers poll which ranked the prophet Mohammad eleventh after President Suharto (who ranked first), Iraq's Saddam Hussein, and the editor of the tabloid. The fact that *Monitor* was published by the largely Catholic-owned *Gramedia* publishing group unleashed a wave of protest aimed at the group and its flagship publication, the mass daily *Kompas*.

Accompanying student demonstrations and a concerted attack by Muslim intellectuals on *Gramedia* were more worrying accusations that the Catholics were 'Christianizing' the country. Christianization has always been a latent fear among Muslims, aware as they are that the Christian church is better equipped to proselytize. In the aftermath of the 1965 killings in Java, it is widely believed that more people were attracted to the Catholic church, which was untainted by extremism and better organized to provide succour and relief to the terrorized peasantry.

The *Monitor* affair alerted moderate intellectuals of all religious persuasions to an emerging trend of intolerance in Indonesian society. It also signalled an alarming degree of traditionalist resurgence among the Muslim masses. On campuses in Central Java conservative Muslim groups were retreating behind sombre beards and Arab headgear. In keeping with the artistic eclectism charactersitic of Indonesian society, Muslims have adopted a variety of overt and demonstrative approaches to finding solace in their religion. There was a growing interest in mystical Islamic tendencies; ritualistic aspects of Islam such as the rigorous practice of daily prayers, religious chanting and Koran reading contests became popular. Schoolgirls went to court in Jakarta to defend the right to wear their *jilbabs*, or head covering, in school. In a surprise move, the government relented and decreed that schools would tolerate the *jilbab*. Even Muslim preachers enjoying popularity among the students feared these new conservative groups. 'They are fearful of outsiders, of anyone who they perceive as less than a true Muslim,' fretted one young popular preacher, whose blunt and often humorous approach to religious matters, drawing liberally on Javanese customs, had made him popular in student and intellectual circles.[15]

It appeared, on the campuses at least, that a stricter, uncompromising Malaysian style of *dakwa* was gaining ground over the more relaxed, syncretic Javanese approach to religious belief. Young Muslim intellectuals began expressing the hope that Indonesia could indeed become more Islamic than it already was. By early 1991 some non-Muslims believed this was inevitable. ICMI helped rekindle hopes of a political role for Islam to a remarkable extent. Despite the transparency of Suharto's patronage, and the uneasiness this generated, a combination of co-optive measures and momentum attracted more members to ICMI. Ultimately even the hardened doubters submitted to the tendency in Indonesian society not to resist the comforts of patronage and dependency. Arguably the organization gave voice to previously cautious types who now openly talked of the need for Muslims to assert their status as a majority. Less than six months after ICMI was formed, a group of *pribumi* (native Indonesian) businessmen formed an organization to promote a greater role for the *pribumis* in business. There was talk of a Malaysian style New Economic Policy, which actively promoted the restructuring of equity in favour of *pribumis*.

Lurking behind these incipient pressures from the Islamic community, was the suspicion that social and economic stress, and the absence of viable secular political alternatives, were driving young Indonesians to seek refuge in religion. Patronage of these social urges by the elite was encouraging the old *santri/abangan* divisions to emerge in erstwhile secular organizations like Golkar and Abri.

Prevailing social and economic conditions seemed the only way to explain why a society as heterogeneous and intrinsically syncretic as Indonesia's could demonstrate a tendency towards piety and intolerance. To some these developments highlighted the dangers of the political sterility which *Pancasila*, as the sole basis of the state, had created. Deprived for so long of a voice in politics, Muslim intellectuals corralled into ICMI believed they had been granted a licence to organize. Sensing political motives, not all of them were very willing. One prominent Muslim political science professor was ordered to join by the Minister of Education. Another Muslim intellectual from Jogyakarta was persuaded after ICMI officials leaned on a relative of his to whom it would have been difficult to say no. Once ICMI was sanctioned by the state, and in keeping with other social organizations the New Order had developed, it was difficult to escape membership.

Despite the New Order's efforts to breed a generation of western-trained Islamic scholars; despite a co-option strategy involving the official defence of Islamic values by building mosques and sanctioning the wider use of religious courts – much to the consternation of Christian leaders – the Islamic community was becoming less passive. Gradually it found it had a voice with which to make demands of the state. Indeed, there were signs that Indonesia was quietly and in a unique way becoming Islamicized. In this context, Suharto's play on the Islamic factor amounted perhaps, calculated or not, to a timely move as far as his own position was concerned.

Suharto pressed home his advantage in early 1991 by announcing he would undertake the pilgrimage to Mecca. Entering his seventieth year, an important stage in the life-cycle of the Javanese, Suharto made the case that he was going to Mecca for purely personal reasons. It was difficult, given the timing – two years before the presidential election – entirely to swallow this reasoning. 'Suharto's journey to Mecca follows his seventieth birthday and could be interpreted as making peace with God. But the visit should be viewed above all as political: as an attempt by the president to demonstrate his Islamic credentials to Muslim voters' wrote one analyst.[16]

On one level, Suharto's haj seemed nothing short of a show of force; a political crusade to the holy land. The president's perambulations around the ka' bah in his humble white pilgrim's robes were brought to the homes of television viewers courtesy of state television. Obligingly, one newspaper editorial remarked: 'there was no difference between one person and another... between the rich man or the poor man.'[17] With the barrage of criticism about his family's wealth growing more intense, perhaps Suharto believed that the sight of him and his children humbled before the holy shrines of Mecca would quell the clamour. It made instead for a great deal of cyncism in intellectual circles. At an open air sermon delivered in Jakarta, a former brigadier-general remarked: 'A thief who goes to Mecca still comes home a thief; a cat will return as a cat.'[18] Others worried that the majority of the population were more gullible. 'This makes the results of the election almost a foregone conclusion', argued a Golkar politician.[19]

On another plane, Suharto's pilgrimage acted as a rallying point for those loyal to the President. A cursory glance at the large group accompanying the President to the holy sites of Mecca, revealed a parade of loyal and faithful retainers. As well as his family and their close business partners, there was Armed Forces Chief General Try Sutrisno, Suharto's brother-in-law, Major-General Wismoyo Arismunandar, who was appointed army chief in 1993, and his son-in-law, Colonel Prabowo Djojohadikusumo. Added to this loosely labelled 'praetorian guard', there were cabinet ministers known to be unquestionably loyal to Suharto. Even close business associate Bob Hasan – an ethnic Chinese who converted to Islam – joined the President's caravan.

Others joined an outer group, keen to be seen on holy ground with the man in whom they saw the nation's stability vested. In practical terms, the hadj acts as another focus of Indonesia's characteristic social networks. On their return, pilgrims who made the haj together the same year form a fellowship under the banner of the *Ikatan Persaudaraan Haji Indonesia* (Association of Indonesian Pilgrims). Suharto has proved a master at manipulating such broad-based social organizations to mobilize support. Indirect inducement from the top prompts the organization to issue a *kebulatan tekad*, or unanimous endorsement. However insignificant the association may be in political terms, this can have a disproportionately important impact. Professional groups such as the national doctors association, teachers association and the like may fail to excite the fancies of political pundits, but the New Order regards them all as 'functional groups'. Their input can be measured in terms of the number of their members who will eventually end up in provincial assemblies, or in key Golkar positions in the towns and villages. Among them will be members of the MPR, which elects the president. Exploiting the tendency of Indonesian society to place inordinate importance on these networks, Suharto has consistently managed to fashion a consensus in his favour, and in this way, as he puts it 'coincidentally', he has been elected five times since 1966.

However cynically Suharto's shrewd manipulation of Islamic symbols is viewed, few can doubt its inherent soundness as a political strategy. If one accepts the growth of Muslim consciousness in the country, there was clearly the need for a new strategy of co-option. Allowed to develop independently of the leadership the voice of a majority could become a dangerous asset in the hands of the wrong people. They needed a signal, though. If nothing else, Suharto's haj acted as a rallying signal. On his return from Mecca, Suharto was almost certainly relieved to hear ulama pro-nounce their judgment: 'Before, I was troubled. Indonesia is the biggest Muslim country in the world, but its president had not been on the haj. Now it is done', declared a 74-year old senior ulama in east Java.[20]

As close as Suharto came to identifying his leadership with the banner of Islam, there was no move to establish expressly Islamic institutions close to the heart of government. The only concrete institutional result so far has been an Islamic Bank – in which Suharto, his family and Bob Hasan all own a significant portion of the shares. Nor was there evidence of government support for the assertion of Islamic law. The New Order has proved adept at creating carefully controlled vehicles for the expression of Islam; all within the heterogeneous framework of *Pancasila*. Indonesia is possibly the only sizeable Muslim country where the state projects itself as a patron of Islam without feeling the need to grant concessions to Islamic zealots.

This structure is essentially unchanging, rooted as it is in the rigid proscription of religious political activity. Though for political ends the nuances can be useful. A Law on Religious Courts, passed in 1989, was widely perceived at the time as a surprisingly generous concession to the Muslim community. In fact, the law was a natural product of a 1970 law granting equal status to religious and civil courts. The new law was merely a clarification of this principle. It did not seek to broaden the jurisdiction of religious courts beyond the areas of marriage and inheritance. In other words, there was less there than met the eye.

There has been no move to define Indonesia as a Muslim polity, and the expression of Islam is likely to continue to be governed by rigid institutional constraints. In this respect, Suharto's appeal to Muslims is to the largest section of society rather than to society as a whole. It is meant as a show of political force, rather than a commitment to social change. In fact, by 1991, signs of a counter-move were evident.

As thousands of students marched in protest against a numbers lottery controlled by Suharto family members in late 1991, the President was hard-pressed to set this profitable but plainly un-Islamic activity against his new-found piety. There were open accusations of military backing for the protests, some of which were so large it is inconceivable they were not granted the army's blessing. Similarly, when Abdurrahman Wahid opted to shun ICMI and set up a 'Forum Demokrasi' in mid-1991, the move was construed as an attempt to undermine Suharto's patronage of the Muslim mainstream. Wahid's influence among the NU membership, suggested his role as the principal spoiler. The army also moved to polish its much-tarnished Muslim credentials by patronizing poets and musicians bent on popularizing Islam as a youth culture through rock music. The move stirred memories of army-backed anti-communist artistic movements in the mid-1960s. For Suharto, the danger was that by making the Muslims a high value piece on the political chessboard, his opponents would seek to place it in check.

Suharto has demonstrated his mastery at anticipating and then co-opting new social forces and the interest groups which define them. In many ways his ability to attract rather than compel new social groups in this way explains the generally non-violent nature of the New Order. As the above analysis indicates, not all aspects of New Order society fall so easily under the New Order's ample cloak. In fact, the rise of Muslim consciousness appears to have been an unintended by-product of the levelling process through which the New Order sought to weed out all the political alternatives. The removal of secular political avenues of expression left the mosque as one of the few platforms from which views could be expressed.

Confronted with evidence of a Muslim community tinged with disaffection, Suharto arguably had no option other than to identify with their interests. In this respect, his apparent tilt towards Islam must be seen as a political device. Whether the move was intended to help him win the presidential election in 1993 is a more subjective – not to say controversial – interpretation. There is no doubt that certain members of the small, urban, intellectual, secular-orientated elite believed this to be Suharto's principle motive. There were also those who saw Suharto pitching the new Muslim lobby against the armed forces. But for the vast majority of rural or small town ulama and their less cynical followers, Suharto's new-found piety has been cast in the cultural context; a man grows old and draws closer to God. By doing so, he grows wiser and more benevolent. Wisdom, benevolence and a degree of piety are all the qualities Suharto needs most as he heads into the final stage of his presidency. The enhancement of such qualities can be worth a great deal in the Javanese political context.

6

SUCCESSION STALKS SUHARTO

I will clobber anyone who tries to unseat me unconstitutionally.
(Suharto, September 1989)

By 1990, Indonesia's sustained economic recovery and liberal investment regime was attracting and holding the attention of foreign investors. 'Today, Indonesia is moving steadily into position to join the club of Asian dragons', acclaimed one observer in typical fashion.[1] Yet just as the economy was revealing its true potential, political problems began to cloud the landscape.

Hard as it was for some to understand why, given the country's admired social stability and improving economic performance, the politics of succession – whether President Suharto should or could remain in office – began first to dominate political debate and then slowly to influence policy. In fact, the succession became the focus of attention to such an extent, that all other issues of political significance in this latter period of the New Order – demands for democratization, widening economic inequalities, and the future role of the military – were subsumed as part of the same problem. That problem was: how was the New Order to renew itself?

To those with more than a passing interest in the country, Indonesia at the start of the 1990s presented something of a paradox. Outwardly a successfully managed economy was bearing fruit, but increasingly the managers of that economy were confronted by internal power struggles linked to the politics of succession. Ironically, this increased the chances of politics interfering with economic policies, which is precisely what the New Order has always sought to avoid. Rumour and intrigue have always accompanied the New Order, but there was a creeping sense of doom shrouding the political machinations which mushroomed in the wake of Suharto's re-election in 1988. Rather like the behaviour of a tight-knit family close to the death of its wealthy patriarch, the mere hint of mortality was enough to set off squabbling over the inheritance.

This was not the first time Suharto's tenure in the leadership had been questioned. As already described, in the mid-1970s, certain senior figures in the armed forces tried to persuade Suharto to step aside and make way for another general. They failed, and it soon became clear that the growing tenacity of his rule reduced the chances of acquiring power for themselves. The apparatus of power Suharto was assembling around him, drew increasingly on non-military expertise. By the late 1980s, provincial governorships, heads of state enterprises and even choice ambassadorships were going to civilian instead of military appointees. 'Suharto is increasingly becoming civilian in his outlook; if not by concept then by association', remarked a junior minister in April 1988.

Gradually, almost imperceptibly Abri was being sidelined; their role increasingly defined as protecting the interests of the state rather than the nation. One suggestion is that close Suharto associates like Ali Murtopo envisaged balancing Abri's role in politics with a pre-eminent political party, probably Golkar. Murtopo's death, and the eclipsing of his circle by a less imaginative bureaucratic clique, allowed Abri to maintain its share of power in the party. None the less, many officers were concerned that close identification with Suharto was prising the army as an institution away from broader sections of the community. There was a feeling that Abri should close the widening gap between itself and the people, rather than submit itself entirely to playing a praetorian role for Suharto.

Outwardly, Abri's concern was ideologically driven. Abri's ideological *raison d'être* was to remain as 'guardians of the state'; positioned above the state and alongside the people. By this reasoning, loyalty to the state could be questioned if the New Order either exceeded constitutional bounds, or became unpopular and a threat to social and economic stability. Suharto's careful definition of his legitimacy in strict legal terms, and the enduring stability of the country ensured that neither of these conditions really materialized. In reality, Abri's doctrinal arguments served to justify political action by senior officers who wished to preserve their stake in the political system. Political manoeuvring over the succession was above all motivated by elite concerns for its own future.

Under the New Order, Abri has employed two strategies for exerting pressure on the leadership: direct, and (its preferred method) indirect persuasion. Indirectly, manipulation of social forces had been attempted before and met with little success. Back in 1977, with tension building up on campuses, Abri confronted a dilemma. The corruption and favouritism of Suharto's New Order was angering students, and Abri was reluctant to

140

be tarred with the same brush. One contemporary student poster read: 'Return Abri to the People.' If there was tacit Abri backing for these protests, it was short-lived. In January 1978, the military leadership abruptly changed course and sent troops onto the campuses, rounded up the student leaders and helped push through a ban on all political activity in the universities.[2]

As was shown in Chapter 3, early ambivalence towards the New Order leadership within the ranks was effectively smothered when Suharto lashed out at the army in 1980. Suharto was alert to Abri's discomfort, and feared its impact on political manoeuvring to ensure his smooth re-election in 1982. Abri appeared to be putting a distance between itself and Golkar and lending tacit support to the disaffected Muslim political parties, now unhappily corralled within the confines of the PPP. At an Abri commanders' meeting in the Sumatran town of Pekanbaru on 27 March 1980, Suharto aimed a body blow at the Abri high command by implicitly challenging their loyalty to the state. He was more specific at a subsequent gathering to celebrate the anniversary of the army's special forces, or *Kopassandha*. By spelling out his willingness to use force to squash his critics, Suharto challenged the military to be loyal and threatened to divide its leadership. There was already concern about the President's use of military intelligence and special forces units to bypass some of Abri's formal functions. To preserve its precious unity and political position, Abri had no choice but to tow the line.

In the wake of the Pekanbaru outburst, around fifty public figures, among them senior retired military officers such as the popular ex-Governor of Jakarta, Lieutenant-General Ali Sadikin and the former commander of the West Java region, Lieutenant-General H. R. Dharsono, drew up a petition expressing their concern at the President's use of *Pancasila* as an 'instrument of coercion against political contenders'.[3] They objected to Suharto's implicit suggestion that criticism of the executive could be construed as anti-*Pancasila* and therefore disloyalty to the state. The open opposition this step marked, also unwittingly aided Suharto, for it physically separated men like Dharsono and Sadikin from the mainstream of the armed forces.

In character with the prevailing political culture, the criticism articulated by this group was mild and politely asserted. None the less they paid for their audacity. Rather than have them arrested, members of the 'Petition of Fifty' group, as they came to be known, were banned from travelling overseas, cut off from lines of credit and access to state tenders, and could not air their views in the national press. Their ability to operate politically, economically and legally within the state was completely circumscribed.

Even socially, they found themselves ostracised as many foreign missions dared not be seen inviting the 'dissidents' to formal receptions and cocktail parties. In effect, the group was placed under state, rather than house, arrest. Some of these restrictions eased as the political climate loosened up after 1988. Yet as late as 1991, all attempts to have the travel ban lifted were blocked by Suharto, who insisted on a full apology from the group.

Aside from this small band of die-hard opposition figures for whom the end of Suharto's rule has become an article of faith, the 1980s saw comparatively little agitation against Suharto compared with the decade before. The country entered a period of economic recession after the collapse of oil prices in 1983. Hard though times were, the opposition, such as it now existed, did little to exploit the situation. Perhaps because the oil crisis was externally driven, it was hard to capitalize on what was seen by the majority of people as Indonesia's unfortunate victimization by circumstances beyond its control. The government's successful response to the crisis, pushed opposition to Suharto's rule even further to the margins. Few could argue with the ameliorative effects of the economic reform programme. Moreover, many would-be grumblers found themselves on the receiving end of the reforms, which unshackled the private sector and fuelled middle-class aspirations.

This forestalling of political pressure on Suharto was, as it turned out, only temporary; and when questions about his rule surfaced again in the late 1980s, the social and economic side-effects of Indonesia's rapid economic recovery were initially employed to good effect by those who sought to replace him. Less easy to determine is to what extent these factors of themselves contributed to the questioning of Suharto's tenure as president. Was Suharto the problem, or was he becoming a victim of his own sucessess? Typically, the latter was argued as follows:

> The Suharto government is in essence facing up to problems arising from its successes in maintaining political stability and economic growth. Its legitimacy is primarily based on its macro-economic success over the past twenty years: strict monetary control, balancing the budget, building infrastructure and debt management. Societal forces against government pressure are increasingly vocal and insistent.[4]

All these factors were present, indeed pressing on the regime by the close of the 1980s; and they were duly exploited, initially by those in the elite who felt that Suharto should be persuaded to step down some time after 1993.

Talk of succession surfaced again remarkably soon after Suharto's re-election in March 1988. With Abri's tacit support, student protests erupted across Java in late 1988 and early 1989, calling for an end to Suharto's rule. In intellectual circles, demands for more political openness and equitable economic growth grew more vocal. It was but a short leap of logic to argue that a change of leadership would help achieve these goals. Newspaper editors and academics found to their surprise that their comments went uncensored; their meetings and seminars obtained licences freely. Even members of the government chimed in with their support for openness. Several prominent New Order officials proposed that it was time Indonesia looked to the future under new leadership. All this chafing at the bit, so soon after Suharto's re-election, and with the next elections still a distant prospect, bore the marks of what was popularly termed 'political engineering'. That Abri personnel participated openly in the new atmosphere of debate over the national leadership, indicated who was doing the engineering. But why?

Social issues provided the context in which argument over the succession was set. Critics of Suharto drew frequently on this context for their political ammunition. But although it was tempting to regard calls for openness and popular participation as the first signs of a wave of political change, what made the succession issue more cogent at this stage was Suharto's age – in 1991 he turned seventy – and the lack of any apparent successor, or tested mechanism for succession.

While the emerging middle class debated the prospects of political change in the broader sense, what really worried the elite was how to preserve the system. For them, the New Order was the bedrock of their existence, and the need to ensure its survival was arguably more acute than any urge to tinker with the basic system. Indeed, it was hard to reconcile the obvious confidence in the country expressed by foreign investors and multilateral donors with the pessimistic political forecasts expressed privately in elite circles. Indigenous perceptions of the New Order's legitimacy are anchored to Suharto rather than his government and its policies. The basic issue was whether Suharto could or should continue to lead the country, and if not, who would replace him. The key concern was the succession process; constitutionally untested and heavily loaded in favour of the incumbent.

Concern about the future was most evident in military circles. The question of succession could not have loomed at a worse time for Abri. Internal debate about the future shape of Abri's role in politics was becoming more strident, and was beginning to have a polarizing effect. As shown above, many younger officers were inclined to leave politicking to the politicians. If not against the dual function, they at least saw the need,

143

as the 1990 army seminar indicated, to re-cast their role in a more contemporary mould. Their elders argued that to strip the army of its political role threatened to sap its spirit. The divide was indistinct. More politically inclined Abri leaders, such as Murdani, who represented the last of the generation of army officers with links to the independence struggle, admitted the need for Abri to foster a 'group of professionals outside the military who can help guide the country'.[5] However, Murdani represented the interests of the Abri old guard; their main concern was to maintain the relevance of Abri's role in politics, not encourage a divorce between the two.

To avoid appearing insubordinate, Abri channelled its views through the still influential retired officer circuit. Typical of them was retired Four-Star General Sumitro. In the 1970s, Sumitro was a senior army commander entrusted with *Kopkamtib* (the command for restoring order and security.) Detainees and dissidents of that period remembered Sumitro as a tough advocate of force and order. In 1989 Sumitro emerged as a leading proponent of Suharto's gentle removal from power.

> Once Suharto makes it clear he is not going to run in 1993 the political situation will be eased. Because right now everything is focused on him and his family businesses.[6]

Sumitro argued that Suharto should be persuaded to take the decision himself – and that the persuading must be done by the military leadership. Sumitro took it upon himself to write letters of advice to all the current military leaders, arguing that as their senior, such advice would be taken in good faith. In March 1990 he told the author he had written to Generals Murdani, Sutrisno, Rudini and Sudrajat, asking them to 'act like presidential candidates'. 'They are not being open with each other,' he complained, 'therefore consensus is hard to achieve'.[7] By early 1992, Sumitro had taken his self-appointed role as chief challenger of Suharto's leadership onto a more defiant plane by openly calling for Abri to distance itself from the New Order leadership.

Here it is interesting to note how Abri was reviving old concerns; its role in politics and position *vis-à-vis* the leadership. There was no unanimity on either point, and a variety of views existed. The older generation appeared to bend their principles according to their political prospects. Sumitro, wedded firmly to the security approach in the 1970s, was now advocating a civilian presidency. Murdani's ejection from the Suharto inner circle apparently convinced him of the need to encourage poiltical openness and look for new leaders. Other senior military leaders, depending on where their loyalties lay, were either all for change or appalled by the thought of it. Lower down the chain of command there were those less exposed to the power struggle within the elite who believed only in Abri's duty to maintain order and the need for a monopoly of power in order to do so. Perhaps as a reaction to the political manoeuvring at the top, younger officers sought refuge in their purely military role. The polarity was therefore multi-faceted.

On one point, however, Abri was united. If the military men failed to manage the succession and secure their nominee for president – or at the very least vice-president – in the next presidential election, not only their traditional role as political commissars would lapse, but the blow to their prestige would be even greater. This explains why senior Abri officers began airing views after 1988, which verged on the heretical.

> We should be looking towards a two term president. Ten years is enough. After the experience of Sukarno and Suharto, we need to examine the terms of the next election. The issues need to be more widely and more openly discussed.[8]

To the casual observer, the military's pre-eminent position in the political hierarchy seemed enough to guarantee it a leading role in the order to come. But inwardly, Abri leaders felt less optimistic. Suharto had demonstrated his ability to bypass the military when he appointed its nemesis in the shape of Sudharmono as vice-president in March 1988. Of the group he hand-picked to advise him on the composition of his new cabinet and policy options for the period 1988–93, only three out of nine came from the armed forces. Civilian Muslim and nationalist tendencies were heavily represented. Shortly before his March 1988 re-election, Suharto blocked a move by Abri to pass a law diluting the president's supreme power over the armed forces. His subsequent intervention to have former adjutants and even his brother-in-law appointed to key military commands in Jakarta left observers in no doubt that Suharto still called the shots in Abri.

There was no guarantee he would listen to his military peers in the run-up to the 1993 elections, and the leverage they had over him – employing strictly constitutional means – had been severely curtailed over the years by his shrewd manipulation of senior appointments. As one civilian cabinet minister remarked in late 1989: 'Suharto has pushed the military into a corner so that all they can do is instigate a crisis'.[9] In the eyes of one of the army's founders, General A. H. Nasution, the armed forces were united in spirit but divided and poorly led at the top: 'The army cannot trust each other enough to talk about the strategy for the future'.[10]

There was another, more widely felt reason for concern. Indonesia's first President, Sukarno, fell prey to a *putsch*. Indonesia's collective allergy to succession grew out of the traumatic manner in which the new Republic experienced it for the first time. Stripped of its anti-communist veneer, Sukarno's downfall – and the events surrounding it – bore the stamp of a traditional succession struggle: it was accompanied by the imprisonment or execution of key Sukarno supporters; the subsequent besmirching of his name and achievements, and a period of chaos and upheaval unparalleled in the nation's modern history. Broadly speaking, the reasons for this are culturally driven and are shared by other South-east Asian states.

A slight digression may be helpful in this context, in order to explore the extent to which traditional concepts of power and authority have become more rather than less potent in the post-independence period. Independence triggered in South-east Asia's former colonies what Lucien Pye aptly describes as a 're-legitimization of traditional values'.[11] The point needs stressing because so much of the analysis of politics in modern South-east Asia assumes that societies are inexorably converging on a western model of democratic pluralism.

In fact, the evidence points the other way. Following, as Pye suggests, 'an initial effort to show the former colonial rulers that their masters had mastered the Western art of government',[12] most new states embarked on a period of intense debate about the nature of power. The consolidation of power was cloaked in the quest for national identity. Having overcome the imperialist overlords, these states redefined nationalism in terms of the resilience drawn from economic development and the fostering of traditional values. It was argued that to achieve the goals of development and preserve the fabric of society and its traditional values, some of the aspects of western government had to be adapted, or suspended 'temporarily'. In their place, indigenous quasi-ideologies were developed: *Pancasila* in Indonesia; the *Rukun Negara* in Malaysia, and more recently, Singapore's 'Core Principles'. By this process, the leadership of each country acquired more power, and the political enfranchisement of ordinary people, indeed their involvement in politics, was diluted. The legitimacy of this power was justified more and more in terms of traditional values, rather than through the ballot box. Elections became progressively symbolic affairs, designed to lend democratic credibility to these regimes, rather than allow the electorate a genuine choice of leadership.

By the end of the 1980s, all of South-east Asia's former colonies had established stable structures of national power, focused on powerful leaders. Suharto held sway in Indonesia, and Dr Mahathir Mohamad in Malaysia. Singapore's Lee Kuan Yew was the first of this generation of powerful leaders to experiment with succession. He stepped down as prime minister in November 1990, but continued to cast a long shadow over the political process by retaining chairmanship of the ruling People's Action Party and offering his views on major political issues in public, when he felt it necessary.

Forty-five years after the end of the colonial era, all these countries were facing the first test of their maturity. Their economies were developed, with growth rates well above the global average. This meant leaders could not expect to shelter behind their developing status much longer. Western donors would soon realize the absurdity of pumping aid and investment out of economies in recession into buoyant and prosperous centres of economic activity, whose very success threatened their own economic hegemony.

The more confident these countries grew, the more they shed inherited western political institutions in favour of traditional models. This drove a wedge between them and the West, shedding the last vestigial colonial bonds. Thus in Singapore, western values were rejected as increasingly irrelevant, and Mandarin Chinese values promoted instead. In Malaysia, Prime Minister Mahathir Mohamad's controversial premiership led to the perceptible adaptation of the country's British-style parliament and judiciary to traditional Malay forms of patronage beholden to a paramount leader. In Indonesia, Suharto's embodiment of Javanese culture, with its emphasis on respect for individuals who hold power, hindered the development of modern executive and bureaucratic branches of government answerable to elected representatives as broadly envisaged in the Constitution. The personalization of power Suharto achieved at the expense of institutionalized checks and balances, or any formal separation of powers, made the process of transferring that power to another individual an uncertain and risky prospect.

The irony is that just as South-east Asian nations began achieving their own sense of national identity within an indigenous context, marking perhaps the final break with their colonial past, they faced a threat to stability which any cursory reading of the region's pre-colonial history reveals to be the single most common cause of political decline.

The history of South-east Asia is littered with conflict born of succession struggles. As a testament to how seriously a change of leadership was taken in historic times, it was the practice of many South-east Asian Hindu-Buddhist kingdoms to shift the location of their capitals once a new king assumed power. (Faintly echoing this practice, Suharto refused to take up residence in any of Sukarno's palatial state residences on assuming power.) Often the new king would order the deaths of every one of his predecessor – or rival's – family on ascending the throne.

Individual leadership is therefore the most potent element of South-east Asian power structure, a phenomenon which seems to have survived the evolution of modern institutions of government since the colonial era. This poses difficulties when it comes to the transfer of power, because the cultural pre-eminence of leadership allows little scope for the survival of a regime once its leader is no longer in power. Moreover, a change of leaders implies marked changes in policy in order to mark out and legitimize the power of the new leader. In the New Order's case, there were real fears among members of the elite that Suharto's passing would threaten the New Order's legitimacy and unleash a political holocaust similar to that which accompanied Sukarno's downfall.

As a leader undoubtedly steeped in the traditions of his own society, Suharto is unlikely to view the succession process in contemporary terms. Rationally, a man who has contributed so much to Indonesia's well-being could expect to be permitted a graceful exit and comfortable retirement. Yet if Indonesians found it easy to castigate the man who proclaimed independence, how difficult could it be to denigrate the father of development? There is also circumstantial evidence to support the view that Suharto considers his own leadership to be a product of divine intervention. The logic is simple: so long as he is there, he must be the chosen leader of his people. Javanese eschatology stresses the importance of *wahyu*, a divine messsage from God to assume leadership. Suharto is not known to have used the term publicly, but the modern Indonesian language has endowed the generic term for leadership, *Kepemimpinan*, with almost as much sacral power. Even allowing for a modicum of rationality in a man whose policies have been nothing else but pragmatic, strong cultural factors give him little scope for speculation about the succession. Almost certainly, this ruled out announcing his retirement.

Alternative candidates were also hard to detect. Indonesian rulers are traditionally not in the habit of pre-annointing successors to prevent creating an alternative locus of power. Constitutionally speaking, the vice-president of Indonesia is the next in succession, should the president be incapacitated. Actually, the position is one of the most impotent components of the national leadership. Under Suharto, the vice-presidency has been conferred on men of symbolic significance, like the late Sultan of Jogyakarta, Sri Hamengkubuwono IX, or patently benign cronies like General Umar Wirahadikusumah. Never has a powerful military figure held the post, for this would place a figure with access to an alternative source of power in a position to challenge the president.

Most Indonesians consider the vice-presidency a largely ceremonial position with almost no capacity to wield power. Crudely speaking, the post is considered a useful place to park either cronies or potential enemies; too close to the president to do any harm, high enough up the totem pole in protocol terms to signify reward and gratitude for services rendered. Even in the event the vice-president does succeed an incumbent president, the system fashioned by the New Order allows for only a short period, no longer than six months, before the MPR must be called to either confirm or replace him.

Short of the vice-president being conferred with temporary powers as president, the Constitution gives few clues about the succession mechanism. Suharto consistently reiterates the role of the MPR in selecting the president, but this obscures the complex web of interests which must first confer behind the scenes in order to come up with a suitable candidate. In theory, the MPR is empowered to decide between more than one candidate. In practice, Indonesia's consensus-driven political system is shy of deciding anything by vote. Voting on issues is regarded as an invitation to political chaos, and therefore a last resort. Preferably, the establishment reaches a unanimous decision on who will be the sole candidate for endorsement and acclamation by the MPR. For the past twenty-five years, Suharto has been the sole choice. This raises another problem, for if the MPR has to endorse a candidate other than Suharto, can the same orderly procedure be guaranteed?

Against all the institutional uncertainties surrounding the succession process, there were those who saw Indonesia's buoyant economic future as a bulwark against political instability. Many people were simply unwilling to believe that traditional and institutional obstacles to a smooth succession could stand in the way of an incipient economic success story. In fact, this is just what began to occur. In a society with a long history of strict distinction between rulers and the ruled, the possibility of instability generated from the centre of power is that much greater.

Compounding the lack of confidence in the ranks of Abri, the cabinet Suharto appointed in March 1988 acted far less monolithically than was customary under the New Order. This is of some significance, as it allowed individual members of the cabinet and related institutions to articulate their own political ambitions more freely. The very disposition of players assembled for his new cabinet in 1988 seemed to undermine their potential as a team. The Home Affairs Minister, General (retd) Rudini, was known to be on cool terms with the Defence Minister, General (retd) L. B. Murdani, whom the latter had dismissed as army chief in 1986. Murdani himself was still smarting from his own ignominious dismissal as Abri chief in February 1988. His replacement as armed forces commander, General Try Sutrisno, was a man of some charm but little imagination. One of

149

Suharto's former adjutants, he was not the best choice to help forge unity and restore confidence in the ranks.

Some of the younger men appointed to key portfolios were unpopular with the military. Mines and Energy Minister Ginanjar Kartasasmita, Attorney-General Sukarton Marmosudjono (who died suddenly in June 1990) and State Secretary Moerdiono were all considered fellow travellers with Vice-President Sudharmono and therefore mistrusted in military circles. In the words of one minister, the cabinet was composed of 'new people with no experience and old people who are too tired'.[13]

Perhaps it was Suharto's intention to weaken the integral unity of the cabinet. Feeling his age, and pressures to step down on their way, Suharto may have deliberately assembled a mismatched team to enhance the lustre of his own wisdom. Was not the wisest king prudent enough to ensure that none so wise rose high enough to threaten his monopoly over power? Perhaps unsure of loyalties in the wake of the 1988 presidential election, he employed his skill at judging people's qualities and where best they could be deployed to cast potential challengers in opposing positions. In the 1970s, when Suharto had more than a handful of loyal retainers at his side, his strategy was to double up on appointments, and appoint key aides to a number of powerful positions. Attrition, due to both natural and political causes, had decimated the old 'inner circle' leaving the president no option but to fall back on principles of divide and rule.

Pivotal in this respect was the gulf which appeared between younger civilian technocrats and Abri. Many of them came from Golkar, where they had gained prominence under Sudharmono's patronage. While some saw the emergence of former Golkar senior cadres in the 1988 cabinet as a healthy sign, the shift undoubtedly intensified Abri's concern about its own political pre-eminence. Traditional Javanese court history was littered with examples of ancient kings playing his courtiers off each other. One story even tells of a king who entrusted his two most trusted generals with conflicting orders in confidence, with the inevitable result that they fought each other to the death. Similarly, within Suharto's cabinet, political alliances are hard to imagine in an assembly of some fifty men which pitted military against civilian ambitions, bureaucrats against technocrats and loyal retainers against progressive free-thinkers. This kind of Javanese man-management strategy appealed to those who admired Suharto's deft manipulation of the country's elite. But others, specifically in the armed forces, felt that it diminished their influence on the executive.

Something else was different. Suharto himself had changed. He was withdrawing, becoming less accessible and in the process more imperious – as well as impervious. Foreign and domestic journalists recalled his jocularity towards the media in the early years of his rule. But by the mid-1980s his rare press briefings were more like monologues. On one occasion, when Suharto was returning from a visit to Beijing and Hanoi, senior editors were advised not to ask any questions after the President's briefing. Not because he mistrusted the integrity of the senior journalists, said State Secretary Moerdiono aboard the presidential flight, but because he was afraid Suharto's responses would create a stir.[14] Suharto still appeared daily on television or in press photos, and the public saw an image of the working president. Gone was the cigar-smoking, sea-fishing informality of earlier years. Suharto's favoured appearance was either seated at his desk dispensing wisdom to his ministers, or at staged discussions with the farmers in the field. Frequently he was seen on his cattle ranch, imparting advice on the latest breeding techniques to hand-picked rural Javanese bumpkins, their faces filled with awe and wonderment. One farmer featured in a television feature filmed at the ranch was seen asking Suharto how he, a poor farmer from Central Java could ever hope to own so many cattle and such a modern ranch. Suharto's reply: only with hard work and application.

These TV appearances provided some insight into Suharto's own views. While his speeches tended to reflect the advice of close advisers and the policies of various ministries, on those occasions where Suharto spoke off the cuff, the president's innately conservative and uncompromising views shone through. As one commentator put it: 'He only reads the speeches, they are not supposed to be taken as his own thoughts'. On one such occasion, being taped for broadcast on state television, a witness relates that Suharto encountered a group of state-housing tenants who voiced mild complaints about the facilities he was opening. Noting that the complainers were non-Javanese he proceeded to give a lecture about the importance of gratitude inherent in Javanese culture. A non-Javanese senior official had the presence of mind to stop the tape at this point, thus preventing Suharto's genuine, and potentially destabilizing, views from being aired throughout the country.

Aside from these periodic televised chats with the farmers, Suharto became less accessible to the public. Citing the need for economy in the midst of the oil-recession, Suharto stopped holding an open house over the annual Ramadan holiday in 1986 – though pressure of numbers might have been a more forgivable excuse. He became more remote from his people in the process. He also began worrying more about his own personal security – at one time in late 1990 ordering a helicopter to pick him up from his office by landing on the roof of the building. There are persistent, but undocumented stories that he sought advice from spiritual advisers, or *dukuns*, that he arranged to appease Javanese spirits before leaving the country, and that he listened more to his children's advice than that of his advisers.

A distinctly regal air wreathed the President of the Republic. Despite a carefully cultivated image showing a working president living a humble lifestyle, the drab safari suit in which he normally appeared at work, and the homespun traditional Javanese family customs he practised were fooling very few people, in urban areas at least. That is not to say they disapproved. Javanese cultural philosophy preaches that wealth and the arrogance which accompanies it, must be veiled by humility. 'It is better for the rich man to work as an ice-porter and go about singing, rather than sit in his limousine behind tinted glass crying', runs a contemporary version of an old Javanese proverb.

The acquisitive proclivities of his wife and children were hardly a secret. Just as the government's economic deregulation programme seemed to have reached its peak in 1990, Suharto's children were solidifying their hold over the most lucrative areas of the economy. Private airlines, television stations, radio, newspapers were brazenly set up under their ownership. New monopolies were replacing those deregulated by his economic ministers. Once established, these companies bent the rules shamelessly. In May 1991, *Rajawali Citra Televisi Indonesia* (RCTI), a private television station owned by Suharto's second eldest son, Bambang Trihadmodjo, was denied a licence to broadcast test transmissions around Indonesia via a transponder on the nation's Palapa satellite. RCTI continued with its test transmissions willy-nilly.[15] Not long afterwards, RCTI obtained the right to broadcast nation-wide using the satellite. At the same time the company announced it was seeking a permit to broadcast using land-based transmitters. The state televison company, *Televisi Republik Indonesia* (TVRI), was powerless to defend its monopoly.

The government's policy of economic deregulation opened up new areas of enterprise for Suharto's family. They also employed nationalist arguments to good effect. Suharto responded to criticism of his family's business activities by pointing out the transfer of wealth from Chinese to indigenous hands it represented. In the case of RCTI, it was argued that while the Department of Information allowed unrestricted viewing of Malaysian, Thai and Filipino television via satellite, it obstructed a domestic private enterprise.[16]

Less easy to defend, it seemed, was an attempt by Suharto's youngest son, Tommy, to hijack one of the country's most lucrative indigenous consumer industries. In early 1991, Tommy set up a new clove-trading monopoly with the ostensible aim of seeking a higher price for clove traders supplying the nation's *kretek* cigarette industry. Initially, manufacturers

152

resisted the scheme, falling back on healthy stocks and their reputation as among the country's most profitable concerns. But when political pressure forced the government to back Tommy's clove monopoly with a hefty state loan, and impose higher minimum prices on the cigarette manufacturers, the tables began to turn.

By July 1991, the third largest *kretek*-maker, Bentoel, declared debts of $US370 million and faced takeover by Tommy's corporate vehicle, the Humpuss Group. Although partly fuelled by long-term financial problems, Bentoel's predicament stemmed from having to buy up extra clove stocks to stave off Tommy's clove monopoly. Bentoel's battle with Suharto's son had a knock-on effect on Indonesia's economy, as the company's decision to fight it out by suspending payment on its debts led some offshore creditors to reconsider their Indonesian exposure.[17] Worse still for the government was the potential loss of excise revenue should other *kretek* firms go under. *Kretek* sales contribute an estimated 6 per cent of national non-oil tax revenue. Concentrated in East Java, the industry supports an estimated four million people. No one could make any sense, therefore, of why Suharto appeared to be backing his son's scheme when revenue, welfare and ultimately social stability were threatened.

It has always been difficult to judge domestic reaction to the Suharto family's 'success' in business. Much of the criticism emanated from business circles; domestic and foreign business groups which had lost out to the family. The fast-growing private sector grumbled about the family's rapacity, but within such a comparatively small section of society, almost as many grew wealthy by the family's patronage as fell foul of their acquisitive proclivities. Lower down the social scale, local feelings in areas subject to land acquisition or development by the family, ran quite high, but with no outlet for expression, they went barely heard. In a small fishing village situated in one of the poorer parts of the island of Lombok, a pearl-farming operation run by one of the Suharto family businesses, meant that local fishermen were denied access to the pearl beds – even to fish for themselves. To make matters worse, labour brought in to collect the pearls was from nowhere near the area, and certainly not from the village in question.

Local officials complained about alleged agents of family concerns harassing them with demands for lands and contracts accompanied by threats if they were not satisfied. It was not always clear in Jakarta, whether these agents were really working on the family's behalf. Suharto's technocrats were aggravated by the demands of the family, which they found impossible to fend off. Trade Minister Arifin Siregar moaned that his job mostly entailed processing licensing requests for family concerns. These

demands either hindered, or conflicted with the economic reform programme. They had little choice but to comply. The ministers vented their
frustration in talks with World Bank officials and foreign diplomats. A row
erupted in 1986, when it transpired that the US embassy had compiled a
confidential dossier on the family's activities – much to their embarrassment. Fact or fiction, stories about the extent and impact of Suharto family's
business interests were fanned by political interests opposed to Suharto.

In the face of such criticism, Suharto withdrew and spent more time
with his immediate family, doting on his grandchildren and listening to the
counsel of his wife and six children. There were complaints in cabinet
circles that he listened more to his family than to his ministers. In late 1989
the governor of East Timor, Mario Carrascalao, came perilously close to
losing his job after Suharto's son-in-law, Colonel Prabowo Djojohadikusumo, reported to Suharto that the governor was sympathetic to
separatist elements in the province.[18]

Prabowo, a man many regarded as a possible contender for senior
position if Suharto managed to stay the course until the late 1990s, was
convinced of plots against Suharto being hatched by certain elements in
the military. He teamed up with other family members to convince the
president of the danger he was in from certain people – principally Murdani
– and offered advice on whom to promote to counter their influence. Hard
as it was to understand how a mere lieutenant-colonel could wield so much
influence, by late 1991 this impetuous and ambitious young man commanded two battalions of the 17th airborne brigade which came under the
Kostrad command of Suharto's brother-in-law. With or without Suharto's
knowledge he had begun assembling a group of army officers loyal to him
outside his unit, using the threat of Murdani and his 'Christian' clique as a
means of attracting Muslim officers.

Faced by a military elite growing increasingly uncomfortable with his
leadership, it seemed odd that Suharto was doing nothing to stem the tide
of speculation about the succession. Rather more strange was the apparent
lack of concern for the damage to his image wrought by his children and
their sycophants. The result was an atmosphere of expectation; would
Suharto react? Or would he become the victim of reaction? Succession
talk bred consideration of the unthinkable; a head-on confrontation
between Suharto and his opponents. However, most seasoned observers
preferred to hedge their bets, arguing instead that Suharto was not a man
to over-react. Indeed, some felt that by not acting at all – or not appearing
to act – Suharto would overcome the situation. Strangely enough, the
reality played out in a mixture of ways.

As political tension intensified, ministers complained that Suharto no longer sought their advice, but instead gave them orders. Having sat before the President in straight-backed chairs with hands respectfully parked between uncrossed legs, ministers left the President's office merely to reel off the President's commands. The substance of these directives mostly reflected advice offered by his ministers, but Suharto never encouraged them to demonstrate their own initiative in public. That many opted instead to voice their views freely in private must have annoyed Suharto. Monthly cabinet meetings were frequently occasions where Suharto reprimanded his ministers rather than invited their counsel.

In May 1989, in an astonishing display of directness, Suharto told ministers to stop speculating about the succession. The language used was blunt; those present at the regular cabinet meeting on 3 May said the President was clearly aggravated. A month later, the text of his remarks was deemed important enough to be issued as a published statement. In it, Suharto warned his ministers not to air their views freely and 'create divsions of opinion between one official and another'.[19] Conceivably, Suharto was referring to views aired by Co-ordinating Minister for Political and Security Affairs, Admiral Sudomo, in mid-April. The jocular admiral had speculated on the possibility of more than one candidate standing for president in 1993. At the time Sudomo claimed the idea had been relayed to him by Suharto himself, a move which greatly intensified succession talk.[20] Suharto may have deliberately aired the possibility of alternative candidates to smoke out his opponents. The strategy was compared with Chairman Mao's 'Let a hundred thousand flowers bloom'. If that was the case, Suharto was clearly not pleased with the extent to which the notion of alternative candidates received public support

> Already there are some who think it is time to make 'softly-softly' approaches to those they think will be their champions.[21]

One of the most curious of these outbursts came in September 1989. Travelling home from an overseas trip which had taken him on a path-breaking first visit to Moscow and a Non-Aligned Movement meeting in Belgrade, Suharto was in a confident and expansive mood. As his autobiography suggests, Suharto takes great pride in being seen among great leaders of the world – and at that time, Gorbachev was on the way to his Nobel Peace Prize. Basking in the international glow, Suharto talked expansively of Indonesia's candidature for leadership of the Non-Aligned Movement. Then he shifted suddenly; nobody, he said, was prepared to believe anything he said unless it came from his own mouth. He went on to say it simply was not possible for him to explain everything all the time. 'Putting it bluntly,' he said, 'I might die on my feet.... Perhaps that is what they want so I can be replaced.' The shift in context was sudden and effective.

But if they want to replace me with someone else using unconstitutional means, I will clobber them no matter if they are politicians or generals.[22]

While many viewers recoiled from their President's use of harsh, impolite language – specifically the term *gebuk* (to clobber) – political pundits wondered whether Suharto was beginning to feel the heat. Was he reacting to persistent sniping by a small but arguably hopelessly divided group of retired generals? Was he alluding to moves against him behind the scenes? Why risk betraying a sense of insecurity when clearly his grip on power was as firm as ever? Perhaps Suharto was only expressing anger at what he saw as certain people's insubordination. Sumitro's comments, coming from a man who had already crossed him, must have rankled. But by now many felt discussing the succession issue had become a pertinent topic for public as well as private debate.

Showing more concern for the future, in an interview with *Time* magazine in April 1991, Suharto seemed to sound a warning of the political turmoil which could accompany any distraction from his programme of development. 'Should development fail, should there be no economic growth, that failure would almost certainly lead to the possibility of seeking other ideological principles'.[23] Many took this to be an implicit threat of chaos should Suharto lose support as President. Western analysts found this hard to believe given the strength of the New Order's edifice. But Indonesians, imbued with the culture of leadership, feared that the New Order rested on Suharto's shoulders. The threat was aimed at them.

Given Suharto's progressive withdrawal from scrutiny, it became difficult to gauge just how confident he was about the future. Curiously, he held back from delivering the kind of threatening blast which set the New Order back on course in March 1980. There is no doubt the failure to do so prolonged and intensified speculation over the succession. It gave rise to wild suggestions that Suharto himself was considering retirement. Had he not hinted at the prospect in his autobiography published in early 1989? There were suggestions that he was fuelling succession rumours himself; or at the very least, allowing them to proliferate, in order to allow divisions within the elite over the issue to solidify.

In the first months of 1990, Suharto switched tactics. Apparently alarmed by moves to promote criticism of his rule, he launched what seemed like an attempt to deny his critics of ammunition. Up to this point Suharto had confined his reaction to warnings against speculation about the succession. Never once alluding to himself, Suharto shrewdly stressed that the next president would be chosen by the MPR – and by no one else. Suharto has consistently diverted all speculation about his personal position down constitutional alleys, underlining the strict legal legitimacy on which the New Order prides itself. But with parliamentary elections due in 1992, the political heat generated by succession talk appeared to compel Suharto to shore up his rule by deploying strategies in other, more controversial areas. The most remarkable of these moves was initiated in early 1990.

Under fire about his close ties with Chinese business interests, he publicly castigated the Chinese for their greed. At the beginning of March 1990 Suharto summoned thirty-one of Indonesia's most successful businessmen – almost all of them ethnic Chinese – to 'Tapos', his lavish cattle ranch in West Java. There, before the cameras of state television, the president called on them to promote social equality by selling up to 25 per cent of the equity in their firms to co-operatives. 'I invite you to prevent the possibility of social unrest as early as possible', Suharto told the businessmen, most of whom in one way or another had accumulated their wealth through his patronage.[24] This extraordinary demonstration of his power, though couched as an appeal, was followed up by a set of guidelines for the divestment of shares to co-operatives. The scheme was hurriedly framed by his economic ministers – none of whom were alerted of the move in advance.

Suharto's action was puzzling to say the least. Just when his liberal economic policies seemed to be reaping the most returns by unshackling the private sector from the bondage of state control, Suharto appeared to be signalling new constraints on private investment. It soon became apparent that the president's ear had been gained by a group of leftward-leaning economists, whose notions of economic democracy included the view that having endowed the private sector through its policies, it was now the government's duty 'to make them pay'.[25]

More worrying still was Suharto's evident intention to highlight the role of the ethnic Chinese, thus legitimizing attacks on their wealth and privilege. 'If necessary,' followed up Suharto's half-brother, Probosutedjo – a rich and successful businessman in his own right – 'financially strong businessmen who enjoyed facilities could be forced to limit their businesses so as not to make small and medium sized businesses go bankrupt'.[26] Home Affairs Minister Rudini jumped in at the same time with concern that the rate of assimilation of the ethnic Chinese was 'deplorably slow'.[27]

Indonesia's comparatively small overseas Chinese population has always been the target of prejudice. Localized anti-Chinese disturbances probably occur more frequently than they are reported – usually sparked off by a Chinese trader accused of mistreating his native employee. The last major anti-Chinese disturbances were in Bandung in the mid-1970s. The public lambasting of Chinese tycoons at Tapos possibly reflected the president's concern about the impact of rampant private-sector growth on the social fabric of the country, but this might be stretching his feel for tensions in society beyond credulity. Nor does it do justice to Indonesia's Chinese businessmen who, always aware of their precarious security, have deployed some of the most generous and efficient welfare schemes in Indonesia.

Even though there was legitimate concern about the extent to which non-indigenous business growth appeared to be outstripping the pace of commercial development in indigenous hands, it was hard to argue with those who saw the motivation for Tapos as intrinsically political – and related above all to the succession question. Suharto seemed to be fishing for support to undermine his critics. He may even have worked out the move in agreement with his Chinese cronies, and indeed there were subsequent allegations that close members of the Suharto inner circle stood to gain from the divestment scheme. One prominent member of the elite described the Tapos meeting as 'an exercise in self-rehabilitation'.

There were certainly grounds to view the Tapos meeting as a response to growing pressures in society. Comments about the threat to stability posed by the untrammelled growth of 'big' – meaning Chinese – business interests began to surface in the press and during parliamentary hearings in the course of 1989. The word 'conglomerate' assumed negative racial overtones. Warnings about their lack of responsibility and selfish ways were flung about freely in the press, and there was now talk of the need to 'regulate' their activities. Suharto's actions may have been driven by concern that the wealth of the Chinese was tarnishing his own image.[28]

Pointing the finger at Chinese business interests is hardly new in Indonesia. Unusually though, Suharto's actions flew in the face of the New Order's tough curbs on the open discussion on racial issues. The use of volatile racial issues during periods of political flux is also common in Indonesian history. Anti-Chinese disturbances flared up at independence and attended the birth of the New Order. The issue was most attractive of all to the Muslim community, whose commercial prowess has never matched that of the Chinese. At the Nahdlatul Ulama's quiennial congress in November 1989, delegates from small towns in Java spoke bitterly of the way 'big business' from Jakarta was behaving in the provinces, buying up land and gobbling small enterprises.[29]

Suharto's public patronage of Chinese business interests made them a target of his critics. His alliance with big business was the soft underbelly compared with the tough legal and constitutional carapace the New Order had built around itself. Sensing that his opponents might be fishing for a way of pinning charges on him of abandoning the Constitution, Suharto fought to seize the moral higher ground on the issue. By all accounts the plan to sell shares to co-operatives was hurried and not well thought out; it bore all the hallmarks of contingency. None of the technocrats were happy with the idea; it sent all the wrong messages to the investors now queuing outside their offices.

Puzzled, many of these investors began to wonder whether Indonesia was contemplating policies to redistribute wealth along racial lines – something akin to Malaysia's New Economic Policy. In fact what emerged was a scheme generated by the bureaucracy to have larger Chinese-owned businesses foster their smaller, indigenous cousins. The prescription was almost as old as the problem itself. Above all, Tapos, and almost everything that has happened since, demonstrate the extent to which Suharto was concerned about political pressures generated by the succession issue.

By the end of 1989, Suharto's public utterances played heavily on the equity theme. There was to be more for everyone via the shares-to-co-operatives scheme. The provinces would have more fiscal autonomy. The neglected Eastern provinces would receive more attention from the central government. In June 1989, Suharto even held a meeting with members of Indonesia's only avowedly socialist organization, the *Marhaenist* group (with roots in Sukarno's idealistic notions of the common man). He reportedly asked them to help him 'socialize' the national leadership.[30]

All this seemed to suggest a desire on Suharto's part to reassess the country's direction. But did it add up to a commitment to fundamental change? Most outsiders liked to think it was a prime example of the New Order's tested pragmatism. Even after a quarter-century in power the regime still knows what is best for the country, they would say. Many Indonesians were more cynical. Some considered instead that the New Order was fighting a rearguard action to save itself from collapsing from moral decay. All this talk of reform and new ideas was seen, perhaps a little too unfairly, as the nearest one could get to vote-buying.

Running parallel with his appeal to the Chinese were moves by Suharto to woo Muslim leaders. As described in the previous chapter, Suharto again took everyone by surprise in late 1990 when he sanctioned a broad-based organization of Muslim intellectuals (ICMI), a decision which appeared to follow some months of subtle probing of their support by a close Suharto ally, former Religious Affairs Minister Alamsjah Ratu Perwiranegara. Alyamsjah was known to be a self-seeking man, but few believed he would have acted without Suharto's tacit acknowledgement. Flying in the face of the New Order's allergy to mass organizations – and specifically those of a religious nature – Suharto encouraged ICMI to set up a nation-wide network, and leaned on those Muslim intellectuals who were reluctant to join.

Both tactics were immediately interpreted as ploys to secure popularity in the run-up to presidential elections in 1993. On the one hand, Suharto seized the higher ground from his critics by publicly appealing to Chinese businessmen to spread their wealth more equitably. This in turn provided him with a credible platform from which to appeal to the Muslim majority. In the preceeding chapter it was suggested that the New Order's emascu-lation of conventional political alternatives gave the Muslim mainstream considerable opportunities to articulate pressing social and economic issues through sanctioned organizations. Suharto probably felt the need to co-opt this nascent political energy; and, looking for a way of channelling it via a government-controlled organization, he seized on ICMI as a suitable conveyance. Subsequent hints of a government plan to centralize collection of the traditional Islamic tithe, or *zakat* (a contribution made personally by all Muslims in aid of the poor) were interpreted in some quarters as a possible source of funding for ICMI. It was as if he conceived of the Muslims, co-opted and organized under a centrally controlled umbrella group, as an alternative to Golkar and a useful barricade against the army.

Certainly, Suharto's approach to the Muslims in advance of the 1992 elections implies a degree of concern about the traditional instititional props to his rule. Crudely speaking, the mainstay of the New Order's electoral machine is Golkar, backed by Abri. As already demonstrated, though, Abri was showing distinct signs of fatigue in its supportive role. This exposed Golkar, with its close Abri links, to possibly dangerous levels of unpre-dictability. In the 1987 elections, Abri's potential influence over Golkar was amply demonstrated when it engineered urban support for its electoral opponents, the PDI. In the run-up to the 1988 Golkar congress, Abri again showed its ability to tinker with the system by engineering Sudharmono's defeat as chairman of the party.

Mounting a country-wide campaign, Abri poured money and personnel into provincial-level elections of Golkar delegates, and secured something like 60 per cent of the delegates at the congress. The strategy served to test Abri's political strength at the 'territorial' level; and also reminded Suharto in the words of one senior general, 'that Golkar was set up to look after the interests of Abri'.[31]

The overall aim of Abri's strategy seemed to be that by focusing on Sudharmono's defeat, the military hoped to remind Suharto of their potential political strength. It was something of a Pyrrhic victory. For in response, Suharto bypassed Golkar and went to the people instead. Neither Golkar nor Abri were consulted or involved in the Tapos appeal and subsequent organization of Muslim support. But the ethnic and religious sensitivities provoked as a result, seemed to many – especially in the military – needlessly to stir the embers of past social conflict, and to threaten stability. Equally, these moves demonstrated the ease with which society could still be manipulated.

It is fashionable in some academic circles to read this another way. New Order society, the argument runs, has undergone important changes since the mid-1980s. The oil crisis and the economic reform programme it precipitated have lent more clout to certain sections of society, particularly in business circles, argues the Australian political scientist Andrew Macintyre.[32] Arguably, the rise of Muslim consciousness was partly a reaction to the enhanced influence of non-Muslim business groups. This was something the New Order neither intentionally promoted, nor felt naturally inclined to support. Equally, though, the ease with which Suharto has been able to exploit these pressures by means of timely co-option, suggests the efficacy of state control has not been seriously impaired. Above all, the security of Suharto's tenure seemed assured by the limited social arena in which politics was acted out.

Behind the intensified politicking and debate in elite circles, however, one key question remained unanswered. Would, if pushed to do so, the military take actions into their own hands and force a succession? Was a coup scenario realistic? The fact that so much of the succession debate emanated from Abri circles made this prospect tantalizingly plausible. Against this, so many of the most outspoken military figures were either long retired, or close to retiring. A retired minister once quipped that the hottest source of political gossip and intrigue was the outpatients wing at the Gatot Subroto Military Hospital! If those retired or on the sidelines clamoured for change, how much support could they rely on from the silent majority still in active positions?

Suharto made Abri the fulcrum of his power, but found he relied less on their support with the growth of his own power base. As already demonstrated, his cultivation of Muslim support after 1990 placed a significant segment of society at his disposal. Significantly, relations between Muslim intellectuals and Abri were poorly developed and fraught with ambivalence, for historical reasons already discussed. It was Abri which fired upon the crowd of Muslim worshippers in Tanjung priok in 1984. But could he be sure of re-election without Abri's backing? Almost certainly not. This probably explains why he opted to stay out of the Abri campaign against Sudharmono, in 1988–9.

Yet since the hand of Abri could be detected at every turn in the succession drama which unfolded after 1988, it is worth speculating on their range of options. The more so since, none of the strategies they employed seemed to work. Initially the military believed in their powers of personal persuasion. As closely identified with the New Order as Abri was, it was the duty of senior officers to act as responsible conductors of opinion for the leadership. This was the tack adopted shortly before Suharto's re-election in 1988. Having failed to convince him of their wishes, Abri turned to the manipulation of social forces: a succession of strategies which drew on Abri's experience countering Communism in the mid-1960s. Students were persuaded to demonstrate, political levers were pulled within Golkar, and threats to stability were concocted. Frequent reminders of the need to be vigilant against forces of extremism – be they on the left or right of the political spectrum – was the accepted coding for Abri's veiled threats.

Suharto skilfully dodged these threats by neutralizing the issues on which Abri-backed agitation was based. Finally, Abri was left with two alternatives: it could go one stage further and actually generate instability, or ultimately intervene. As the preceeding analysis of Abri and its doctrine implies, the inherent dangers accompanying the latter course almost certainly ruled out a coup scenario. Suharto's careful climb to power avoided any action which set precedents for his own removal. Abri was saddled with a Constitution which it was sworn to defend. Any change of leadership had to be conducted within its bounds.

Abri was in a position, however, to demonstrate its indispensability. To do so in Jakarta, however, was fraught with risk. The Malari incident in January 1974 demonstrated the difficulties of controlling even engineered popular disorder. While Suharto successfully co-opted forces at the political centre, Abri remained the key to order at the fringes of the nation. Abri operations against rebel remnants in Irian Jaya, East Timor and Aceh intensified perceptibly in the period 1990–1. The zeal with which Abri's duty to defend the state from all threats to unity was prosecuted struck domestic political observers as mildy demonstrative. Of course to the outside world, it assumed brutal overtones. This in itself drove a point home to Suharto, once he began promoting himself as an international statesman after 1989.

By 1991 the succession issue was no less captivating, but seemingly no nearer breaking point. If anything, Suharto's shrewd manipulation of political forces set up a counter wave. Endorsements for Suharto filled the air, even though there were over two years to go before the presidential elections in 1993. Alamsjah Ratu Perwiranegara claimed to have collected the names of hundreds of petty Muslim figures in East Java who wanted Suharto to serve another term. Rumour had it that an earlier petition to this effect, signed by some twenty-one notable Muslims, had only come to light because the military saw to it that the document was made public.

Alamsjah's chief weapon in persuading the Muslim faithful again highlights the extent to which individuals rather than social forces dominate the political scene. Alamsjah spread alarm among the Muslim clergy by casting Benny Murdani as the only alternative. Murdani's Christian faith, tied to his implication in the brutal suppression of a Muslim riot in Tanjung Priok in September 1984, was effective in persuading many Muslims that Suharto had to remain in power to prevent the Republic being ruled by an 'infidel'. By this time, Murdani had become the chief nemesis of Suharto's family, who cast him as the leading plotter in the campaign to bring about their father's downfall. However appealing the scenario was to those aware of Murdani's attractive and not so attractive qualities, he was being used as much as a device – a conveniently obvious bogey, which did not reflect the reality of his own position – or his own inclinations.

Meanwhile, the search for consensus on the succession went on in the upper levels of the elite. Slowly their deliberations led them to the conclusion that, though desirable, Suharto's departure from office would exert too much strain on the political system and could pose a threat to stability. Acutely aware that a sudden change of leadership would not be in anybody's interest, a compromise scenario emerged along the following lines. Suharto was to be gradually phased out. He would be elected for another term in 1993, but be persuaded to appoint a powerful vice-president and minister of home affairs – both from the military. This would ensure effective control of the state was ceded to the generals – a situation comparable in many ways to the structure of power imposed on Sukarno after October 1965. Above all the elite wanted to avoid a chaotic power struggle which was potentially beyond their control, and because of this they dreamed up a comfortable scenario.

The reality was more complex. As the following chapter will show, the political undercurrents generated by the succession question were increasingly interfering with Indonesia's internal development and external image. Events leading up to elections in 1992 would inevitably be interpreted in terms of their effect on Suharto's position. Arguably, though, the fundamentals were still in his favour. The army was weak and divided, and Suharto had placed loyalists in key military commands. The principal social and political groupings were under his control. Foreign aid donors and

INDONESIAN POLITICS UNDER SUHARTO

investors had faith in Suharto, and were as wary of sudden political change as the domestic elite. More fundamentally, Suharto could still depend on a political culture, steeped in Javanese values of respect for authority, which was as unlikely to support a direct attempt to usurp power now, as it was in the mid-1960s.

This left the possibility of either Suharto himself choosing to step down, or to borrow an earlier analogy, for some catastrophic event – small or large in scale – indirectly to weaken his claim to power. With the army as weak and divided as it was, one possibility was an internal military power struggle – not explicitly directed at the leadership – which could damage his credibility. For all the battering Abri's pre-eminence suffered under the last two decades of Suharto's rule, the institution has managed remarkably well to preserve the illusion of power and influence. But this has left Abri in a potentially dangerous state of disillusionment, as an institution from which much is demanded, but very little effectively delivered.

7

DRAGON APPARENT OR ROGUE TIGER?

We are trying to reorder and reform.
(Suharto, 1989)

Against a background of political uncertainty over the succession – if not who would succeed Suharto, then at least how smoothly will Suharto succeed in refashioning his mandate for another term – Indonesia's economy at the turn of the decade continued to flourish. Economically speaking, the country could consider itself a nascent newly industrialized economy. On the political front, if critics saw the President become more aloof and steadily less receptive to the advice of his peers, their concerns seemed at odds with the New Order's apparent attempts to present a face more acceptable to the contemporary political mood in the country, raise its international profile, and outwardly conform to the obstinate democratic proclivities of its major trading partners. The government embraced the popular slogan *keterbukaan*, or political 'openness', but it was not an evident component of policy. Beneath the impressive array of economic reforms prepared by the New Order technocrats, which seemed to invite social and political change as well, lay an imposing conservative edifice remarkably resistant to corrosion.

The paradoxical picture Indonesia presented at the start of the 1990s is worth examining. On the one hand it demonstrates the potency of the New Order even as it veered towards a possible political crisis. Stability pervaded even while the guardians of that stability began tinkering with the mechanism. A society as regulated as Indonesia's has a high threshold of docility. There was neither evidence of economic decline nor mismanagement to fuel popular discontent. The paradox dwelt at the centre. Unease about the coming post-Suharto era pervaded the elite just as everything seemed to be going so well.

In the foreign diplomatic and business community there were wild extremes of opinion. Boundless optimism coloured the views of the mainly Hong Kong-based stockbrokers who, after exhausting opportunities in Bangkok and Kuala Lumpur, collectively declared Jakarta 'an interesting bet'. Their optimism was not always repaid with rich dividends, but the potential was enough to keep them interested. By contrast, gloom and foreboding began to set in at the chanceries of some foreign embassies, where political officers were reporting that the·chances of political turbulence over the succession were much increased. Optimism about the business scene was tempered by doubts about the capacity of the existing political structure to sustain a healthy commercial environment. By early 1991, the financial adventurism of some of the larger Indonesian business groups with political – or filial – connections to the leadership was exposing flaws in the private sector, and Indonesia's credit-rating among offshore lending institutions began to slip perceptibly.

Meanwhile, having headed out of depression into something of a mini-boom in 1989–90, the period thereafter ushered in some retrenchment. GDP growth, which peaked in 1990 at 7.4 per cent, was expected to fall off. Global recession was setting in, and there were fears of protectionist sentiment in Europe and the United States affecting two of Indonesia's key export markets. Higher inflation, nudging 10 per cent by late 1990, was considered an inevitable side-effect of the economy's rapid growth in the late 1980s. The massive increase in borrowing which accompanied this growth pushed interest rates as high as 30 per cent in early 1991. The needs of Indonesia's burgeoning private sector escalated the volume of imports, and the current-account deficit increased over 100 per cent to somewhere near $US5 billion from 1990 to1991. These were all necessary evils, market economists argued, but the New Order's meticulous economic managers feared that any sign of a downturn in the economy would affect donor country perceptions, and they kept a tight rein on monetary policy and a watchful eye on the size of the foreign debt.

With no sign of any official move to lower interest rates, businesses began adopting a more cautious stance. Domestic social and political issues were also exerting contractionary pressures on the economy and breeding caution in the business community. Having embraced all the opportunities thrown their way by the technocrats in the reform packages of the late 1980s, the Chinese business community found themselves being accused of greed. The spectre of racial tension loomed. Suharto's blunt appeal to the richest of the Chinese to share their wealth in March 1990 stopped many people in their tracks. Some saw in this the danger that the Chinese might revert to the old ways – seeking government favours to protect their businesses and funnelling the profits overseas. There was alarm over an independent report that as much as $US26 billion worth of Indonesian private capital was placed in Asian Currency Unit funds in Singapore.[1] Overall, the government appeared to be resorting to policies which juggled political contingency driven by oncoming elections with economic priorities, and some Indonesian Chinese were growing uncomfortable.

Yet for the most part, tensions afflicting the New Order remained hidden from the outside world. Not everyone wished to play them up. Rising domestic political temperatures in Indonesia came at a bad time, for example, in Australia's ministry of foreign affairs and trade, where a new era of warmer bilateral ties with their northern neighbour were being toasted as a personal success for Foreign Minister Gareth Evans. Demonstrating almost perfect affinity with the ostrich, the alarm raised by Australian diplomats in Jakarta was buried in Canberra's bureaucratic quicksand.[2] Outwardly at least, there was a reluctance to see the looming succession issue as a serious threat to stability. Impatience and disgruntlement within the ranks of the armed forces were dismissed in the belief that as a more professional army, Abri would be less inclined to intervene in a succession crisis. Even the growing chorus of demands for democracy was considered evidence in itself that Indonesia was becoming more democratic.

Before the end of the cold war, followed by the Gulf War, consumed all of what little time the US has ever had for the region, privately at least, Washington was growing concerned about Indonesia. The state department, kept particularly well informed by Ambassador Paul Wolfowitz before he left for the Pentagon in May 1989, was aware of mounting political pressures. This, again with prompting from Wolfowitz, translated into a lame attempt by Vice-President Dan Quayle in 1989 to persuade the Suharto government to democratize. Quayle's June 1989 meeting with a group of well-known, Jakarta-based dissidents raised eyebrows in official Indonesian circles and marked a tacit departure from Washington's blinkered approach to the voice of opposition against Suharto. In a broader context, as Communism waned, so did forbearance of Washington's former allies in the battle against Communism.

Japan, traditionally aloof from domestic politics in South-east Asia so long as it did not affect the investment climate, was also demonstrating mild concern about the future. Prime Minister Toshiki Kaifu raised the succession issue with Suharto during a visit to Jakarta in late 1989. Japanese diplomats, under pressure elsewhere in the world to show more commitment to ideals other than profit, made tentative contacts with Indonesia's small dissident circle for the first time. Significantly, in a May 1991 policy statement he delivered in Singapore, Kaifu spoke of co-operation with

Asean countries based on principles of 'freedom and democracy'. Subsequently, Japan announced that its overseas development assistance would be governed by four principles, one of which was progress towards democratization.

By saying Tokyo wanted to see the reins of political power eventually pass smoothly and with minimum impact on the economy, Japanese officials were coming as close as they could to hinting at potential external pressure on the regime. As Japan is Indonesia's major donor, the potential impact of such pressure was considerable. However, many Japan watchers – specifically those of the so-called 'revisionist' school who are suspicious of the new, globally oriented Japan – felt that Tokyo's new stress on democracy as a factor in aid disbursement was a calculated ploy to ward off US pressure on Japan; an exercise in window dressing rather than an expression of heartfelt moral principles. Japan yearned for stability in Indonesian political life, above all. So long as Suharto remained an asset rather than a liability in this context, Japan would back him to the hilt.

The European Community was calling a somewhat different tune. The sudden end of the cold war after the failed August 1991 coup in Moscow brought to a climax the sense of moral self-righteousness which had been building up in Europe since the collapse of the Berlin Wall in 1989. The disintegration of the Soviet system, as *New York Times* columnist Anthony Lewis put it, was the victory of an idea – the West's idea: democracy. 'Whatever difficulties follow now... we are entitled to this moment of celebration', he wrote.[3] Celebrating the triumph of democracy, the West pressed boldly for the idea to be more stringently enforced in other areas of the world. At a meeting hosted by Luxembourg between European and Asean foreign ministers in May 1991, there were acrimonious exchanges when the Europeans proposed joint sanctions against the military regime in Burma. Asean stood firmly behind the principle of non-interference in the affairs of neighbouring countries. To make matters worse, at the prompting of some smaller European countries, the Community advised Asean of its intention to insert a clause on human rights observance and the environment in the new EC-Asean co-operation agreement scheduled for 1993.

It is too early to say whether such outward posturing on human rights from the West will have any impact on Indonesia. To some extent, Jakarta has responded. Despite the fierce defence of Indonesia's culture of stability, Foreign Minister Ali Alatas stated in late 1990 that 'it is time that Indonesia addressed this issue (of human rights) in international forums in a more active way, and not in a reactive or defensive fashion.'[4] On 1 January 1991, Indonesia joined the UN Commission on Human Rights in Geneva.

168

Subsequently, Alatas persuaded the government to draw up a charter of Indonesia's position on human rights, a document which is none the less expected to fall short of recognizing the inalienable rights of the individual. At the same time, there were attempts to persuade the military to become more conscious of human rights. Foreign ministry and civilian officials were encouraged by their initial contacts with Abri over this issue, but as events in Aceh and East Timor demonstrated, the armed forces still adhered to a 'might is right' philosophy in dealing with the low-level insurgencies in these areas.

In true mercantilist fashion, few governments with a commercial stake in Indonesia were bent on becoming too insistent on progress towards democratization, and the ostriches multiplied. The total value of foreign investment approvals in the first six months of 1990 already exceeded the $US4.7 billion achieved in calendar year 1989. Overall figures for 1990 exceeded $US8 billion. January to June 1991 figures totalled $US6 billion.[5] The size of some of these capital investments, in petrochemicals, in pulp and paper, and in extractive industries, was large by regional standards.

There was also a regional dynamic. Fortuitously, Indonesia's economic growth was picking up at a time neighbouring Asean economies were beginning to groan under the strain of higher labour costs and overloaded infrastructure. Institutional and commercial donors were also impressed by the way economic liberalism was being implemented in Indonesia. Many were banking on the possibilities after harnessing Indonesia's racially tolerant, secular society to the modern age. Less openly, they were also happy with a state which administered policies of economic rather than political liberalism. What they wanted to see was the development of an open, competitive economy founded on private enterprise. Few cared to peer too closely at the confusing reality beneath the surface; the whiff of 'NIC-dom' was enough. Jungle though it may be, the economic landscape was yielding a bountiful harvest for those with the temerity to venture forth.

From an elite Indonesian standpoint, there was less cause for optimism. 'You have to understand that we are genuinely concerned about the future', remarked a senior military figure in early 1991.[6] What a curiously morbid outlook given the country's impressive economic performance. From an elite standpoint, however, the stability so admired by foreign investors rested on the shoulders of national leadership. While outsiders admired the system bred by the New Order, the elite worried about the system's capacity to survive Suharto, or a power struggle to replace him. The army, traditionally regarded as the safety net in times of national crisis, was politically weak and divided. Civilian political institutions, neglected under the New Order, were not yet in a position to take up the slack.

Suharto was not making an open bid for another term. Nor was he acting as a man preparing for retirement. The suspicion was he would like to stay on after 1993. While his continued presence assured many, particularly in the business community, of stability, no one could be certain that at 72, Suharto's age would not become a liability. Another term would grant Suharto's family an extended licence to acquire the most profitable areas of the economy for themselves – and therefore further reduce the amount of that pie available for others. The lack of any institutionalized mechanism for succession, and more importantly the absence of any recognizable or credible alternative candidate, began to persuade many they were better off with the incumbent.

Compounding uncertainty over the succession in elite circles was concern about the changing nature of the society over which they presided. Many were conscious of a growing middle class with political aspirations of their own. The paternalistic ties which traditionally held these social forces in check were running up against the powers of consumption and education. 'The more educated the people are, the more disposed to criticism they will become,' concluded participants at an army seminar in December 1990. The fear of popular demands for participation and accountability transcending the culturally acceptable norms of respect for those in positions of power and authority was perhaps just as deep as their frustration with an ageing Suharto. Aligning these two factors, the sce-nario-seekers could build up quite a gloomy forecast. Opening up the political system to broader participation would not solve the succession problem, and there seemed little hope for political change if Suharto was re-elected.

Outwardly, the dragon-like qualities of Indonesia's economic perform-ance masked political problems which many believed, if not addressed in time, could launch Indonesia on a path to chaos and instability. An important question, therefore, is which description – dragon apparent or rogue tiger – best fits reality. More crucially, which can act as a guide to the future?

Healthy macro-economic indicators have a misleading charm about them, and Indonesia's have been very charming indeed. GDP growth in 1989 was a respectable 7.4 per cent. Set against the country's diverse manufacturing base, wealth of natural resources and the lowest labour costs in the region, the government's much trumpeted commitment to reform had alerted investors to new possibilities in Indonesia. More importantly, the government was user friendly. When it came to wooing foreign investors, few countries in the region could match Indonesia's talent for spreading the welcome mat. A series of measures in the late 1980s simplified investment procedures to the bare minimum, bringing the time taken for approvals to within thirty days.

The government's deregulation programme signalled a a long overdue shift towards bureaucratic empathy with the private sector. Law No.1 1987 governing the Chamber of Commerce and Industry was the New Order's first formal recognition that the private sector had a role to play in the country's development. The law recognized that a high cost economy buttressed by the state's stewardship of capitalism was more of a hinderance than an advantage. In January 1987, the National Chamber of Commerce (KADIN) recognized the principle of profit-making for the first time.[7] It appeared, wrote the Australian social scientist Andrew Macintyre, 'that social attitudes towards business are altering and that some of the traditional ideological stigma attaching to it are receding'.[8] Indeed, some New Order officials began to acknowledge the drawbacks of regarding the private sector as something to be managed and frequently milked by the bureaucracy. 'Like a golden goose, they have seen the need to feed the private sector and let it grow, rather than grab it by the neck and strangle it' was how one foreign aid official in Jakarta put it.[9]

There were, however, limits to how much could be changed. By the end of 1989, the pace of reform had slackened. Only two economic reform packages were announced in 1990 – one long-delayed series of measures covering the stock market was issued only just in time to reinvigorate a market the government seemed about to strangle because of its tight squeeze on liquidity. Plans to privatize the stock market were shelved in 1991. Though anticipated, the backwash from the October 1988 liberalization of the banking and financial sector threatened to send some pretty sizeable private banks to the wall. There were calls for some re-regulation and, as always in Indonesia, the state was poised to intervene. In fact, it did so to prevent financial confidence in the country from draining away because of the ineptitude of some private financiers.

The reformers were running up against the political issues which were loading up the other side of the national equation. Criticism of the rapacity of Chinese-owned conglomerates and demands to address the widening socio-economic gap in the country were fast becoming too politicized to dismiss as intellectual nit-picking. By late 1990 the question of equity became entangled with the rather more delicate issue of race. The Chinese were singled out as enjoying the most wealth.

The fact that influential members of the elite spoke openly of these issues, raised the tone of debate above the circumspect and deferential level to which Indonesian newspaper readers were long accustomed. Instead of crowing about growth in the non-oil sector, economists began to talk about *pemerataan* – 'equity'. The use of terms like 'social gap' took on distinct racial connotations. The gap referred to was the gulf between rich Chinese and poorer indigenous Indonesians. Objectively, there was concern that the private sector's gains were generating resentment among those ill-equipped to benefit from the reforms. Traditional norms and values were invoked. A government minister complained that Indonesia's current growth strategy encouraged too much 'materialism'; that what Indonesia wanted was industrialization but not 'westernization'.[10]

In tandem with the articulation of volatile social issues, the economy became the subject of bureaucratic conflicts. The questioning of liberal reform policies in political circles allowed those who had a stake in defending the state's role in the economy to cry foul with impunity. The government sought to balance measures aimed at strengthening the private sector with concessions to the still powerful state sector. Thus, amid the first signs that the private sector was gaining the upper hand in policy terms, chairmanship of the National Chamber of Commerce (KADIN) passed to a bureaucrat, Sotion Ardjanggi.

In 1989, Professor B. J. Habibie, the German-trained Minister of Research and Technology, persuaded the President to corral several industries of 'strategic' importance into a new secretariat under his command. These included steel, arms, ship and aircraft production – in fact most of the promising areas of hi-tech production which were already under Habibie's stewardship. Talk of privatizing state enterprises died down. In an interview, Finance Minister Johannes Sumarlin could not even be persuaded to use the term. Instead there was plenty of talk about the government's commitment to Article 33 of the 1945 Constitution, the enduring quasi-socialist ethic wherein the state's role in key sectors of the economy is enshrined. By the end of 1990, Habibie's anti-economic notions about productivity and technology were being actively patronized by Suharto because they fitted in with his plans for reaping support from the Muslim and *pribumi* community.

The appeal to Chinese businessmen to divest shares to co-operatives in March 1990 demonstrated how easily the powerful executive could swing the pendulum the other way. In fact, the idea was first proposed by a professor of economics at the University of Indonesia, Sri Edi Swasono. Swasono had come up with the idea in a study funded by the Canadian Cooperatives Association. The President liked the scheme, and inserted the vague outlines into his January 1990 budget speech without informing his economic ministers. Swasono, an ambitious man imbued with the quasi-socialist ideas of the country's early economists, harboured designs on a ministry for himself. He now claimed he had the President's ear. The foreign business community was baffled.

The racial connotation of Suharto's appeal was what most worried investors. Indonesia's record of racial harmony was enviable. The Chinese were not generally perceived as a threatening minority; their economic success was regarded more as an asset than a liability. The fact that some social resentment smouldered just beneath the surface was recognized. But this made the government's earnest attempts to suppress racial sentiments all the more appreciated. So when Suharto appeared to ignite those very sentiments with his appeal to the Chinese, it came as a surprise and a shock to many.

The fallout from the Tapos meeting was considerable. It scared the Chinese and threatened their commitment to domestic investment. The government's reform programme also implicitly lost momentum as the state wore its interventionist mask. The political implications for the Chinese compounded the stimulus the government's tight monetary policy was giving to capital flight. But for Suharto, the move also opened up fresh areas of political support. His co-operatives appeal was popular in Muslim circles. It also gave a voice to a group of young, aggressive *pribumi* businessmen bent on benefiting from sizeable government tenders, so many of which they had seen pass to well-connected Chinese business groups. Suharto not only moved to confound his critics, he created as a by-product a fresh pool of supporters. The danger lay in the latent social tension he generated in the process.

On another level, Suharto moved to reassert some of the very aspects of political economy the reformers were hoping to do away with. As well as being driven by political considerations, apparently the influence of nationalistic elements in the bureaucracy remained strong. Indeed, if Suharto's 1989 autobiography was any guide to where his sympathies lay, he had much warmer praise for this group than for the technocrats. The nationalists; men like Habibie whose ministry of research and technology always obtained healthy increments in the annual budget, were described as men of vision. The economists were all but dismissed as 'servants' of the state.[11]

In short, the reality of Indonesia's political economy began to catch up with the liberal myth. In his annual National Day address to the nation in August 1990, Suharto seemed to apply the brakes by putting the reforms in perspective: 'Deregulation and de-bureaucratization are precisely aimed at re-awakening public initiative, creativity and participation in development,' he said, 'They are certainly not measures to abolish the role of the state. It is definitely not a step towards liberalism.' With general elections in the offing in June 1992 and pressure on him to solidify support for the presidential contest in 1993, Suharto highlighted the relationship between economic liberalization and political stability. Or, as one regional economist put it: 'The extent of government intervention is positively correlated with the degree of political uncertainty faced by the ruling regime.'[12]

Was it ever Suharto's intention truly to liberalize the economy, or were the economic reforms of the 1980s merely a device to secure the economy after the collapse of oil prices? Contingency or grand strategy? Many observers of the post-oil-boom decade in Indonesia have assumed the latter to be the case before probing the New Order's foundations, and the personal beliefs of its creator, Suharto. It would be over-simplistic to picture Indonesia being pulled along by economic developments elsewhere. This ignores the New Order's commitment to preserving at all costs the supremacy of the state. Suharto's contemporaries, it must be remembered, consider Suharto less the strategist and more the tactician.

Suharto's generation was imbued with a fundamental belief in the state's role in the economy. So long as the 1945 Constitution remains in force, this is unlikely to change. Crudely speaking, it is the best way to ensure that the state preserves its limitless power. Grant the economy autonomy and it is but a short step towards demands for the state to be accountable to those who own the means of production. In Malaysia this problem was circumvented by granting key political institutions the lion's share of the nation's corporate ownership. Indonesian capitalism also vests the state with the power of patronage over the private sector, but it is less institutionalized than in Malaysia and, more importantly, concentrated in fewer hands.

Suharto was not inclined to unleash the economy entirely. More plausibly, he allowed his ministers to liberalize just enough to guarantee annual infusions of foreign aid and investment. The extent to which the technocrats were acting under restraint is clear from a succession of annual World Bank reports in which 'fine so far but where is the rest' always seemed to the message.

No Indonesian economist can be faulted for adopting a cautious approach. The social consequences of economic change in a country the size of Indonesia are easy to neglect if one's perspective is oriented solely towards the market-place. But stability is not something the Indonesian ruling elite takes for granted. The country's transformation from the protective, import-substituting, commodity-exporting economy inherited by Suharto in the mid-1960s, to a state-capitalist economy with a substantial industrial base and free foreign-exchange controls, has indeed been remarkable. Growth in the industrial sector in the period 1983–8 galloped along at a remarkable 13 per cent per annum. The social and political problems this transformation has thrown up in its wake have been slow to emerge, but for the government they are not difficult to envisage. As Indonesia's senior economist (also a former minister) Mohammad Sadli wrote:

> The major policy reforms in China after 1979 and the culmination of events leading to the Beijing tragedy [May 1989] ring a familiar bell in our minds. If a strongly controlled economic regime relaxes and gives market forces a greater role in reviving the economy, some backlash will occur sooner or later.[13]

Some of the tinder which could potentially light the fires of social unrest was already evident. Aside from a growing consciousness of the racial divison of wealth, employment was becoming a primary concern. More and more of the jobless were found in urban areas, where the risk of unrest is always greater. By official estimates, Indonesia's 72.4 million-strong work-force was growing by more than 3 per cent a year. Actual unemployment is pegged at a reasonable 2.64 per cent, but underemployment – measured as those employed for less than 35 hours a week – is thought to account for as much as 40 per cent of the work-force.[14] The New Order's successful education policies fuel the problem. The number of school-leavers with higher aspirations but no job to go to is climbing at a frightening rate. Those living below the poverty line are undoubtedly fewer – estimated at around thirty million people, or 20 per cent of the population – but in urban areas the perception is that economic development has brought with it spiralling inflation and a credit squeeze which in turn has squeezed the consumer.

Inflation hovering around 10 per cent by official measures – though probably exceeded 18 per cent in urban areas by 1990 – was in part the price to be paid for a fiscal regime more liberal even than in neighbouring Malaysia. A measure of just how liberal the authorities had become, were all the calls for tighter supervision of the banking system and nascent stock market by the early 1990s. On a social level, the fear was that these issues, though not of themselves a serious destabilizing influence, had none the less exerted a strain on the country's fragile social fabric.

Contributing also to the shallow impact of the reformers were the bureaucratic and institutional shortcuts the government took to achieve the rapid shift away from an oil to a non-oil base. These papered over real shortcomings in the country's legal and bureaucratic infrastructure. Company law in Indonesia pre-dates independence, and is badly in need of reform. Copyright and patent agreements are only now being worked through – and they are riddled with loopholes. Thus, while the regime was content to allow the technocrats a reasonable free hand to attract investment, more fundamental issues such as the need for legal certainty in a reformed and more complex economy were proving more difficult to address.

For a while the country was swept along with the drive to boost non-oil exports. Few questioned a strategy which diversified the country's revenue base to guard against another oil shock. There was even forbearance when, in the name of boosting exports, the government introduced restrictions or total bans on the export of certain products, primarily unprocessed or semi-processed commodities such as rattan and timber. The logic for reinstating monopolies the liberal reforms were designed to do away with, was that restrictions of this sort promoted downstream industries and generated a higher added value. In reality, business interests close to ruling circles exploited the export drive to strengthen their grip on new-found monopolies. In all the most profitable areas of Indonesia's new-look economy, cronies and members of Suharto's family led the field. Others followed, but only at their discretion.

Indonesian society is more complex than the dragon-seekers would have it. The technocrats made enormous efforts to shape a new economic landscape, but were unable to alter fundamentally the socio-political context governing the environment. In private discussions, they would admit they were up against a bureaucracy unwilling to accept change, vested interests who demanded impossible quid pro quos, and ultimately an uncertain political future. What they created was an impressive façade.

The foremost obstacle to fundamental change was the New Order's firm resistance to far-reaching institutional reform. The collapse of oil prices in 1982 convinced Suharto of the need to adapt, but not fundamentally alter, the structure of the state. The fact that foreign donors were willing at the same time to provide a cushion of aid meant the financial autonomy of the regime was never threatened. Development spending was sustained. Socio-economic conditions, far from deteriorating in the early 1980s, actually improved through the course of the oil crisis. It was therefore only really necessary to tinker with the fringes of the system in order to insulate the state from another external shock.

The most striking evidence of this remains the fact that the majority of reforms effected since 1983 have yet to be enshrined in law. Most were introduced, and continue to exist, as presidential decrees. Because they have yet to acquire a standing in law, they could be replaced just as easily with other presidential decrees reversing their effect. The tenuous regard for legal structures this suggests, is seen as a key obstacle to Indonesia's performance in the future.

Although they may have wanted to, the economic ministers faced enormous problems translating their policies directly into law. The process of legislation in Indonesia is hamstrung by the competing demands of government departments. The legal department of the state secretariat in Jakarta is stuffed with draft laws which have waited years before proceeding further because various government departments cannot agree on a final version. For Suharto's economists the safest way to proceed was by decree, followed by vague promises to formulate laws at a later stage. So long as the reformers hid behind the handy sobriquet of 'deregulation', the need for clear and unambiguous regulations to govern the new-look economy could be brushed aside. Indonesians are inclined to consider regulatory flexibility as a virtue rather than a vice. The legal process, the courts and statutory procedures, are all considered institutions to avoid. Everything 'can be arranged'. A Jakarta lawyer once asserted that the quality of his services was measured by his ability to evade the legal process.

In the foreign business community, this almost pathological disregard for legal certainty can be considered an advantage. Foreign investors concerned about the required divestment of a minority shareholding over a period of time, are reassured by senior officials that the regulation is loosely and even rarely enforced. But as James Castle, an experienced business consultant in Jakarta, pointed out:

> Because of this emphasis on flexibility – on pragmatism, rather than on rules – most new business visitors will see Indonesia as very much a developing country with a long way to go, and where many compromises must be made with efficient business practices if one wishes to participate successfully. These compromises are palatable because of opportunities, but they are compromises nonetheless.[15]

By the end of the 1980s, the World Bank began to qualify their glowing praises for the economic reforms with faint but distinct warnings about the lack of attention being paid to the legal and bureaucratic institutions needed to underpin the economy. The Bank's 1990 annual report pinpointed administrative reform as crucial: 'The shortage of highly qualified and motivated management and staff is one of the most serious impediments the government is facing at every level and in every sector', droned the report in what most people took as a sanitized call for a better trained and less corrupt civil service.[16]

Legal reform was also badly needed, and again politely advocated by the Bank. The Bank cited the system of law enforcement, interpretation of the law by courts and the general efficiency of the legal process as areas in need of improvement. 'In many important areas,' the 1990 report said, 'the existing commercial laws are outdated and do not meet the requirements of a modern economy'.[17] Many, if not most, of the basic laws in current use are based on Dutch colonial ordinances.

In late 1989 Indonesia's major donors moved to address the issue of human rights, popular participation and a broadening of the political base. The annual meeting of Indonesia's aid donors in April 1990 took 'popular participation' as that year's special topic. The original intention was to discuss democratization, but bowing as ever to Indonesian sensitivities, an awkward cloak was assumed. 'Participation' was the coded but less adequate form of words eventually agreed upon. No one was surprised when, in the end, little was said which could be construed as pressure on the government to change. No one expected the lack of democratization to result in the withholding of any aid, either. Rather, donors earnestly hoped the hint might be taken.

Flexible when it came to preserving the financial integrity of Indonesia, Suharto could not be convinced that any aspect of the political system needed changing. He was fond of telling visiting dignitaries that Indonesia's stability was ensured by the democratic process developed by the New Order. If there were shortcomings in the legal and bureaucratic area, these were because of Indonesia's developing country status. Hiding behind this vague and increasingly transparent notion of underdevelopment, Suharto would argue that more aid would help develop the country and ameliorate the problems. The argument was apparently convincing. Mindful of investment opportunities, the aid poured in. The façade held up.

Meanwhile, concern was expressed in domestic circles about the impact of all this economic vigour on Indonesian society. Even if the principles of the 'trickle-down' school of development economics applied, vibrant growth and enhanced national prosperity was generating resentment in certain elite quarters. Just as the private sector was freeing itself from the shackles of state control, its leading proponents became the object of criticism. The larger and mainly Indonesian Chinese-owned conglomerates were held up as symbols of greed and rapacity, widely seen as feeding off the people and ploughing their profits overseas. Interviewed in March 1990, Indonesia's most powerful ethnic Chinese tycoon, Liem Sioe Long (alias Sudono Salim), was reluctant even to divulge the number of companies owned by his group: 'it might cause a public outcry,' he said.[18]

The ferocity of criticism directed at the country's larger business interests seemed at odds with their evident contribution to national GDP. Liem Sioe Long's Salim Group, for example, accounts for roughly 5 per cent of Indonesia's GDP. The group's turnover in 1990 totalled around $US8 billion.[19] Foreign investors flocked to set up joint ventures with Indonesia's nascent corporate giants. Many of the latter launched their most ambitious expansion plans financed by joint ventures with Japanese and European companies; others have access to Hong Kong, Taiwanese and increasingly South Korean capital. Their flotations on the stock exchange attracted millions of dollars' worth of overseas funds.

Lower down the scale, medium-sized business concerns were making a real contribution to export revenues. Indonesia's cheap labour (costing just over a $US1 per day compared with $US4 a day in Thailand) was employed to develop new light manufacturing areas south of Jakarta and around Bandung. Indonesia's exports of garments and shoes grew exponentially. By the end of 1990 the value of training shoe exports to the US market alone was worth $US270 million, up from $US50 million two years before.[20] Most of the capital for these ventures originated from Hong Kong, Taiwan and increasingly Singapore.

Government officials, some of them alarmed by the threat to harmony posed by increased racial tensions, tried hard to modulate the problem. Perceiving economic imbalances as a racial problem was a dangerous generalization, they said. There were some Chinese who behaved too exclusively, and lending a bad image to the majority of Indonesian Chinese – not all of whom were rich and so well connected. Some blame was also laid at the door of the bureaucracy, which tended to favour certain rich Chinese businesses in return for commission. Left unsaid, of course, was the fact that the many of the excesses practised by the Chinese community, stemmed from New Order patronage.

No one could deny that rapid economic growth would not be accompanied by minor problems and undesirable side-effects. The organization of and treatment of labour, for example, was the subject of an AFL–CIO petition to the US trade representative for three successive years (1987–90). Wildcat strikes began to hit some of the new light-industrial growth areas on the fringes of Jakarta, where some employers felt no compulsion to enforce the minimum wage. Even the government admitted that enforcement of the minimum wage was below par. The only state-sanctioned union, the SPSI, was dominated by Golkar party officials and was led in 1990 by one such official whose wife owned a garment factory in North Jakarta. The SPSI, following government guidelines, frowned on strike action, preferring to mediate through so-called 'collective labour agreements' between management and workers. To help 'guide' the work-force in some of the industrial areas around Jakarta, the government engineered the appointment of ex-military officers as local SPSI chiefs.

Land was another potential source of unrest. Indonesia's economic boom, in the classic fashion, increased the degree of land speculation.

Consequently, respect for legal title declined and incidents of land-grabbing increased. The chief culprits were, again, said to be the 'conglomerates' and their cronies in the bureaucracy. Surprisingly enough, land has never been a particularly volatile issue in Indonesia. Despite impossibly high population densities in some areas of Java, the stability of tenure was impressive. Indeed, some of the disputes which received publicity demonstrated laxity on the part of the authorities where those occupying the land for more than thirty years had never possessed legal title, nor were they in strict legal terms eligible for it.

None of these factors might have counted for much in the scheme of things had they not become grist to the political mill. Sustained foreign aid and investment insulated the state from most of these issues. Instead, different factions within the regime chose to exploit them for political ends. Official patronage of Chinese conglomerates was initially targeted as a weak spot in Suharto's armour. Land disputes were played up by the Abri faction in the DPR to highlight the business activities of Suharto's children. Even more remarkable was Suharto's own behaviour in this respect. Far from sheltering behind the New Order's battery of devices to suppress communal emotions, he chose to harness and drive them clean through the political forces ranged against him.

Another way Suharto appeared to be altering Indonesia's image was through a conscious display of international statesmanship. When Suharto assumed the national leadership in 1966, he vowed never to mimic the reckless and bombastic foreign policy of his predecessor, Sukarno. Instead, he declared, Indonesia would give priority to fostering regional stability and co-operation among South-east Asian states, and to ensuring that relations with the outside world yielded what he called 'real material benefits for both parties, and particularly for Indonesia'.[21] Sukarno's arrogant pursuit of non-aligned and developing world leadership resulted in Indonesia being viewed as a pariah in the West, and as an aggressor in the region. Alliances Sukarno forged with North Korea and China fuelled fears that Indonesia would be the next domino to fall into Communist hands after Vietnam. Suharto's more pragmatic approach restored a sense of security to the region and prompted the flow of much-needed foreign aid from the West.

Over the next twenty years, Suharto steered a bland, low-profile foreign policy. Yet it served Indonesia's interests well. Suharto helped establish Asean in 1967, a step unthinkable under Sukarno's more confrontational foreign policy regime. Suharto agreed to the formation of the fourteen-member Inter Governmental Group on Indonesia (IGGI), which governed until 1992 the amount of foregn aid pledged to Indonesia on an annual basis. Suharto's low profile on the international stage and commitment to regional co-operation persuaded both his neighbours and the world beyond, that Indonesia had opted wisely to contain its considerable potential as a regional power.

Sukarno's abandonment of the country's neutralist principles in the early 1960s led to the slide into confrontation with Malaysia. Ostensibly, Sukarno's excuse for attacking Malaysia was his suspicion of the plan to confederate the territories of Northern Borneo, Singapore and the peninsular states. Sukarno saw in the plan the hand of former colonial masters, and an encirclement of Indonesia by potential foes. Subsequently, these suspicions translated themselves into overt action, and by April 1963, clashes with British forces in Sarawak were reported. In 1964 several air and sea-borne landings on the Malayan peninsula were made – and repulsed. Ineffectual as these military actions were, they embedded the notion of Indonesia as a threat deeply in the Malaysian and Singaporean collective psyche. Regional concerns about Indonesia's expansionist potential were subsequently addressed by the formation of Asean.

Suharto's deliberate policy of self-imposed containment and unflinching commitment to Asean, has in no small measure contributed to the security and stability of the region for the past twenty-five years. However, the sense of nationalism which powered Sukarno's rhetoric was never entirely extinguished; it lay dormant, often frustrated by Suharto's policy of self-restraint. These latent emotions are now to some extent being tapped by Suharto to raise Indonesia's profile on the world stage. It is easy to mistake the confidence of Indonesians for ignorance and inward-looking obsessions. Yet at heart, Indonesians perceive themselves as a regional power with a role to play, and increasingly like to be considered as such.

In September 1991, Indonesia was chosen to lead the Non-aligned Movement. That the movement's meaning had been undermined by the end of the cold war seemed to matter little to Foreign Minister Ali Alatas. He believed, perhaps too passionately, in the role Indonesia could play as a mediator among newly developed nations; and as a bulwark against the marauding interests of the North. Were he still alive, Sukarno might well have smiled. The ghosts of the 1955 Asia Africa Conference in Bandung rustled faintly. The question is, why did Suharto consciously opt for this, albeit benign and more purposeful, reassertion of Indonesia's self-perceived pre-eminence?

Part of the answer to this question presupposes that Suharto himself directs the country's foreign policy. Knowledge of the precise nature of any aspect of policy-making under the New Order is at best patchy. Suharto is not a leader prone to allowing his ministers and advisers to take credit for a particular policy. If there is wisdom in the guidance of the state, it flows from him. If mistakes are made, they are the fault of its servants. The model is not unique, but in Indonesia it is practised almost to a fault. Surrounded by men of ideas and burning ambitions, there is no shortage of policy options. Only the timing is his.

The timing in this instance seemed at least partly related to Suharto's need to burnish his mandate and contradict those who claimed new leadership was needed for new times. Suharto has never been strictly isolationist in his outlook; the foreign ministry has always conducted an active, if low-key diplomacy. Part of the problem was Suharto's reluctance to join the growing circuit of perambulating developing world leaders. His English is poor, and his preoccupation with domestic politics and development dictated an inward-looking emphasis.

Suharto's long years of shunning the international limelight began to wane with the international recognition of his domestic achievements. In 1985, Suharto travelled to Rome to receive an FAO Ceres award for his achievement of rice self-sufficiency. In 1990, his population policy won him recognition at the United Nations. In his autobiography, Suharto demonstrates little modesty and an understandable degree of pride in listing these achievements. Perhaps this boosted his confidence. Another factor was the country's emergence from the oil crisis as a robust, promising economy. In August 1990, Suharto declared that Indonesia was economically strong enough to begin playing a responsible role in world affairs.

By the close of the 1980s, Indonesia had already begun to play a more active role, at least on the regional stage. Asean's dogged pursuit of a policy aimed at ousting Vietnam from Cambodia placed Indonesia in an ideal position to mediate, and its Asean partners appointed Jakarta as 'interlocutor' with all parties to the conflict. Indonesia feels close to Vietnam both because of their common anti-colonial struggle and a shared apprehension of China. Unlike Thailand, Indonesia is also remote enough from the South-east Asian mainland not to have a geopolitical stake in Cambodia's future. Indonesia's offer to host the first round of negotiations between Cambodia's warring factions and interested regional states in July 1988 was therefore credible. The move struck the right tone for those in the foreign ministry who were eager to see Indonesia shed its inward-looking image, but at the same time find a niche as a constructive mid-sized regional power.

In tandem with the Cambodian initiative, were efforts to achieve chairmanship of the Non-Aligned Movement, a goal which would place Suharto in the post less than a year before his current presidential term expires in 1993. Indonesia's stubborn refusal to discuss the status of East

Timor, annexed by Jakarta from Portugal in 1975 and still regarded as a Portuguese possession by the United Nations, gave way to negotiations over the issue with Portuguese diplomats at the UN. This paved the way for Indonesia's broader acceptance in Non-Aligned circles, as did permitting Palestinian Liberation Organization diplomatic representation in Jakarta, donating $US10 million to the African National Congress, and establishing diplomatic relations with China and Libya.

Suharto himself began to travel more often, and to more effect. Until the mid-1980s, his most significant overseas trip was to Eastern Europe. By 1991, his visits to the Soviet Union, the US, Europe and Latin America cast the President in a more contemporary mould. Suharto's September 1989 visit to Moscow followed by his attendance at a Non-Aligned heads of government meeting in Belgrade, was described by the leading Jakarta daily, *Kompas*, as the beginning of 'a new phase' in the development of the country's foreign policy.[22] The last time Suharto attended a Non-Aligned heads of government meeting – 1970 in Lusaka – he was put off by questions about his anti-Communist and seemingly pro-western stance. His return to the Non-Aligned forum in person in 1989, made a deep impression on him, as other leaders assembled in Belgrade paid him compliments for the achievements of his policies. According to cabinet sources, the experience convinced Suharto that he was able to play a more prominent role in international affairs.

The pivotal decision he made, however, was to unfreeze relations with Beijing. China's support for the PKI, and an alleged plot to smuggle arms to Indonesia in 1965, resulted in the New Order's freezing of ties with Beijing in 1967. The stance had an important impact domestically and in the region. Singapore took the view that its own diplomatic relations with China would not be established until Indonesia took steps to normalize the situation. Brunei followed suit. Once Jakarta normalized relations in August 1990, China felt it could secure more assured relations with Asean, begin mending fences with Vietnam and finally unblock the deadlock over Cambodia.

Until the mid-1980s, it was assumed that Suharto's political legitimacy drew too heavily on the events of 1965 to mend fences with China. However, in 1985 a memorandum of understanding, to initiate trade links, was signed with Beijing. A visit to Jakarta by the Chinese foreign minister a few months later to commemorate the 1955 Asia Africa Conference in Bandung seemed to offer little hope of movement on the diplomatic front. Suharto would not budge from his position. Then in February 1989, a meeting with Chinese Foreign Minister Qian Qichen was arranged in

Tokyo, where he and Suharto were attending Emperor Hirohito's funeral. The move seemed to take the foreign ministry in Jakarta by surprise.

By this stage, Suharto himself seemed intent on normalizing ties if the right formula presented itself. Opposition to the move was now heard in military quarters. Either there was a genuine belief that China still aimed to destabilize Indonesia, or the generals were concerned about the domestic political implications of finally burying the myth of the Communist threat. Again, there seemed no clear unanimity within the ranks. More significantly, Suharto was prepared to allow the process of normalization to be conducted with a fanfare. Soon after the agreement with Beijing in August 1990, Chinese Premier Li Peng was invited to Jakarta. A visit by President Yang Shangkun followed less than a year later. All this suggested Suharto hoped the decision would burnish his credentials as a statesman overseas and enhance his relevance at home.

Ironically enough, it seemed that Suharto was borrowing the very device Sukarno employed to boost his popularity when his power was threatened. Sukarno's most audacious and reckless feats of international diplomacy were launched in the last two years of his rule. Echoes of the past can also be detected in the tone of the foreign policy Suharto now seems to be favouring: Non-Alignment and the championship of developing nation issues. Like Sukarno before him, Suharto is proving adept at deploying powerful symbols to enhance his grip on power. In this case, however, most of the policy decisions made sense: the higher international profile they are giving Indonesia was seen in nationalist quarters as long overdue.

There was one area where Indonesia's higher international profile made Suharto more vulnerable. Closer international scrutiny of the way Indonesia dealt with internal security problems revealed that the methods used were far beyond the boundaries of international acceptance – even in some Non-Aligned and developing world circles. In the former Portuguese colony of East Timor, where an indigenous separatist movement had been smouldering with varying degrees of intensity since 1975, the army's methods of counter-insurgency were at best heavy-handed, at worst brutal. In the North Sumatran province of Aceh, a new flare-up of irredentism in 1990 focused international attention on these methods more closely. Human rights organizations estimated that hundreds of people disappeared, presumed dead or incarcerated, within a year in the province.[23]

The point was driven home on 12 November 1991, when Indonesian troops fired on a crowd of 3,500 mourners in the East Timorese capital, Dili, killing dozens and wounding many more. The army claimed only nineteen people were killed and alleged foreign instigation of a riot.

Independent reports put the death toll as high as 115. Witnesses said the shooting was unprovoked.[24] It was the third such incident where the army's response to local discontent was to shoot and kill unarmed civilians. In September 1984 the army's response to a disturbance outside a mosque in North Jakarta left dozens dead. Another confrontation with Islamic malcontents, in the Sumatran province of Lampung in March 1989, saw the army use a similar approach. Officially forty-nine villagers died.

The government was divided over these issues. On the one hand there was recognition of the need to clean up Indonesia's human rights image, on the other there were real fears that conciliatory policies towards local discontent, of a separatist nature particularly, could encourage other areas with a history of strong separate identity to reassert demands for autonomy. In this respect, Indonesia is captive to its definition as a unitary state; a framework which allows for no assertion of regional autonomy or incipient federalism. Abri's role as guardian of the state puts it at the forefront of the defence of unity, and therefore of a harsh, uncompromising approach. Unlike neighbouring countries, where strong internal security acts guard national unity using civil authorities and the courts, the Indonesian armed forces place their faith in the stopping power of automatic weaponry.

The Indonesia that sought a global diplomatic role and advertised itself as a haven for investment contrasted sharply with the Indonesia that brooked no dissent. The contrast in image was reflected by divisions within the establishment. By the end of the 1980s, the foreign ministry, aided by more enlightened advisers to Suharto, persuaded the President that there was little point in seeking international laurels if there were to be no concessions to international opinion. But the military establishment still believed that in matters of internal security, it was above the rule of law.[25] Commenting on the 12 November shootings in East Timor, Abri Commander General Try Sutrisno said: 'It is necessary to fire on those who do not follow the official line. Abri is determined to eliminate whoever disturbs stability'.[26] Gradually, though, the balance of opinion was shifting in favour of those advocating concessions to international opinion, and Sutrisno's stout defence of the 'security approach' before the DPR after the Dili shootings temporarily cost him his standing as a political figure.

Before the November incident in East Timor, and yielding to diplomatic pressure, some efforts had been made to soften the approach to East Timor. After fifteen years of virtual army rule, in late 1989, East Timor was declared an open province, and Abri implemented what it called 'a smile policy'. However, the difference was more apparent than real. Instead of brute military force, Abri sought to control the populace by exploiting local divisions in Timorese society using a network of spies and local provocateurs. As a result, disaffection among a younger generation of more educated Timorese youth escalated. Demands for self-determination began to be heard from a generation who were supposed to have been raised to forget the past and enjoy the fruits of better access to welfare.

The government also tacitly admitted to human rights abuses in Aceh, citing poor military training and the ferocity of local rebels as the cause. The International Red Cross was granted access to Acehnese detainees, despite opposition from Abri quarters. None of this seemed to have a moderating impact on the military's strategy, which stuck obstinately to the credo that any threat to the unity of the state must be ruthlessly dealt with. The upper levels of Abri high command were not blind to the wider diplomatic implications and the negative impact on Indonesia's overseas image. Either they regarded the security approach as too effective to abandon, or, as some suggested, there was a limit to how much discipline and control the senior ranks could extend to poorly trained and often frightened Javanese soldiery led by ambitious field commanders.

By the time Suharto embarked on a three-week trip overseas in November 1991 to promote his international profile, it was apparent that centrifugal tendencies were re-emerging in the foreign policy establishment. Ranged on one side was the military; either unable or unwilling to modify their security policies to international tastes. Favouring a more accommodating approach were civilian diplomats in the foreign ministry under Ali Alatas. Between them stood Suharto, who in early October made it clear to Abri officers that 'internal stability' was an essential precondition to ensure the success of the Non-Aligned heads of government meeting in September 1992. Because Indonesia wishes to play a role in the changing global order, he said, the success of the Non-Aligned meeting was important.[27]

To what extent Abri was willing to oblige Suharto in this respect, seemed in doubt after the shooting incident in East Timor. There was some speculation in political circles about the possibility that the Dili tragedy and the timing of renewed student unrest (thousands marched against a government-sponsored lottery at the end of 1991 in Java and Sulawesi) were not somehow part of a co-ordinated strategy to sabotage Suharto's election manoeuvres; to undermine his influence overseas, and among the Muslims.[28]

Abri may have felt provoked but this is unlikely. Abri sources have since insisted the army was not entirely to blame for the tragedy. At the end of their annual commanders meeting in September 1991, Suharto as usual met the assembled Abri command. This time, instead of an invitation for a quiet tea at the palace, seventy senior officers were called to the imposing

Tapos ranch outside Jakarta. After taking them on the requisite tour of the ranch – the same tour given to awe-struck Javanese farmers – Suharto sat them down with a boxed meal and proceeded to lecture them while the cameras rolled. It was the president's favourite theme: the merits of *Pancasila* democracy. The calmness and authority with which the homily was delivered contrasted sharply with the anger he could barely conceal at Pekanbaru in 1980. The fact that this, like the Tapos meeting with the Chinese magnates, was later broadcast (twice) on national television, suggested that the intended effect was little different: dare not threaten the state; *l'état c'est moi.*

The embarrassing Tapos lecture delivered a blow that was hard to respond to by turning the other cheek. Afterwards a military spokesman instructed editors of the Abri organ *Angkatan Bersenjata* not to run any story about the meeting.[29] The president's office supplied its own video-tape of the meeting to the state television station. The incident was a clear demonstration of Suharto's power over Abri. This did not mean, though, that Abri had lost its power to influence the preferred course of events. Certainly, regarding East Timor, senior Abri personnel could barely conceal their delight over the cancellation of a visit to the territory by Portuguese parliamentarians, which senior officers had opposed strongly, but on which the foreign ministry had pinned hopes of a settlement of the issue.

Whether Abri anticipated it or not, international reaction to the shootings was unusually fierce, resulting in calls to reassess East Timor's case for independence. 'It is time to dust off the question of East Timor and give it the priority that justice, and now international sentiment require', declared an editorial in the *Washington Post*.[30] In an instant, Indonesia's new image as a burgeoning economy, preparing itself for a more responsible global role, was defaced by a smear of ugly repression. Worse still for Suharto, several governments suspended foreign aid disbursement. Facing pressure at home, after a video of the shooting was shown on national television, even the Japanese government was forced to act. In a private meeting with Defence Minister Benny Murdani, the Japanese ambassador to Jakarta warned that the incident may have an effect on Japanese overseas development assistance to Indonesia.

Although probably not premeditated, Abri's actions in East Timor showed how difficult it was for the New Order to acquire a new image, saddled as it was with anachronistic methods and dogma concerning internal security. Commenting on the significance of the East Timor shootings, Asians themselves initially tended to see it either as Indonesia's Tiananmen Square or Suharto's Benigno Aquino (a reference to the

187

murder of the Filipino opposition politician which set off the train of events which eventually brought down the Marcos administration.) Coverage of the tragedy in the normally tame regional press was unusually detailed and persistent – a lack of regional solidarity which clearly annoyed Indonesian officials. More seriously, for the first time the spectre of donor countries witholding foreign aid as a means of exerting pressure on the New Order came a step closer to reality. Canada and the Netherlands were the first to suspend aid in December. The political significance of this is that so much of Suharto's power hinged on his ability to deliver development, and half of the development budget was composed of foreign aid.[31]

By sacking two generals and backing an official enquiry which contradicted Abri's sanitized version of events in East Timor on 12 November, Suharto turned a potentially dangerous situation to his advantage. Returning from his overseas trip, sounding defiant about threats to cut off foreign aid, he neverthless ensured that international opinion was satisfied, while Indonesia retained national honour. In the process, he achieved a show of strength on the domestic front by implicitly rejecting the stand taken by the Abri commander, General Try Sutrisno, and by sacking two generals.

More significantly, at the 28 December meeting with Abri commanders where the two generals were sacked over East Timor, he invoked for the first time his notional constitutional status as Supreme Commander (*Panglima Tertinggi*). This marked another milestone in Abri's declining political fortunes. As earlier stated, Abri had attempted in 1987 to adjust the soldier's oath to mark a clear separation between loyalty to the state and the government of the day, in accordance with pure Abri doctrine. They failed then, and now Suharto's actions proved their fears justified.

The past three years have seen Indonesia's stature as a dynamic regional economy grow, but the limits to economic reform and institutional change have somewhat dampened early enthusiasm. Similarly, political manouvering over the succession has alerted a widening circle of observers to Indonesia's major weak point; the uncertain process of transferring leadership. The fact that Suharto appeared happy to emasculate Abri's political status but was reluctant to grant more autonomy to civilian institutions to compensate, raised alarm because it pinpointed a fundamental structural flaw that has plagued Indonesia since independence. Historically the army's role in politics was justified in terms of making up for the weakness of civilian institutions. Now that succession loomed, the army was poorly placed to play its traditional role.

Yet, on the surface, heading into the 1992 elections, the New Order had regained much of the composure it seemed to be losing when, buffeted by calls for democracy from below and a mood for renewal of its leadership prevailing in the ranks of the elite, it completed its third eight-year cycle (or *windu* in the Javanese calendar) in 1990. Outwardly, Indonesia's stability and prospects under the leadership of President Suharto stood firm. Even his re-election in March 1993 was now being predicted with more confidence, as early engineered endorsements of his candidacy began to trickle in. Suharto had skilfully hijacked most of the ammunition collected by his detractors to garner support for another term.

Several potentially dangerous snags still lurked below the surface. In the process of disarming his critics, Suharto unleashed some of the very social forces the New Order traditionally struggled to contain. Issues of race and religion were now debated openly. The Chinese community felt less secure in the face of demands for more equity. Non-Chinese businessmen were calling for legislation to allocate them a fairer share. Politically minded Muslims were gaining confidence in the wake of patronage extended to them by the President in the course of 1990–1. Some even optimistically envisaged the re-formation of an expressly Islamic Party.[32]

Most dangerous of all was Suharto's firm handling of Abri. Intentionally or otherwise, Suharto, by the end of 1991, had thrust Abri to the back of the political stage and altered the complexion of the regime. Saddled by the dilution of its political power over the years, Abri made vain attempts in the period after 1988 to bring influence to bear on Suharto. At every stage, Suharto fended Abri off, and in the process, the army lost even more power. In 1989 Abri relinquished its special powers after the dismantling of *Kopkamtib*. The security body replacing it, *Bakortsanas*, was a pale shadow of its predecssor. Appointments approved by Suharto in the course of 1990 undermined Murdani's pervasive influence and moved loyal Suharto supporters into key staff positions. By 1991 his brother-in-law and three former adjutants filled key commands in Jakarta. His son-in-law commanded potentially important military units in the capital, Jakarta.

Weakened institutionally and now under the thumb of Suharto loyalists, Abri was forced to abandon its political strategy of promoting criticism of Suharto in late 1990. A series of service seminars held in 1990–1 produced disappointing results, and further diminished Abri's political credibility. By its own admission, one of Abri's weaknesses was the poor grasp of politics by its junior officers. This bred disappointment among the general staff, and undoubtedly further divided the ranks. The danger here lay in the threat of an internal Abri power struggle, and the knock-on effect this would inevitably have on the executive.

Most frustrating of all for an institution which has maintained the spirit of struggle at the core of its doctrine for almost half a century, avenues for expression of that struggle were becoming more and more constricted. If the army entertained any thought of abandoning its long-standing aversion to mounting a direct challenge to the executive, the cultivated legal tenor of the the New Order more or less ruled out the use of force to make its point. Just as Abri's low fiscal budget limited its acquisition of sophisticated weaponry, so prevailing political conditions militated against Abri's turning its guns on the state. Moreover, firing on unruly sections of the populace boxed the army into an even tighter corner, because of the threat this posed to the New Order's standing with important economic partners.

Abri's actions, together with the increasing tempo of domestic politics driven by oncoming elections, were starting to affect Indonesia's image in the region and overseas. Indonesia was in no sense threatened with the pariah status Burma was acquiring in the West; President Suharto was still considered an asset rather than a liability to his country. But in the process of securing guarantees for his own political survival, Indonesia's outwardly optimistic prospects became riddled with potentially volatile tensions.

8

DEMOCRACY ON HOLD

There is a basic contradiction between the tolerant nature of Pancasila and its actual intolerance in practice.

(H.R. Dharsono)

Suharto's position by the end of the 1980s has been compared to a man riding a tiger. If he stays on he runs the risk of being devoured; the same fate naturally awaits him should he decide to get off. This handy metaphor was very popular on the Jakarta cocktail circuit at the close of the 1980s. It neatly captured the choice Suharto apparently faced, between staying in office another term and inviting even more intense speculation about the succession, or stepping down and having to answer the critics of his rule. Like most issues discussed over canapes, the tiger scenario is attractive but perhaps a little too simplistic. Would Suharto envisage his own situation in such a way? Psychologists might suggest that a leader as strong and as confident as Suharto rarely, if ever, views himself from a distance. The Javanese culture into which he was born, for all its purportedly collective ideals, fosters at the same time an insular view of one's self and well-being.

After twenty-five years of jockeying a country as vast and as complex as Indonesia, Suharto might have become accustomed to the ride. In one sense, Suharto's tongue-lashing in cabinet meetings, the threats to 'clobber' those who tried to depose him, and his decisive moves to counter critics, gave no hint of insecurity. After years of shunning the international limelight, he was taking command of a more active foreign policy. At home he was making his peace with his fellow Muslims. These moves betrayed a keen sense of political timing. Viewed through the Indonesian culture of leadership, they were the acts of a man in control, rather than a mark of weakness. Indeed, those who claimed to be close to him, insisted that Suharto never felt stronger in political terms. Javanese politicians make an art-form of feigning invulnerability.

Quite possibly Suharto was not even fully aware of political pressures building up around him as he grew older. No one brought him bad news anymore, and those in whose interest it really was for Suharto to stay on – his family, corporate cronies and their hangers-on – might have been telling him what great things he still had to do for his country. By some accounts, his wife, Tien, favoured early retirement on the grounds of health – she herself was periodically unwell. Other members of the family, conscious of a degree of popular resentment of their sizeable business empires, were thought to be less enthusiastic about their father's early retirement. At the same time, they ploughed on with their ambitious, cash-hungry schemes, ignoring a government campaign to put the brakes on overseas borrowing.[1] Behind the scenes, their unparallelled access to Suharto enabled them to promote those who were loyal and viscerate those who were not.

Suharto's view of the country he ruled is probably taken at two distinct focal lengths. The most distant is that of the nation, which under his policies and guided by ministers he appointed, seemed to be on course. There was need for encouragement and inspiration, but little more. Suharto probably did not see the need for far-reaching political changes, a belief confirmed by his moves to prevent more vocal members of parliament being re-elected in the 1992 elections. In August 1991, Golkar's list of candidates was scrutinized by Suharto and some of the party's more outspoken members either dropped or placed too far down the list to be assured of election. As far as Suharto was concerned, the political system embraced by the New Order worked – a point he never failed to make to visiting dignitaries.

Closer to his eyes, and therefore a bigger preoccupation, were arrayed the elite, among them potential contenders for power. Some of them had hounded his presidency from soon after the birth of the New Order. Behind the Malari incident in January 1974, the student disturbances of 1978, and more recently criticism of the Chinese conglomerates and calls for more openness, the hand of certain officers – some retired, others not – was discernible. The membership of this group was fluid and not always apparent. The more outspoken among them were referred to generally as *Barisan Sakit Hati*: 'The group of discontented'. Others were less easily identified, either feigning loyalty, or unable to bring themselves to be disloyal. Most were Suharto's former army colleagues. All of them had been rewarded amply enough, but mutterings in the wings could always be heard. Suharto was careful to make sure the most powerful of them was removed before any real harm could be done. It suited his own position

192

to have less effective contenders squabbling among themselves, allowing his strength to shine even more brightly.

Many Indonesians believed – Suharto possibly among them – that the real threat to his position was posed by this small and so far hopelessly divided clique of military men. So long as the New Order still recognized Abri as a key element in the power structure, it was perceived by all as the most powerful component, even if in real terms this power had been effectively diluted over the years. One former General who opposed Suharto from early on, Kemal Idris, believes Abri's dual function served Suharto's purposes better than the army's: 'Because of the dual function the army has lost sight of its aims and purposes and became involved in business'.[2]

Realizing they were gradually being made redundant, certain military officers began to use their influence and patronage to generate criticism of Suharto. The army seminar of December 1990, though considered disap-pointing because of its elliptical conclusions, none the less clearly signalled a desire to limit the tenure of senior officials and also recommended that:

> those officials which have failed in their duty or are no longer able
> to carry out their duties, must be prepared to step down to avoid
> harming the national interest.[3]

Strict interpretation of this kind of thinking was difficult to pin down. Either Abri was issuing a subtle warning to the palace, or wished to be considered more progressive in advance of the coming political struggle over the leadership. Calls for democracy and equity were the sheep's clothing donned by these ambitious wolves of the inner political circle. It was by no means clear whether they actually believed the system needed reform so much as a change of management. By the same token, Suharto's response should be seen less as genuine commitment to creating a more open system, and more as a means of neutralizing his irritating critics. In other words, all the debate and the political energy generated at the turn of the decade could easily be taken as a move towards a more open democracy generated from the top. More realistically, it was a by-product of palace politics.

Arrayed below the battling elite was a body of Indonesian intellectuals and businessmen – if you will, the nascent civilian middle class – many of whom genuinely hoped that one way or another progress towards democratization and an open economy could be achieved. As students in the mid-1960s, many of them took to the streets and helped bring Suharto to power. Now in their late forties, most had prospered under a regime which breathed life into the economy and fostered a class of professionals.

They were torn between a desire to promote their own participation in the system, and the fear that in doing so they might undermine the stability Suharto represented.

It is not easy to place the political problems facing the New Order in a social context simply because of the extent to which the regime has de-coupled the bulk of society from the formal political process. On the other hand, historically, the political impact of Indonesia's middle class was considerable. The nationalist struggle grew out of the disaffection of Dutch-trained native civil servants and wealthy Muslim merchants – both groups with arguably bourgeois pretensions. The bourgeois values and liberal western educations with which nationalist leaders like Mohammad Hatta and Mohammad Natsir were imbued, ensured that Indonesia was governed under a constitutional democracy – albeit fragile – for the first decade after independence. In the mid-1960s, after the failure of Sukarno's flamboyant authoritarian 'Guided Democracy', the New Order drew initial support from urban students and intellectuals, not from the masses.

Yet beneath this '1966 generation' riding the coat-tails of the New Order, the majority of professionals in their thirties are more or less apolitical. They were reared on depoliticized campuses in the late 1970s. Many were themselves the beneficiaries of New Order patronage. Shirking the underpaid bureaucracy and presented with no viable political role beyond sycophantic youth and business groups in Golkar, an entire generation born under the New Order is steeped in their own selfish pursuit of self-gain and pays almost no heed to the politics of their elders. Instead, one newspaper editorial saw:

> the emergence of another middle class whose members are privileged people, whose sense of nationalism is not so high. These people have set up for themselves an affluent society and demonstrated its class consciousness by enjoying vacations abroad.[4]

Objectively, therefore, government spokesmen were not far wrong in assessing opposition groups calling for more democracy as merely a vocal minority.

By 1990 the picture of political impotency among the middle classes seemed to alter somewhat. Ironically, Suharto himself lit the touchpaper; first by explicitly sanctioning the airing of more opinion in August 1990, then by encouraging Muslim intellectuals to form a group to discuss social issues in December of the same year. His appeal for wealth to be shared in March 1990 galvanized a younger, previously apolitical generation of young entrepeneurs and invited them to join the fray. As has already been demonstrated, the actual degree of expression these moves allowed was limited. The extent of openness was more apparent than real.

Suharto's principal aim was to grab the higher ground on issues which he suspected his opponents would use against him. As a useful by-product he picked up early endorsement of his continued leadership. It would be naive to assume he intended the power structure to change, or become any less focused on himself. The existing formula was too successful. This fact, however virulently the politics of succession seemed to threaten the *status quo*, weighed heavily on the conscience of the elite, as well as on that of foreign governments with a stake in Indonesia's stability. Above all, Suharto succeeded in maintaining himself as the central body in the political constellation.

Suharto's response to demands for more democracy was therefore misleading. As political pressures built up in the late 1980s, the President appeared to sanction more openness. In his August 1990 national address, he called on people not to be afraid to express different views. Following his lead, ministers chimed in with assurances of a more open system, inviting previously shunned dissidents to tea, and not over-reacting when these same dissident groups began mimicking Eastern Europe by forming 'forums' for democracy. Abri had its own agenda. In the struggle to influence the executive office, it needed the flickering flames of dissent to act as a bargaining chip; some hint of a threat to the state with which to enhance its own role as guardian and protector of stability.

But there were those who were less sanguine. It soon became apparent that Suharto's tacit acceptance of openness had been interpreted too literally. The President was said to be angered when the DPR invited the dissident 'Petition of Fifty' group to the parliament in June 1991.[5] Some of those involved found their names dropped from the Golkar candidates list for the 1992 elections. Suharto's interpretation of openness was more guarded in his 1991 national address; it required responsibility. Responsibility carried connotations of control. In early October, Suharto warned:

> There have been people who... have been influenced by other systems and who consider that political development here has not yielded anything.... Political systems based on other systems must be viewed with caution lest our resolve is undermined by those who have other intentions those who aim to use other systems.[6]

Once again, he emphatically ruled out any changes to the system. Slowly, the clock was being turned back, a move which seemed logical in the run-up to elections, and implied little change to the cyclical nature of New Order politics.

195

What did Indonesians actually want? Was there in any sense a ground-swell of support for a change of direction? First of all it is important to remember that Indonesia has experienced a period of constitutional democracy in a more or less genuine sense. Describing this period before Sukarno imposed his more authoritarian 'Guided Democracy', Herb Feith argues:

> The operation of Constitutional democracy in the period of the first four cabinets was reasonably effective. Cabinets were accountable to the parliament of the day for many of their actions, although this was not an elected body. The press was exceedingly free. Courts operated with considerable independence of the government. Demands for national loyalty were rarely used to silence the critics of cabinets. And non-political administration characterized at least some major parts of the government apparatus.[7]

If this was so, then it is ironic that many Indonesians reflect on this period as one of ever-changing, weak government, dominated by unconstructive party politics and resulting administrative chaos. Another important point made by Feith is that no ready alternative presented itself at the time. There was no overarching state party as such; neither was the military cohesive enough in the 1950s to seize the reins of power. This reinforced the validity of the Indonesian political equation; a poorly developed and mistrusted civilian establishment set against the more idealistic but also fractious military elite, allowing a single powerful leader to dominate. Not much has changed.

The New Order rode to power with the full acquiescence of an elite left battered by the last years of Sukarno's rule. Democracy was put on hold with the support of the majority of those in a position to argue about it. For twenty-five years, the New Order has sought to perpetuate a state of constant vigilance, arguing that economic development must take precedence over political freedom. Those who protested too loudly were subject to mild but effective sanction. However, it was possible to detect by the late 1980s a broader basis of support for political liberalization.

Broad in the New Order context, cannot in any sense be interpreted as a majority. For the structure of society was such that in the absence of widespread social unrest, only a small section near the top of the social structure could effectively bring influence to bear on the leadership. Yet, noticeably, larger sections of this educated and economically enfranchised elite demonstrated a tendency to question the current power equation. Education, exposure to the outside world, prosperity, and the inevitable desire to protect more valuable personal assets, all contributed to demands for greater accountability in government, for more input to policy, and for a freer, less controlled society. In effect, the historian Kuntowidjoyo concluded, Indonesia was becoming subject to the same social urges born of industrialization that the West experienced a century before:

> An industrial society requires a critical society. The Industrialization of the Western world was accompanied by the appearance of (political) opposition forces to ensure that society's needs were looked after. A conformist, affirmative attitude embraced by a bureaucratic culture is not capable of supporting the critical approach required.[8]

None of these urges was easy to quantify or judge qualitatively. There were also those who argued that the increasing spending power of Indonesia's urban middle class fuelled support for the *status quo*. Yet, the period roughly spanning 1989–91 also saw the press become bolder and less subject to sanction, opposition figures spoke more freely, and the private sector articulated its own interests relatively free of state control.

But as we have seen, many of Indonesia's new democrats found shelter under the wing of disillusioned or embittered contenders for the leadership. Old patterns of patronage persisted, and many were gambling more on the benefits from a change of leadership than striving for far-reaching political reform. Suharto also found it expedient to tolerate more debate about the system, so long as politeness and respect softened the tone of such debate. By doing so he appeared magnanimous and wise. A cabinet minister remarked that Suharto posessed a talent for giving people what they want.

> Giving people what they want is one of the hallmarks of Suharto's tenure. He gave the Muslims their religious courts, Abri has been granted a more creative role, Golkar a more independent role. This way he keeps everybody happy and preserves harmony. But it's all going to lead to some hard bargaining, pay-offs and claims of primacy.[9]

Another handy generalization on the cocktail circuit was that the New Order was falling victim to its own success. That by pursuing sensible policies of economic development, and being committed to allowing those policies to bear fruit, an intrinsically statist regime ran up against the demands of its more liberal-minded subjects. Objectively, it is too early to say if this attractive generalization will prove valid. However, there was a sense in which, not just in Indonesia but elsewhere in the region, the logical extension of policies committed to trimming the role of the public sector and enfranchising the private sector, was for more private individuals and institutions to have a say in the running of the state. Eager as they were to increase productivity, attract investment, and ease the financial burden of government, most of the region's leaders were not quite ready for the broader power-sharing all this implied.

One reaction was for government's to fall back on the rhetoric of nationalism or, in the case of Malaysia, on divisive issues of race. Many observers were taken aback by the ferocity of the ruling National Front's attacks on the opposition in the 1990 election campaign. The opposition blamed their eventual defeat on the National Front's deployment of the race issue. In Indonesia, the New Order's most faithful prop, in the shape of the Communist threat, had been made redundant by Communism's global retreat and the restoration of ties with Beijing. Certain figures in Abri still brandish the threat of a 'Communist comeback' in order to justify their role as guardians of the state. Other, more progressive officers were aware that Abri needed a *raison d'être* more in tune with contemporary conditions. But in Indonesia too, the old and trusted nationalist rallying cry was far from being abandoned. In the wake of the East Timor incident, many of those who may have felt inclined to join the international community to condemn Abri for its action, susbequently rallied behind the army to defend the country's honour in the face of the fierce international reaction.

A common approach in the region was for the leadership to set itself new and more distant goals in order to justify and reinforce the grip on power. Malaysia's Dr Mahathir Mohamad fashioned nine 'central strategic challenges' into the concept of 'Vision 2020', by which time Malaysia would become a fully industrialized and developed nation. The slogan bloomed into a political talisman, against which the opposition in Malaysia appeared virtually powerless.[10] Singapore, under the uncertain stewardship of Prime Minister Goh Chok Tong, outlined a programme for 'Singapore: the next lap', which aimed to make Singapore 'more prosperous, gracious and interesting'.[11] The New Order opted for a second 'long term development period' of twenty-five years (*Era Pembangunan Jangka Panjang Kedua*) beginning in 1990, culminating in a second 'National Reawakening'.

All these exercises in boosterism shared a common goal: they were attempts to protect and revitalize the successful political formula which so effectively maintained a strong executive style of leadership in the region. How can this formula be defined in general terms? After the upheavals of the Second World War and the struggle for independence, the newly independent states of South-east Asia found that nationalism, which so effectively motivated people to overcome colonialism, could serve useful political ends once the colonial masters had departed. Neither was independence proving to be the elixir of life and prosperity. In Indonesia, regional revolts and a Communist uprising threatened the fledgeling Republic in its early years. These were deemed a threat to the nation fuelled by the dying embers of imperialism. Malaysia, launched from a Malay core in 1957, struggled to forge unity between its three major ethnic communities. Singapore needed to emerge from the shadow of its larger neighbours and survive as a city state. In all cases, the leadership prescribed vigilance, discipline and order as the necessary formula to hold the nation together. Replacing the goal of independence, but with the same stress on collective or corporate loyalty and the suppression of individual rights, was the goal of national development.

Invariably, as outlined in Chapter 6, this goal was presented to the people as a struggle, consciously echoing the struggle for independence. In the 1950s and 1960s, Sukarno deployed overtly anti-imperialist themes to justify the harsh suppression of regional revolts, the acquisition of West Irian from the Dutch and even the portrayal of the federation of Malaysia as a western plot to destabilize Indonesia. In his speech to the MPR after his re-election for a third term as President, Suharto observed:

> That the struggle during the forthcoming five years will not be less arduous than the struggle of the past five years. Also it does not have lesser significance than our previous struggle for independence.[12]

The new struggle would also require sacrifices. 'There is no struggle without victims', an Indonesian slogan from the pre-independence period runs. Implicitly, if not explicitly, one of these sacrifices was the right to question authority. In the process, local definitions of the democratic institutions adopted at independence altered accordingly. Malaysia began to distinguish between its own and the 'Westminster' style of parliamentary democracy. Singapore's People's Action Party allowed its original Marxist-Leninist-like cadre structure to subsume its modern parliamentary form. Indonesia's New Order defined democracy in terms of '*Pancasila*', the 'Floating Mass' and an allergy to the '50 plus 1' definition of a majority.

As a recipe for stability, the formula has worked well. Undoubtedly it laid the foundations for the region's economic success. But having achieved a level of development that has pushed these countries far beyond the shadow of the colonial period, where next? What role for a strong, paternalistic leadership once the subjects have achieved a measure of confidence and self-reliance? These questions teased the leaders of these countries just as the cold war, and fifty years of Communist tyranny in the Soviet Union, ended.

The sense of relief in South-east Asia once the threat of a superpower confrontation passed at the turn of the decade was all too brief. For it was superseded by alarm over the way the triumphant West brandished its values in their faces. Not content with securing democracy for Eastern Europe and the Soviet Union, the West now questioned the democratic credentials of its former anti-Communist allies in Asia. The threat of conditionality on issues of human rights and the environment attached to aid and trade from the European Community was dangled before Asean countries.

Asean leaders saw this as an unfair imposition of western values, and a stream of anti-western rhetoric ensued. After Lee Kuan Yew of Singapore stepped down as Prime Minister in November 1990, Malaysian Prime Minister Mahathir Mohamad eagerly assumed the mantle of speaking up for the region. 'People talk about Democracy very freely without waiting to define or understand it', he said in October 1991. In his view, the West considered democracy a religion to be imposed on everyone, regardless of their beliefs. This view, shared – if not so stridently expressed – by other leaders, was that South-east Asia had its own set of values to defend, and it was unjust for the West to transpose western definitions of democracy and human rights onto an Asian context. Indonesian Foreign Minister Ali Alatas, himself a shade liberal by New Order standards, led the Asean onslaught against the European Community's suggestion that a human rights clause be written into the new Asean-EC trade agreement at the May 1991 joint ministerial conference in Luxembourg. The irony of the end of the cold war and East-West polarization, was that in its place antipathy between the North and the South was intensifying.[13]

Against this background, Indonesia was entering the uneasy period just before the quiennial 'festival of democracy', the culmination of which for the last quarter-century had been the ritual re-election of President Suharto. An air of nervousness and expectancy prevailed. However, this was not the first pre-election period coloured by restlessness and a questioning of the system and its progenitor. The dynamics of each five-year cycle in the New Order's history share certain similiarities, the most common of which was early, but ultimately ineffectual manoeuvring to persuade Suharto to step down. There were periods before the 1970, 1978, 1983, and 1988 presidential elections where the libertarian demands of critics could be heard, and the plots of disgruntled military men uncovered and smothered. In all cases, Suharto's deft co-option of the disenchanted left them exposed as weak or uncommitted.

Was this last five-year period any different? Suharto's fifth term, 1988–93, can be regarded as the most consistently questioned, the least monolithic. Calls for Suharto to make this term the last were heard almost as soon as it began in 1988. The cabinet was more divided and fractious than any other in the New Order's history. Suharto's age, the loss of so many of his former inner circle, his family's commercial avarice, even the words of his own biography; there was a plethora of persuasive explanations why Suharto might step down or be forced out in 1993. This survey ends before any final conclusion can be safely drawn. But there are two advantages to what might seem to some as a somewhat premature retro-spection. The first is that when Suharto's long shadow is eventually lifted, the potential for distortion of both his good and bad qualities as a leader will inevitably intensify. There is a danger, as with Marcos in the Philip-pines, that the popular political energy harnessed to replace a once-popular leader will obscure not only the achievements of his rule, but also the way it should be assessed. For in many ways, Suharto is less the political genius he is often painted as and more an expression of Indonesian, or more specifically, Javanese political culture and society.

The Javanese concept of power, as the scholar Benedict Anderson has shown, fosters the reification of traditional symbols, myths and history. For the analyst trying to understand Suharto, the need to shuttle between universal concepts of power politics and those which are specifically Javanese is a constant and baffling concern. The logic or rationale of the one often conflicts with the latter. What MacDonald calls the 'traditional substrata of of Indonesian politics'[14] doggedly pursues the rational analyst, especially when it comes to Suharto himself. Does Suharto consider himself a leader in the modern, nationalistic sense, or as a *pandithu ratu*, or wise king in the traditional Javanese sense? Does he believe his rule is mandated by the MPR, or protected by a *wahyu*, or divine blessing? Lack of access to Suharto's personal views about his leadership makes it hard to answer these questions. One suspects that he himself would rather keep people guessing, but a good guess would focus on his instinctive talent for deploying traditional symbols of power.

Indonesia's passage through the latter half of the twentieth century under two powerful leaders, neither of whom have devoted close attention to the restructuring of the basic rights of the people and obligations of the state in a recognizably modern framework commensurate with the coun-try's stage of economic growth, has naturally led many Indonesians to believe their leadership is modelled on the past. Despite the belief in some quarters that the New Order has installed fundamental principles of popular sovereignty and the institutions of democracy, it is hard to see how the Indonesian people really have a say in how their government rules. Elections, the manifestation of the people's choice, tend to be played out as rituals – their smooth, orderly running is considered more important than the actual results. Strict control over the three sanctioned political parties, and the government's final say in who is appointed to the MPR, makes the choice of presidential candidate a foregone conclusion. Any questioning of this system is met with the argument that Indonesia has blended traditional culture with modernity and produced its own form of democracy. The New Order has been conspicuously successful in perpetuating traditional forms of paternalistic leadership through the manipulation of modern notions of nationhood and sovereignty. That the mixture has extended a measure of security and welfare to a majority of people is unquestioned. The focus of debate within Indonesia is on whether changes must now be introduced, and if so, how best can change be managed without inviting chaos.

The two major political problems Indonesia has faced more openly in the past five years remain unsolved. The mechanism for succession remains a source of concern, and the degree to which a wider section of society should be granted a political role has not been addressed. The key questions are: will Indonesia's stability be threatened? Will the measurable economic progress achieved over the past decade be jeopardized?

By way of supplying an partial answer to these questions, the absence of two major scenarios from this overview are perhaps significant. First the prospect of a military coup has not been highlighted. Rather, the military has been portrayed as a key political component of the New Order which is itself in a weak and divided state. Nevertheless, unity is not a necessary prerequisite for launching a *putsch* – indeed the lack of unity in the ranks probably explains why a small group of officers from the presidential guard were able to act the way they did on 30 September 1965. However, only a united Abri could safely wrest power from Suharto. Deeply ingrained, almost institutionalized suspicion pervading the upper echelons of the armed forces has been one of Suharto's chief assets in his handling of military politics – and this, together with his judicious manipulation of appointments, explains more than anything else the inability of Abri to move against Suharto.

The common understanding is that Abri will refrain from intervening unless the unity or stability of the state is threatened. 'The only factor which might create problems for the Armed Forces', wrote Brigadier-General Nugroho Notosusanto in 1980, 'would be a setback in the economic field which would cause unrest and endanger the stability of the country.' If this comes close to defining Abri's doctrine of action, Notosusanto's ominous conclusion is:

Then the armed forces would be compelled to use force which in turn would create civil-military friction.[15]

If a coup were to be launched, almost certainly it would result, as before, in a successful counter-coup. Current levels of suspicion and disunity in the ranks of Abri would almost guarantee this sequence of events. One difference might be the indifference of the West. The final round of shadow-boxing between Bear and Eagle has been played out; therefore who becomes a proxy of a superpower or bloc is less important. As a result the world is more immune to changes of government by military means. But like before, a coup or counter-coup could result in a change of leadership – one hopes without the incidental bloodshed witnessed in 1965.

So far, all the indications are that Abri has opted to stick to constitutional means of politicking, even if this does stray into small demonstrations of its might on a local scale. As with Suharto's own position in 1966, Abri is acutely aware of the dangerous precedent even a clean and successful coup would pose to any future president chosen from among its ranks. Suharto's legalistic ways and the New Order's longevity has served to confound those who saw the country on the verge of a long cycle of coup and counter-coup in the mid-1960s.

This reluctance to make a precipitous bid for paramount leadership could explain why so much of the recent debate over the succession has focused on the rather less powerful position of vice-president. Possibly it served to divert the competition among ambitious contenders for power into a less contentious arena, thus defusing somewhat a potentially destabilizing political confrontation. More realistically, the race for pole position in the vice-presidential stakes could be seen as a typical expression of Indonesian political culture, where the premium is on politeness and non-confrontation. Few of those who watched the antics of a figure like Rudini in the run-up to 1993 believed they were witnessing anything other than a campaign to burnish presidential credentials. It is, in any case, hard to imagine a situation where Suharto would tolerate the appointment of a vice-president openly acknowledged as his heir-apparent. In Indonesia, power is absolute, or not considered power at all. Rather, speculation over the vice-presidency in the run-up to March 1993 served to deflect attention from the real problem of deciding on the presidency.

The prospects for political change are more difficult to guage. The regional atmospherics are confusing. Burma's Aung San Sukyi was awarded the Nobel Peace Prize in 1991. But at the same time, opposition to the West's more aggressive propagation of human rights and democracy was building up, even in erstwhile democratic societies like Malaysia, let alone

Indonesia. For the time being, an air of pragmatism reigned on both sides of this new ideological divide. The West's considerable economic stake in Asia's prosperity almost guaranteed a soft approach to domestic political issues. Experience showed that violent or sudden popular overturning of undemocratic regimes did not necessarily result in a more democratic alternative. While gentle pressure and friendly criticism aimed at the existing regimes preserved stability, economic growth fostered the liberalizing tendencies the West wishes to see emerge. For their part, Asean countries valued trade and aid from the West too highly not to show a willingness to contemplate political reforms – on their own terms. The effect was to give an impression of change while disguising the tension between the forces of change and continuity.

In the case of Indonesia, all the energy and rhetoric expended on calling for openness and institutional change at the end of Suharto's fifth term looked like exhausting itself. By late 1991 Suharto's ability to absorb, co-opt and in some cases concede to his detractors appeared to have smoothed over what looked like a crack in the mould. Also because when it came to the crunch, even the most liberal-minded of Indonesia's small and comparatively comfortable elite, was unwilling to induce chaos. Whether it was the risk of derailing the economy, or the lack of any obvious alternative to Suharto's steady leadership, or the fact that the elite had been co-opted, the momentum for change slowed as the elections approached.

Instead, another focus of political confrontation emerged. If Suharto could not be persuaded to step down, the political and military establishment would try and persuade him to appoint a vice-president they found acceptable: a figure with the potential to assume the reigns of power at some point before the end of 1998 – implying a mid-term transition without elections. Such a scenario suited the Abri establishment for two reasons. First, it sidestepped the issue of Suharto's re-election in 1993, by allowing him to continue in office. Second, and perhaps more crucially for the army, a vice-president of their choice could be appointed, with the likely eventual task of assuming the leadership, peacefully and without a messy power struggle. As a dividend, Abri's political role would clearly be enhanced as well as preserved.

Neat as this sounds, it was far from easy to achieve. As pointed out earlier, Suharto has always perceived the vice-presidency as a useful siding into which to shunt either his loyal cronies or potential opponents. Never has the position been conferred on a military figure of any real importance. As the military appeared to increase the pressure on Suharto to heed its advice in late 1991, keen observers could make out the vague shadow of the group which would play an important role in the political manouevring before 1993.

The group consisted roughly of all the retired senior officers in cabinet: the Defence Minister, General Benny Murdani; the Minister of Home Affairs, General Rudini, Admiral Sudomo, the Co-ordinating Minister for Security and Political Affairs; and General Soepardjo Rustam, a veteran of the war against the Dutch in Central Java and former aide to the late General Sudirman. Because of his powerful position as State Secretary, the younger but ambitious Major General Moerdiono, could also be considered a key player. This was no cohesive group; their common interest born only of proximity to power and a stake in the future leadership and the preservation of the New Order. They were all destined, however, to play a key role in the immediate future of the country – insiders dubbed this group 'the kingmakers'. Suharto himself betrayed no hint of concern about his future; no obvious preference for a successor.

The dilemma for some of Indonesia's most progressive politicians was rooted in the unprepossessing political structures in which they sat. A number of the student hotheads from the late 1970s had found themselves given senior positions in the Golkar hierarchy. Much to their surprise, the relaxed atmosphere of the late 1980s provided them with an opportunity to exercise their liberal tendencies. Some began talking of turning Golkar into a political party with aspirations of its own. But as elections approached in 1992, Golkar's intended purpose became more difficult to disguise. With its funding tied directly to Suharto, and its only leader capable of independent action, Sudharmono, safely removed, Golkar emerged as what it has always been intended to be; the chief vehicle for ensuring the elections would be run smoothly and above all predictably. 'Golkar does not anticipate or entertain any idea of departing from the present system', said its secretary general, Rachmat Witoelar in late 1990. Witoelar, along with a growing number of capable politicians with a modern outlook, hope that by surviving the system, they may contribute to its gradual change. 'We are sitting out the inevitable end of Suharto's rule, after which we shall be in a good position to share power with his successor'.[16] Witoelar's remarks are perhaps a shade more optimistic than realistic. Others suspected that all they would be required to do will be to stand up and applaud his successor.

9

THE FRAGILE STATE

Anyone without military support cannot make it.
Major General Sembiring Meliala, October 1993

The morning of the June 1992 general election, there was a minor earthquake in Central Java. Everyone in the city of Jogyakarta felt the mild tremor that struck just as the polls opened in the morning, but few dared guess what it signified. In earthquake-prone Java such mild tremors are common, but when they coincide with major events they are believed to be pregnant with significance. A local *dukun*, or seer, would only say that the quake, coming as it did on the day of the election itself, could portend either good or bad things – he would not say which.

The earth may have moved on 9 June, but Indonesia's almost 100 million voters made barely any impact on Suharto's New Order. Golkar's share of the vote declined slightly – from 73 per cent in 1987 to 68 per cent. The minor parties, the PPP and PDI, made modest gains. 'The electorate was tired of the same party winning for the fourth time and above all Golkar could not really defend itself against criticism of the deficiencies of the government which are generally associated with Golkar', suggested a pro-government analyst.[1] In East and Central Java, Golkar lost 18 parliamentary seats. Wahono, the chairman of Golkar, later dryly observed that Golkar fared badly in the election because there was now more democracy.

There certainly was evidence of a demand for more democracy. Large numbers of younger, mainly first-time voters indicated their desire for a more open political system by abstaining from the polls. These so-called *golput* or 'white groups' highlighted the wide gulf between what was articulated during the campaign and the election itself. The campaign saw issues like nepotism, corruption, and the New Order's stifling of political expression raised openly. Young first-time voters were more articulate, considerably more restless, but utterly disorganized. A few days before the election, young people in Jogyakarta gathered in small angry groups discussing the futility of these views. 'The people are ready for change, only the leaders are not' said one young activist. 'Where is our Chamlong?' asked another – referring to Bangkok's populist mayor who had helped to mobilize popular action again the Thai military in the streets of Bangkok only a month before. [2] The problem, as columnist Emha Ainun Najib put it, was the inability of any of the three 'contesting' parties to reflect these aspirations and frustrations:

> It is very simple, you have the urge for change running strongly below the surface... there is a new polarization. But it is not attached to any one party – there is no connection. The link is missing. [3]

On balance, a muted point was made but not taken. The election results did not have any bearing on the culmination of the process, which was the March 1993 re-election of President Suharto for a sixth term of office.

This presidential election was if anything more orderly than the ritual endorsement of Suharto in 1988. There were no surprise candidates for vice-president at the eleventh hour; no interruption from the floor – only a muted demand for debate on electoral reform from the PDI, which MPR chairman Wahono rejected. Opening the MPR on 1 March, Suharto listed the economic achievements of his long rule: an average of 6 per cent growth in GDP per year over the past quarter century, per capita income up from US$70 to US$600 over the same period. These facts are hard to argue with. The quibbling was over Suharto's style of rule, the lack of openness, and the corruption which many feel has held the country back from even better economic performance. As Indonesia began to play a more active rule in international diplomacy, there were those who found it hard to reconcile the country's desire to be taken seriously as a medium sized regional power with a government that told its people that full democracy was a still distant goal.

Even those content with the political system, or who derived generous dividends from it, were feeling uncertain. Another five years, then what? Then who? The central question in contemporary Indonesian politics remained unanswered. The New Order was dusted off and set back on the mantelpiece, but the flaw which made it so intrinsically fragile was even more conspicuous. The question of who would succeed Suharto was still unresolved.

There was some comfort for the armed forces in this respect. A small triumph which set the stage for political manoeuvring in the early part of Suharto's sixth term. Remarkably, Abri managed to impose their candidate for vice-president on Suharto. Although it is not clear who Suharto favoured in the run-up to March 1993, he certainly did not want the decision made for him. In 1988, Sudharmono's name only emerged shortly before the MPR got underway – and was clearly Suharto's choice. In this case, several senior Abri officers indicated that armed forces chief Try Sutrisno was their choice well ahead of the MPR. The PDI nominated Try as early as January. One by one the other factions of the MPR followed suit, presumably at Abri's behest.

By all accounts, Suharto was displeased. One view is that Try was considered for the job, but Suharto was wary of his links to the Abri high command, defence minister Benny Murdani in particular. By the end of Try's tenure as Abri commander it was clear that he was being managed and groomed for higher office by Murdani's group in the Abri high command. But Suharto could hardly tamper with the consensus already reached by all the MPR factions, and Try was duly selected.

The boyish-looking 57 year-old former office boy from East Java was not considered the brightest prospect in Indonesian politics, but Abri needed a candidate who was both loyal to Suharto and the military. As a former presidential adjutant and armed forces chief, Try fitted the mould perfectly. According to Murdani:

We took the decision five years ago. We decided after Sudharmono was elected vice president in 1988 that Abri must decide the next Vice-president. So we decided on Try. [4]

Abri's nightmare was that Suharto favoured Professor B. J. Habibie. The 57 year-old German trained engineer (whose ambitious plans for developing a hi-tech industrial base in Indonesia appealed to Suharto) enervated the cost conscious Berkeley technocrats. He had long been regarded with suspicion in military circles because his procurement plans were tailored to the needs of his hi-tech industries rather than to Abri's military needs. This suspicion turned to dislike when, out of the blue, the German-speaking, opera-loving physicist was appointed head of the Suharto-backed Muslim Intellectual Organization (ICMI) in December 1990.

From the start Abri considered Habibie's leadership of ICMI as a violation of its 'golden rule' that civilians should not be allowed to build up personal power bases. [5] Using Islam as a platform made Habibie even more unpopular with the generals because this threatened religious harmony. Having deployed Habibie to garner Muslim support for his re-election, many Indonesians were convinced that Suharto would consider him for promotion. This seems unlikely, since Suharto was already unhappy with Habibie's rather un-Javanese manner of self-promotion ahead of the MPR. In the end, it seems hardly credible that Suharto seriously considered anyone other than an Abri candidate at this stage.

By placing Try at Suharto's side for the next and possibly last five years of his rule, Abri — but more specifically Benny Murdani and his group — was counting on managing the succession and checking the rise of anti-military political influence. Abri also calculated that Try could be managed — a perception which betrayed little support for more political pluralism in military quarters. Suharto was aware of this strategy and did his best to play up Try's credentials as a former presidential adjutant rather than military commander. He was in no hurry to groom anyone, and he certainly did not want his hard-won independence from Abri eroded.

Abri's triumph at the MPR was therefore short-lived. Countering Abri's move to secure the succession, Suharto continued to sow the upper ranks of the military with his own men. Most observers saw the far-reaching changes as a move to undermine the pervasive influence of Murdani and his supporters. This explains why General Edi Sudrajat — a Murdani protégé — found himself promoted out of the Abri commander's position to be defence minister barely three months after he was appointed. Sudrajat's successor, General Feisal Tanjung, a Muslim from North Sumatra, was considered more sympathetic to Habibie and the ICMI group. Of eight key positions reshuffled in the period after mid-1992, four of the incoming appointees were considered Suharto's protégés. These included the army chief of staff, Lieutenant-General Wismoyo Arismunandar (Suharto's brother-in-law, since promoted to four star rank), Major-General Kuntara as KOSTRAD commander, Major-General Hendro Prijono as Jakarta garrison commander, and Brigadier-General Tarub as special forces commander. Attempting to dismiss the *praetorian* loyalties of the new guard, Murdani remarked: 'most of these officers represent people whose time to be promoted had come'. [6] In reality, it became even more difficult to distinguish those who served the President, Abri, or both.

Following up the military reshuffle, Suharto also reduced the level of Abri representation in the cabinet. The number of active senior officers in the new cabinet appointed in March fell from eleven to nine. Suharto also chose a new cabinet which allowed his own long experience in government to shine at the expense of veterans who had overseen a decade of economic development and reform. While ICMI activists and civilian politicians cheered the new team for being less military and Christian, businessmen and foreign investors worried about the implications for economic continuity. Almost gone were the Berkeley mafia. In came over half a dozen of Habibie's nominees. The new faces prompted concern and even a parallel with the last cabinet of 100 ministers selected by Sukarno in the final years of his rule – a patronage free-for-all with no real direction or drive. As one experienced businessman put it: 'The private sector is now concerned that deals will have to be made with all these new people. It is a strange time to be experimenting with new faces.'[7] It was, however, a good time for Suharto to draw on younger blood. At 72 he was growing conscious of his age, and perhaps feared giving the impression that he was simply on automatic pilot. For the first time he called smaller groups of his new ministers for regular working group meetings – he was projecting a 'hands-on' image.

Predictably, observers lauded Suharto's ability to emerge from the election stronger and politically invigorated. His choice of cabinet ministers and vice-president superficially looked like another shrewd balancing of the political forces. A more Muslim, less military cabinet found favour with his new civilian and Muslim support base; Try's accession to the vice-presidency appeased Abri. Balancing the forces was indeed Suharto's strongest political skill, except that the forces he now had to manage consisted of a more complex and volatile brew.

By introducing ICMI to the political equation, Suharto played the Muslim card which worried the small but influential Christian elite and Abri. Habibie's influence over economic policy created a stand-off between the technocrats (whose policies had never been openly questioned before) and the more nationalistically-minded *technologues* who favoured more state management of resources. Suharto's apparent patronage of both ICMI and Habibie's *technologues* encouraged civilian political forces opposed to Abri's role in government. Add to this the increasing role Suharto's family played in politics, and the New Order began to look like a much more complex political organism. As predicted by Sarwono Kusumaatmadja in the preceding chapter, the claims of primacy this more diverse political spectrum generated were about to roll in.

From this array of political forces, the two most obvious protagonists and contenders for power in the post-Suharto era were Abri and the civilian political elements gathering around Habibie. These battle lines appealed to political pundits, who saw the forces competing for power divided between the military and civilians, with Vice-President Try Sutrisno as Abri's candidate, and Habibie as the civilian choice for president after Suharto left the scene. Many saw the prospect of intensified civilian pressure on Abri to relinquish its claim to power as the most likely theme of Suharto's sixth term. Never before had Abri's role in politics looked like being challenged so effectively.

Events in the first few months of Suharto's sixth term seemed to bear this out. Soon after the MPR, Habibie began to make his moves. By inviting well known dissident and Petition of Fifty leader Ali Sadikin to a ship-launching ceremony at his PT Pal shipyard in June, Habibie forced the military onto the defensive. It was a bold stroke – at once claiming to support the liberal winds of change, and at the same time flouting his favour with the executive office. Habibie made it plain that this new détente with dissidents had Suharto's full approval.

Abri's counter move was clumsily executed and fraught with contra-diction. Newly appointed armed forces commander General Feisal Tanjung insisted that Habibie's overture to Sadikin was not a sign of reconciliation between the government and its critics. Sadikin's Petition of Fifty group still represented a threat to security because they were 'still launching political moves which are a danger to stability'.[8] In a classic example of KISS[9] politics, Tanjung also claimed he had secured Suharto's full backing on this. Yet barely a month later, a smiling Tanjung posed at the hospital bedside of none other than the doyen of Indonesian dissidents, General A. H. Nasution. Abri too, it seemed, could tack into the liberal winds of change.

Abri seemed to be tacking all over the place. Stressing threats to security one day, supporting student demonstrations against the state-backed lottery the next. The question at this point was who in Abri had control of the tiller. Was it an Abri initiative to engineer the first meeting between Nasution and Suharto in over twenty years? [10] Was this meant to be a slap in the eye for Habibie – a demonstration of where the real roots of the New Order lay? Why did Abri try to upset the re-election of PDI chief Suryadi in July – a move which backfired, but embarrassed the government all the same? Fingers were pointed at Murdani who, despite having lost his cabinet position in March 1993, remained a force to be reckoned with in the eyes of the Jakarta power elite.

Stripping away all the myths shrouding Murdani's career, there re-mained the fact that retired from active service and now out of office, the 61 year-old general maintained a conspicuously high profile and a loyal following. Barely a month after Suharto's re-election and his ejection from the cabinet, Murdani declined the offer of an ambassadorship overseas – the New Order equivalent of falling on one's sword in the wake of defeat. Rather than withdrawing gracefully to a large house in one of Jakarta's leafy suburbs, like other spent generals, he occupied an office and played politics from behind the scenes. In fact, he took Ali Murtopo's old office in the Centre of Strategic and International Studies – the same office, and the same desk, from where Murtopo had planned *opsus* (special operations) on Suharto's behalf in the 1970s. From here, chomping on expensive cigars and wielding a mobile phone, Murdani received a steady stream of visitors and supporters, claiming that he was enjoying his retirement.

To those who knew him, Murdani was incapable of retiring. Barely weeks after Suharto's re-election Murdani presided over the glittery launch of a book on his career ghost written by a local journalist. The event brought the Jakarta elite out in force, a demonstration of influence – if not power – which completely reversed the prevailing impression that he was a spent force. The book itself was too subjective to reveal any hidden secrets. That was not the point. The book's message was simple: Murdani is the country's most senior military officer, a 'superlative example of national service', with leadership qualities few can rival. In an introduction that some people considered more significant than the text itself, Muslim leader Abdurrahman Wahid, a staunch ally of the General, described Murdani's style of leadership as 'essential' to Indonesia.[11]

The book, the book-launch, and his daughter's wedding later in the year (which was attended by, among others, the Sultan of Brunei and president Ramos of the Philippines) were all fine examples of the diffuse projection of power in Indonesia. Demonstrations of power need not assume recognizable or obvious forms. The New Order's suppression of meaningful political institutions allowed manifestations of power to be expressed in rather more personal, even quirky ways. Murdani's opponents even coined the term 'De–Bennysisation' to describe the process of ridding the government of his influence.[12]

Instead, Murdani bounced back in the course of 1993 to convince everyone that he was Abri's Godfather. A senior local journalist described him as the 'only alternative leader in Indonesia today'.[13] In Javanese cultural terms, he projected himself as the model 'warrior knight', *ksatria* of the 'wayang' drama. Those prone to Javanese symbolism, argued that the country was divided between two 'republics'; Republic 'A', under Suharto (a play on the title of a pro-ICMI newspaper, *Republika*), and Republic 'B'; under Abri led by Murdani. Taking the imagery a stage further, it was even suggested that the two 'republics' were a reincarnation of the historical rivalry between the sultanates of Jogyakarta (from where Suharto came) and Solo (near where Murdani was born).

Against this fanciful suggestion were set hard realities that even the most sympathetic to Murdani's role could not deny. His *Bais* military intelligence apparatus had been downgraded to a passive rather than active role. The extensive re-shuffle of key military positions dislocated Murdani's network in the chain of command. By moving Edi Sudrajat smartly out of the Abri commander's position, Murdani was tricked. He lost direct access to the high command. Or so it seemed, for there were also those who saw a safely neutralized, but still influential Murdani as a useful foil for Suharto to wield against the powerful forces gathering around Habibie. (In September, Suharto made attempts to foster closer co-operation between Abri and ICMI – a move Abri read as more an attempt to persuade NU to endorse ICMI and unite the Muslim community.) If Suharto was out to balance the forces, he needed personalities to represent those forces. As before, Murdani was careful to project a loyal, if not entirely passive attitude towards Suharto. He could not be drawn into open criticism of the President. Like the classic *ksatria* he preferred to project his power as a moral, conscience-pricking force in the background.

If Murdani was indeed still involved with formulating Abri strategy in this new and challenging period for the armed forces, he and the other generals faced the biggest test of their political ingenuity ahead of the third act of the New Order's quiennial political cycle; the Golkar elections.

Well ahead of the October 1993 Golkar Congress, rumours circulated that Suharto was considering the appointment of the party's first civilian chairman in its nearly 30 year history. That such rumours were taken seriously indicated how low Abri's political stock had sunk. Abri once again fumbled; at first asserting their own candidacy, then saying they would not interfere, and finally mounting a fierce campaign to secure Abri domination of the regional Golkar chapters. In a replay of their 1987–8 strategy to prevent Sudharmono and his civilian cohorts from dominating Golkar, Abri managed to place retired or active officers in 80 per cent of the regional seats. At the Congress itself, Abri pitched retired general Susilo Sudarman as their candidate. But it was too late.

Abri may have had the floor and packed the hall, but Suharto still called the shots in a political organization that he never intended to function more than symbolically. There were hopes for a compromise with Abri – an acceptable civilian at the very least. Instead Suharto opted for what by New Order standards was almost a confrontational move. Not only was Information Minister Harmoko made Golkar chairman, but Habibie dominated the seven man 'team of selectors' which presided over the election (he was already appointed to the powerful Golkar advisory board headed by Suharto), and two of Suharto's children were given executive board positions. Although the appointment of retired Major-General Ary Mardjono as the party's secretary-general conceded one senior post to Abri, the message was plainly and bluntly sent. Even advice not to harness the family to the formal political process was ignored. The President appeared to be circling the wagons.

Abri's rearguard campaign highlighted the threat it now faced from those favouring more civilian political influence. Even if he had no intention of doing so, Suharto helped make this seem a possibility. Already two-thirds of the provincial governors were civilians – a position dominated by Abri members in the preceding five year period. Suharto also appointed fewer military officers as ambassadors. The cabinet was only 'greener' in the Islamic sense. 'Suharto is consciously civilianizing the government', commented a retired senior general.[14] In the process, he was inviting a re-assessment of the once unquestioned 'dual function'.

> To face the challenge of service to the nation in the future, Abri must provide assistance and leadership from outside Abri circles. In the field of socio-political affairs, there are functions better served by officers retired from active service, rather than active duty officers.[15]

Suharto's message to a gathering of retired officers in October was unequivocal. On another occasion in the same month he emphasized that whether in its military or political role, 'Abri does not stand alone.' It was the closest the former general who inaugurated military rule in 1966 had ever come to ordering Abri out of politics. The reconciliation with Nasution helped. In an article he wrote for Armed Forces Day, Nasution cited Suharto repeatedly in reminding Abri 'that the process of development has become difficult and complex, and it is impossible for Abri to deal with it alone.'[16]

With encouragement like this, latent divisions of opinion within the armed forces about their role in politics were harder to suppress. There were those who felt that Abri needed to adapt the dual function to new realities. The Abri seminar in 1990 had concluded that Indonesians were no longer content to accept the status quo. Now those doubting voices were heard more openly. Some felt that Abri should re-cast its role in politics in a more consultative, advisory capacity, leaving the implementation of policy to the existing government structure.

Meanwhile, popular feelings against the military were being aired more freely. More significantly, these anti-military voices were mainly coming from Muslim quarters. It is hard to measure the potency of the Habibie factor which came into play after the 1993 election, but clearly it galvanized a latent political force the New Order had long suppressed. Muslim political consciousness was awakened by Habibie's stewardship of ICMI. The new slogan was *Penghijauan*, or the 'greening' of political institutions. Encouraged by Suharto's patronage, Muslim intellectuals argued that their participation in politics was an assertion of the numerical majority, and thus struck a blow for democracy. They now had the tools to do so; a newspaper staffed by ICMI members (*Republika*) and a think tank, 'the Centre for Information and Development Studies'. It seemed like the stage was set for a substantive revival of the Muslim factor in Indonesian politics.

Less clear is whether this is really what Suharto intended. As suggested earlier, the formation of ICMI in December 1990 may have been conceived as a device to thwart Abri's power. But clearly Muslim intellectuals saw ICMI as an opportunity to revive Islam as a force in national politics. For many Muslims this was long overdue. They resented being shut out of New Order politics and branded as 'extremists' who wanted to turn Indonesia into an Islamic state. There was perhaps room for a modern Islamic nationalist ideology. The New Order's lean political diet of development and *Pancasila* was running foul of its own success. After reaching a certain level of development and social stability, many Indonesians thirsted for political stimulation. There were now special interests to serve and socio-economic imbalances to correct. In the absence of the secular ideologies stamped out by the New Order, Islam had begun to fill the vacuum.

Rather than opting for a fundamentalist route, the new Muslim lobby represented by ICMI sensibly looked to a revival of the Islamic nationalist ideology from the Republic's early years. The link between nationalism and Islam had been broken when the Mohamad Natsir's *Masyumi* party was disbanded in the early years of the New Order. Those with strong family ties to *Masyumi*, or those who were attracted to its modernist, nationalistic Islamic ideology, now flocked to ICMI.

The trend also reflected a primordial polarization in Indonesian politics. The tension Herb Feith detected in Indonesian nationalism between the 'Javanese aristocratic pole' and the 'Islamic entrepreneurial pole' – something like the *santri* and *abangan* streams in Indonesian society. Certainly there were signs that the New Order's manipulation of traditional concepts of Javanese power and authority was increasingly resented by more enlightened elements of society. The inherent populism of Islamic teaching appealed to those who felt the New Order had become too feudal. There were more secular pro-democracy thinkers arguing the same point, but their intellectual approach appealed to a narrow strata of society. The New Order's reliance on foreign aid was at odds with the exclusivism of Islam, so there was also scope for nationalist appeal. Of course, like any other New Order proto-political grouping, idealists mingled with opportunists.

In Habibie, these neo-*Masyumi* types saw a vehicle rather than a new Muslim leader. Habibie's close ties with Suharto offered ICMI the shelter it needed to acquire institutional strength. Habibie could also command a loyal following, having sent some 3,000 students on scholarships overseas since becoming research and technology minister in the mid-1970s. Those who worked closely with him insisted that he genuinely favoured political change and was not afraid to stick his neck out for a more open, genuinely democratic society. Put simply, they saw ICMI as a nascent Islamic political party with Habibie as its temporary figurehead.

Their aim was to build up political strength so that they could field a candidate in the next presidential election in 1998, by which time they expected the field to be more open. 'If Suharto died in office today, the army would step in, and ICMI is lost. That is why we need more time', was how one ICMI member assessed the situation. And why not groom Habibie for the presidency in 1998? Might not the world be intrigued by a German-trained aerospace scientist as president of the world's fourth largest nation? Might it not be feasible to have Habibie selected as a candidate by a civilian-led and Muslim-dominated Golkar? Against this background, ICMI activists began to take bolder stands against the abuse of military power.

When four villagers were shot dead by security forces after protesting against a local dam project on the island of Madura in September, 1,500 students demonstrated in Jogyakarta chanting Islamic slogans. A letter to Suharto signed by 40 *ulama* from East Java called for the 'people to be humanized and for the violence to stop.'[17] At around the same time *Tempo* magazine reported an eyewitness account of where a 'truckload' of Muslim worshippers gunned down by the army during the Tanjungpriok incident of September 1984 were buried.[18] The Sampang incident dragged up memories of the Tanjungpriok shootings in 1984 and Lampung in 1988. The press published pictures of Muslims praying in front of armoured cars; the innocent faithful cut down by Abri bullets. These were potent images which threatened to set Muslims as the country's largest religious community against Abri, the country's largest political organization. Such images confirmed the worst fears of those who saw the seeds of ethnic and religious polarization in the formation of ICMI and its subsequent patronage by Suharto.

Unfortunately for Abri, its clumsy handling of dissent did little to foster public sympathy. The November 1991 massacre of mourners in East Timor may have done little to change official attitudes towards the people of East Timor, but it shocked an Indonesian public now much more aware that in a modern society soldiers should not fire on the populace. For many Indonesians, Abri was becoming a 'specter in the eyes of the people', and not the guardians of social order and sovereignty its doctrine preached. The generals were being looked at more objectively, and their virtue as *ksatria* was seen to be wanting.

Behind the selection of a civilian as Golkar chairman, therefore, lay the much larger issue of Abri's future role in politics, now more questioned than at any other time under the New Order. Golkar was no stronger a political institution, but having a civilian chairman would probably make it harder for Abri to persuade the country that the next president should be a military officer. Some elements in the military were already sensitive to this. In the wake of the Golkar Congress, a senior officer insisted that whatever the composition of the Golkar leadership, Abri remained the 'largest and most popular organization in the country. Anyone else lacks support.'[19]

The contra-variable here was the possibility of a popular swing in Abri's favour should all the political manoeuvring around the succession threaten stability. It might be a little far-fetched in the wake of incidents in Lampung, East Timor, and Sampang to believe that Abri could be popular, but the military was still considered the most organized political force in the country. What if religious and ethnic tension surfaced because the civilian forces lining up against Abri were aligned with the new Muslim power base fostered by Suharto? If the only viable political alternative to military power were the *ulama* and Islamic activists, what room would they give to notions of religious tolerance?

Abri's principal political asset was its doctrinal dedication to the pluralistic principles upon which the Indonesian state was founded and a track record of containing centrifugal forces. Abri could still find potentially acceptable national leaders from among the ranks. After playing a dual role for over a quarter of a century, the distinction between military and civilian roles had become ambiguous in some cases. A man like State Secretary Murdiono, who held the rank of Major General, was not widely perceived as having roots in the military. Ginanjar Kartasasmita was considered by some as a potential presidential candidate for 1998. (The former Mines and Energy Minister was appointed head of the National Development Board [Bappenas] which carries cabinet rank in March 1993.) Still in his early 50s, the Japanese-trained engineer who held the airforce rank of Air Marshal, was never considered part of the core group in Abri. Long seen as marginal in purely military circles, men like this could conceivably play a bridging role in any future power struggle between civilian and military political forces.

Although it looked like Abri's political influence was on the wane, and although it seemed that Suharto had found a new political anchorage for the New Order, it would be misleading as well as premature to predict the end of Abri's 'dual function'. For what Suharto had still not done was allow civilian political institutions to replace Abri. Instead of broadening the political basis of the state and allowing civilians to wield power, the focus of political competition and debate was still the presidency. It was still, in the words of Juwono Sudharsono, a fragile state:

> You get the feeling that all this talk about civilianising is just among educated civilians and educated officers. They are using this to strike at the leadership. The way to civilianising is a strong state. Indonesia is still a fragile state. [20]

If anything, it seemed that the New Order's political base was narrowing. Under the Berkeley technocrats, apolitical as they seemed, there was a logic to stabilizing the economy and that economic development would eventually broaden the level of popular participation in government. Many of the technocrats were closet democrats. Habibie and his ICMI followers seemed to be playing a more strictly political game. 'They are bypassing economics and using politics to come to power.'[21]

Abdurrahman Wahid's view is not entirely objective – or fair. ICMI activists were just as concerned about the future shape of Indonesia's democracy, some rather more impatient than the technocrats had been.

> Economic development has progressed relatively well, so it is already time attitudes towards popular participation were changed.[22]

Suharto himself was forced to acknowledge – not for the first time – that Indonesians were no longer content with the limited degree of political freedom the New Order allowed. In his August 1993 Independence day address, Suharto conceded that '... differences of opinions in our life as a nation are legitimate', and that 'socio-political organizations, mass organizations, representative bodies and other state institutions are gradually becoming more aware of their respective missions and functions.'[23]

Perhaps one sign of change was the greater freedom granted to the press to comment on these remarks. 'Could it be that Suharto believes that our society is now more mature and strong enough to launch and pursue a more democratic system? Does the promise, thus, constitute the first step toward a more open society? Or is it the sign of an aging leadership and a desire to make peace with old foes? Or could it be part of a grand strategy to move away from reliance on the military?'[24] Here, the *Jakarta Post's* editorial writer blended appropriate measures of optimism and scepticism. Yes, there was less official pressure on the press. Journalists were receiving fewer calls from the authorities, who promised more tolerance of criticism. The government had promised more freedom and appeared to be acting on its word. But was this all in the name of more democracy, or for Suharto to buy political space and pursue a more limited imperative of power?

By the end of 1993, Suharto was still struggling to balance the forces competing for power near the end of his long tenure, rather than making any move to build a more open society. In this respect, popular demands for more openness seemed to serve the limited purpose of containing military power, which Suharto probably saw as the main threat to his position. It has been argued in earlier chapters that Suharto's chief political skill was as a tactician, not a long-term strategist. Neither is there much evidence to support the view that Suharto had too much time for western models of democratic pluralism. Nevertheless, Suharto's moves to preserve his position left in their wake opportunities for longer-term political change. These could be exploited as long as the military remained committed to acting within the boundaries of the Constitution, and the ethnic and religious fault lines within Indonesian society remained in a stable state.

NOTES

1 SUHARTO

1 Pramoedya Ananta Toer, *Anak Semua Bangsa* (Child of All Nations), London, Penguin, 1980, p.209.
2 *Jakarta Post*, 15 September 1990.
3 Development Foundation of Indonesian Youth (YPPI). A group consisting of members of the 1966 generation of Students which helped bring Suharto to power. Cited from their report to President Suharto quoted in *Tempo*, 19 January 1991.
4 H. Crouch, *The Indonesian Military in Politics*, Ithaca, Cornell University, 1978, p.26.
5 Suharto, *Suharto: My Thoughts, Words and Deeds*, Jakarta, PT Citra Lamtoro Gung Persada, 1989, p.8.
6 Ibid., p.10.
7 Personal communication, 21 July 1990.
8 Suharto, op. cit., p.11.
9 O.G. Roeder, *The Smiling General*, Jakarta, Gunung Agung, 1970, p.3.
10 Suharto, op. cit., p.5.
11 M. Vatikiotis, 'Directing the Debate', *FEER*, 17 August 1989.
12 Roeder, op. cit., p.98.
13 Ibid., p.101.
14 Suharto, op. cit., p.24.
15 Ibid., p.26.
16 Ibid., p.69.
17 Roeder, op. cit., p.124.
18 General Abdul Haris Nasution [interview by the author] 11 November 1989.
19 H. MacDonald, *Suharto's Indonesia*, Sydney, Fontana, 1980, p.25.
20 Also known in corporate circles as the Salim Group. Liem took the Indonesian name Sudono Salim.
21 R. Robison, *The Rise of Capital in Indonesia*, Sydney, Allen & Unwin, 1986, p.346.
22 A cabinet minister revealed to the author how Hasan would write to economic ministers concerning the plywood and rattan industry and imply that his advice be accepted without question.

23 M. Malley, 'Sœdjono Hœmardani: A political biography', unpublished M.A. thesis, Cornell University, 1990, pp.240–50.
24 Ibid., p.36.
25 Ibid., p.36.
26 Ibid., p.32.
27 This is probably because Suharto's ignominious dismissal from central Java is not mentioned in official New Order historical accounts of his career.
28 General T.B. Simatupang [interview with the author] 26 April 1989.
29 Former 1966 student leader [personal communication].
30 Former 1966 student leader [personal communication] 21 July 1990.
31 Former 1966 student leader [personal communication] 21 July 1990.
32 General A.H. Nasution [interview with the author] 11 November 1989.
33 General Kemal Idris [interview with the author] 16 January 1990.
34 R. McVey, and B. Anderson, 'A preliminary Analysis of the October 1 1965 Coup in Indonesia', Cornell University Modern Indonesia Project No. 52, 1971.
35 F. Bunnell, 'American "Low Posture" Policy Towards Indonesia in the Months Leading up to the 1965 Coup', 1990, p.42.
36 General A.H. Nasution [interview with the author] 26 July 1990.
37 General Kemal Idris [interview with the author] 16 January 1990.
38 Suharto, op. cit., p.146 [draft version].
39 Ibid., p.136.
40 R. Kapuscinski, The Emperor, London, Picador, 1984.
41 A.H. Nasution, Opening Speech at the Vth Special Session of the MPRS, cited in U. Sundhaussen, The Road to Power: Indonesian Military Politics 1945–67, Kuala Lumpur, OUP, 1982, p.250.
42 J.D. Legge, Sukarno: A Political Biography, Sydney, Allen & Unwin, 1973, p.406.
43 Suharto, op. cit., p.260.
44 Tempo, 19 October 1991, p.21.
45 A. Malik, In the Service of the Republic, Jakarta Gunung Agung, 1980, p.313.
46 Personal communication November 1989.
47 Suharto, op. cit., p.165.
48 Personal communication, 28 January 1988.
49 General A.H. Nasution [interview with the author] 11 November 1989.
50 Kemal Idris [interview with the author] 16 January 1990.
51 Suharto op. cit., pp. 231–2.
52 Centre of Strategic and International Studies (CSIS) source 1990. [Murtopo and Hœmardani set up CSIS as their own think-tank. Their former subordinates and supporters still staff and run the institute.]
53 CSIS Source.
54 Butir Butir Budaya Jawa: Mencapai Kesempurnaan Hidup Berjiwa Besar Mengusaha-kan Kebaikan Sejati (Javanese Cultural Proverbs: In search of Perfect Life, Noble and generous mind; In quest of the essence of goodness.) A collection of 'moral guidance' and 'prohibitions' given as guidance by Suharto and his wife to their children. Compiled and published by Suharto's eldest daughter, Siti Hardiyanti Hastuti Rukmana, on the occasion of their fortieth wedding anniversary on 26 December 1987. A limited edition, not designed to be widely distributed.
55 General T.B. Simatupang [interview with the author] 26 April 1989.

2 ORDER AND DEVELOPMENT

1 Sukarno, *Biography As Told to Cindy Adams*, Indianapolis, 1965, p.39.
2 J.D. Legge, *Sukarno: A Political Biography*, Sydney, Allen & Unwin, 1972, p.399.
3 Figures from State Investment Board of Indonesia (BKPM).
4 Gelb (1986) 'Adjustment to Windfall Gains', cited in A. Booth, *Agricultural Development in Indonesia*, Sydney, Allen & Unwin, 1988.
5 Radius Prawiro, Speech to APCAC, Jakarta, 19 April 1990.
6 World Bank, 'Indonesia: Poverty Assessement and Strategy Report', May 1990.
7 Bank Indonesia: Monthly Report.
8 Bank Duta was bailed out after cash donations of $US200 million each from Liem Sioe Long and Prajogo Pangestu were given to the Bank.
9 Johannes Sumarlin [interview with author] 14 September 1989.
10 Data from Asian Development Bank.
11 Figures from State Investment Board (BKPM).
12 'Suharto Son, Partners Form Plastic Firm', *AWSJ*, 20–21 July 1990.
13 Edwin Soeryadjaya [personal communication].
14 H. Soesastro, (1989) 'The Political Economy of deregulation in Indonesia', *Asian Survey*, 1989, vol. XXIX, no.9.
15 Gunawan Mohamad [personal communication].
16 Anwar Nasution [pesonal communication].
17 World Bank: Indonesia Country report, 1990.
18 Vatikiotis, M. (1989) 'Order in Court' *FEER*, 15 June 1989.
19 J. Sumarlin [interview] 14 September 1989.
20 Yoon, Hwan Shin, 'Demystifying the Capitalist State: Political Patronage, Bureaucratic Interests, and Capitalists-in-Formation in Soeharto's Indonesia', unpublished Ph.D. thesis, Yale University, 1989, pp. 389–90.
21 *Pusat Data Bisnis*, cited in *Media Indonesia* 30 November 1989.
22 Sarwono Kusumaatmadja [interview with author] 13 July 1990.
23 R. Robison, *The Rise of Capital in Indonesia*, Sydney, Allen & Unwin, 1986, p.295.
24 M. Mas'oed, (1989) 'The State Reorganization of Society under the New Order', *Prisma* 1989, no.47, p.11.
25 R. Robison, 'Doing it their way', *FEER*, 8 February 1990, p.36.
26 K. Yoshihara, *The Rise of Ersatz Capitalism in Southeast Asia*, Singapore, OUP, 1988, pp.3–4.
27 Suharto: Budget Speech, 4 January 1990.
28 J. Sumarlin [interview with author] 14 September 1989.
29 W.L. Collier, 'Emplyment Trends in Lowland Javanese Villages', Jakarta, US-AID, 1988.
30 Figures from Department of Manpower, Jakarta.

3 TWO FUNCTIONS, ONE PURPOSE: THE INDONESIAN ARMY IN POLITICS

1 General Chaovalit Yongchaiyudh, quoted in *Singapore Straits Times*, 22 March 1991.
2 This figure breaks down as follows:

Army	220,000
Navy	40,000
Air Force	23,000
Police	170,000
Student brigade	80,000

Source: Armed Forces HQ Staff: 1988

3 Cited from the Clarification on the Military Bill before a plenary session of the Indonesian House of Representatives (DPR) presented by General (retd) Poniman, as Minister of Defence.

4 Interview with foreign student attending SESKOAD, Bandung, 1989.

5 Written response to questions put by the author to Major-General Feisal Tanjung, Commandant, SESKOAD, 9 December 1988.

6 T.B. Simatupang, 'Indonesia: Leadership and National Security Perceptions' ISEAS (unpublished), Singapore, 1987, p.21.

7 D. Jenkins, *Suharto and His Generals*, Ithaca, Cornell, 1984.

8 L. Penders and U. Sundhaussen, *Nasution: a political biography*, Leiden, Leiden University Press, 1985, p.45.

9 U. Sundhaussen, *The Road to Power: Indonesian Military Politics 1945–67*, Kuala Lumpur, OUP, 1982, p.57.

10 Simatupang, op. cit., p.52.

11 J. Legge, *Sukarno: A Political Biography*, Sydney, Allen & Unwin, 1972, pp.254–6.

12 Y. Sugama, *Memori Jenderal Yoga*, as told to B. Wiwoho and Banjar Chaeruddin, Jakarta, 1990, pp.138–9.

13 General A.H. Nasution [interview with the author] 11 November 1989.

14 Simatupang, op. cit., p.39.

15 Ibid., p.52.

16 Jenkins, op. cit., p.3.

17 Ibid., p.198.

18 General Sumitro [interview with the author] 6 February 1988.

19 General A.H. Nasution: Interview given to FEER 2 August 1980.

20 Dharsono was released in 1990.

21 General A.H. Nasution [interview with the author] 11 November 1989.

22 General Sumitro [interview with the author] 2 March 1990.

23 A. Yani, *Profile of a Soldier*, Singapore, Heinemann, 1990.

24 J. Boileau, 'Golkar: Functional Group Politics in Indonesia', Jakarta, CSIS, p.43.

25 Brigadier-General Abdulkadir Besar [interview with the author] 19 February 1990.

26 Jenkins, op. cit., pp.157–8.

27 L. Kaye, 'Operasi Regenerasi', FEER 15 September 1983.

28 FEER, 24 October 1985.

29 *Tempo*, 31 March 1983.

30 FEER, 17 March 1988.

31 Marsillam Simanjuntak [personal communication] 12 March 1991.

32 M. Vatikiotis, 'Siege Tactics', FEER, 29 November 1990.

33 For the background on Sudharmono, I am indebted to senior Golkar officials.

34 Bunnell, op. cit., p.43.

35 General L.B. Murdani [personal communication] 14 January 1991.

36 *Indonesian Observer*, 5 December 1989.
37 Results of army seminar, December 1990 [document in author's possession].
38 *Kompas*, 2 August 1990. *Indonesia Observer*, 2 August 1990.
39 Indebted for this point to Dr I. Amal and Dr Y. Muhaimin of Gaja Madah University in Jogyakarta.

4 NEW ORDER SOCIETY

1 M. Lubis, *Indonesia: Under the Rainbow*, Singapore, OUP, 1990, pp.20–1.
2 Law on Ormas, 1985.
3 L. Suryadinata, *Military Ascendancy and Political Culture: A Study of Indonesia's Golkar*, Athens OH, Ohio University, 1989, p.70.
4 Sarwono Kusumaatmadja [interview with the author] 4 January 1991.
5 Suharto: Speech to parliament, 7 January 1991.
6 Ibid.
7 J. Mackie, 'Changes in the Power Structure, 1966–89', paper presented at a Conference 'Indonesia's New Order, Past Present and Future, Australian National University, Canberra, 8 December 1989.
8 L. Pye, *Asian Power and Politics*, Cambridge, MA, Belknap-Harvard, 1985.
9 *Kedaulatan Rakyat* 8 October 1989.
10 Pol. Colonel Roekmini Soedjono, cited in *Kompas*, 8 January 1990.
11 A. Mahasin, 'Culture and Power: Changing the Mirage', *Prisma*, 1989, 46.
12 Hari Tjan Silahi [personal communication] 7 August 1990.
13 H. Leuthy, 'Indonesia Confronted', *Encounter*, 1965.
14 *Jakarta Post*, 27 October 1990.
15 *Reuters*, 26 February 1991.
16 General A.H. Nasution, 'Pledge by the 1966 New Order to achieve Pure and consistent implementation of the national Constitution of 1945', re-issued 27 June 1984.
17 General L.B. Murdani, 'Speech of the Abri Commander on National Discipline and Development of our democracy', 20 May 1987.
18 Ministry of Political and Security affairs: Explanation of Ideological screening. 8 September 1988.
19 *Tempo*, 12 January 1991.
20 General Yoga Sugama [interview with the author] 24 July 1990.
21 'Human Rights in Indonesia', an Asia Watch Report, 1989, p.208.
22 S. Awanohara, 'Suharto's Kingdom', *FEER*, 9 August 1984. p.33.
23 D.K. Emmerson, 'Bureaucracy in Political Context', in K. Jackson and L. Pye (eds) *Political Power and Communications in Indonesia*, Berkeley, University of California, 1978, p.107.
24 Personal communication with Taufik Abdullah.
25 A. Reid, *South-east Asia in the Age of Commerce, 1450-1680*, New Haven, Yale, 1988, p.120.
26 Ignas, Kleden, 'The Changing Political Leadership of Java', *Prisma*, 1988, 46, pp.21–32.
27 Umar Kayam, 'Transformasi Budaya Kita', cited in M. Vatikiotis, 'The Open Question', *FEER*, 16 November 1989, pp.42–4.
28 J. Ball, Indonesian Law Commentary, Sydney, 1981, p.359.

29 International Labour Organization, 1988.
30 Murdiono, 'Continuation, Enhancement, Revitalisation and Constant Renewal', Introductory remarks by the Minister/ State Secretary, Murdiono, at a dialogue with 'Business International' on 2 November 1989.
31 General L.B. Murdani, cited in *Jakarta Post*, 15 June 1990.
32 Author's interview with US AID Director, 8 July 1990.

5 TOWARDS AN ISLAMIC IDENTITY?

1 N. Tamara, 'Indonesia in the wake of Islam', ISIS, Malaysia, 1986. See also S. Awanohara, 'The New call to Prayer', *FEER*, 24 January 1985, pp.26–31.
2 Abdurrahman Wahid [interview] 16 November 1989.
3 Abdurrahman Wahid [interview] 16 November 1989.
4 Tamara, op. cit., p.3.
5 Data from Survey Research Indonesia (1991).
6 M. Vatikiotis, 'One Code for all Courts', *FEER*, September 1989, pp.28–9.
7 There was tension between the Vatican and the church in East Timor in the wake of the Papal visit as it seemed Pope John Paul was reluctant to jeopardise the Church's wider interests in Indonesia for the sake of East Timor's problems.
8 Data from Ministry of Religious Affairs, Jakarta.
9 'Violence in Lampung', an Asia Watch report, 16 March 1989.
10 Ibid.
11 I am indebted to Sydney Jones of Asia Watch for this point.
12 Jalalluddin Rachmat [interview] May 1990.
13 Mohtar Maso'ed [personal communication].
14 Confidential communication.
15 Emha Einun Najib [personal communication] January 1991.
16 M. Liefer, 'Suharto's Pilgrimage to Mecca: Is there a Subplot? *IHT*, June – 1991.
17 *Media Indonesia*, 24 June 1991.
18 Slamet Bratanata [personal communication] 24 June 1991.
19 Marzuki Darusman [personal communication] 25 June 1991.
20 *Tempo*, 6 July 1991.

6 SUCCESSION STALKS SUHARTO

1 E.B. Mihaly, 'Indonesia: A new Dragon?', *World Today*, 1990, August/ September.
2 The ban on student political activity held until the late 1980s, when the army again tacitly began promoting student political action as part of a similar political strategy.
3 *Human Rights in Indonesia and East Timor*, Asia Watch Report, March 1989, p.53.
4 Professor Juwono Sudharsono, cited in *Jakarta Post*, 22 June 1991.
5 Benny Murdani [personal communication] 13 June 1989.
6 General Sumitro [interview with the author] 6 November 1989.
7 General Sumitro [interview with the author] 2 March 1990.
8 Major–General Soebiakto, 13 September 1988.

9 [Personal communication] 6 September 1989.

10 General A.H. Nasution [interview with the author] 11 November 1989.

11 L. Pye *Asian Power and Politics. The Cultural Dimensions of Authority,* Harvard, Belknap, 1985, p.91.

12 Ibid., p.91.

13 [Personal communication] 7 February 1990.

14 [Personal communication].

15 'Siapa Memperdaya Siapa', *Tempo* 11 May 1991, p.84.

16 Ibid.

17 A. Schwarz, 'Credit Stubbed', *FEER*, 12 September 1991, p.55

18 Lieutenant Colonel Prabowo Djojohadikusumo served in East Timor with an infantry battalion until 1989.

19 M. Vatikiotis, 'Spiking Speculation', *FEER*, 22 June 1989, p.25.

20 M. Vatikiotis, 'Succession Talk', *FEER*, 27 April 1989, p.28.

21 Ibid.

22 M. Vatikiotis, 'Succession Scenarios', *FEER*, 28 September 1989, p.31.

23 *Time* 8 April 1991, p.26.

24 *Tempo*, 10 March 1990.

25 Sri Edi Swasono [interview with the author], 17 January 1990.

26 *Antara*, English bulletin, 13 March 1990.

27 Cited in *Straits Times* 13 March 1990.

28 In an interview with Reuters, Probosutedjo indicated that this was the reason. (*Reuters*, 23 July 1991).

29 Interviews with petty traders and businessmen from the Cirebon area attending an NU conference in Jogyakarta in November 1989.

30 Brigadier-General Abdulkadir Besar [personal communication] 22 June 1989.

31 [Personal communication] September 1988.

32 A. Macintyre, *Business and Politics in Indonesia*, Sydney, Allen and Unwin, 1991, p.3.

7 DRAGON APPARENT OR ROGUE TIGER?

1 *Straits Times*, 6 August 1991.

2 Political officers at the Australian embassy in Jakarta complained that some of the pessimistic aspects of their reporting were being suppressed.

3 *International Herald Tribune*, 31 August–1 September 1991.

4 Indonesian Foreign Ministry End of Year Statement, December 1990, p.34.

5 Cited in *Tempo*, 5 October 1991, p.22.

6 General L.B. Murdani [personal communication] February 1991.

7 A. Macintyre, *Business and Politics in Indonesia*, Sydney, Allen & Unwin 1991, p.225.

8 Ibid., p.255.

9 US AID official, Jakarta [personal communication] 7 July 1990.

10 Professor Emil Salim [interview with the author] December 1990.

11 Suharto, *Suharto: My Thoughts, Words and Deeds,* Jakarta, P.T. Citra Lamtoro Gung Persada, 1989, p.429.

12 Mohammad Ariff, 'Liberalization works under stable government', *The Star* (Kuala Lumpur), 26 March 1991.

NOTES

13 Professor Mohammad Sadli, keynote address delivered at the Conference on the New Order, Past, Present and Future, Canberra, 4–9 December 1989.
14 M. Vatikiotis, 'Worrying about idle minds', *FEER*, 13 October 1988.
15 James Castle 'Deregulation or Re-regulation: Private Business, regulation and development', paper resented to an international conference on the economic policy-making process in Indonesia, Bali 7 September 1990.
16 World Bank Annual Report on Indonesia, May 1990, p.98.
17 Ibid., p.66.
18 *Tempo*, 10 March 1990.
19 A. Schwarz, 'Empire of the Sun', *FEER*, 14 March 1991, pp.46–52.
20 Figures sourced to US Embassy in Jakarta.
21 Suharto: Speech to MPRS, 1 December 1967.
22 *Kompas*, 15 September 1989.
23 Estimates from Asia Watch (December 1990).
24 A. Schwarz, 'Over the Edge', *FEER*, 28 November 1991, pp.15–18.
25 A point made by a senior Abri staff officer to an ICRC delegate in Jakarta.
26 General Try Sutrisno's comments were made at a gathering of Abri officers and reported in the Abri-backed daily, *Jayakarta*, cited in AFP report of 21 November 1991.
27 *Tempo*, 5 October 1991, p.22.
28 Allusion to Abri's engineering of demonstrations in East Timor and Java was made in an interview with Home Affairs Minister Rudini in *Tempo*, 28 December 1991, p.21. (Rudini denied the allegation.)
29 Personal communication.
30 *International Herald Tribune*, 21 November 1991.
31 Foreign aid accounted for 52 per cent of the Development budget in the period 1991–2.
32 Nurcholis Madjid, quoted in *Tempo*, 21 September 1991, pp. 24–5.

8 DEMOCRACY ON HOLD

1 A. Schwarz, (1991) 'The Team Spirit', *FEER*, 3 October 1991, p.51.
2 Kemal Idris [personal communication] March 1991.
3 *'Strategi Pembangunan Sumber Daya Manusia Dalam Pembangunan Jangka Panjang Tahap Kedua'* Results of the Army Seminar, 15–19 December 1990, p.47.
4 *Jakarta Post*, 21 June 1991.
5 Golkar MP [personal communication] 21 June 1991.
6 *Straits Times*, 9 October 1991. Suharto made the remarks at a gathering of top Abri commanders at his Tapos ranch outside Jakarta.
7 H. Feith, 'Dynamics of Guided Democracy', in R. McVey, (ed), *Indonesia*, New Haven, Yale, 1963, p.314.
8 Kuntowidjoyo, 'Contemporary Indonesian Culture', paper delivered at inaugural meeting of the Soedjatmoko Foundation, January 1991, p.16.
9 Personal communication.
10 Datuk Seri Mahathir Mohamad, 'Malaysia: the way forward', speech delivered on 28 February 1991.
11 *Singapore: The Next Lap*, Singapore, Government of Singapore, 1991, p.14.
12 Suharto,: speech before MPR, 11 March 1983.

13 M. Vatikiotis, 'Dollar Democracy', *FEER*, 26 September 1991.
14 H. MacDonald, *Suharto's Indonesia*, Sydney, Fontana, 1980, p.7.
15 N. Notosusanto, *The National Struggle and the Armed Forces in Indonesia* (2nd edn) Jakarta, Department of Defence, Centre for Armed Forces History, 1980.
16 Rachmat Witoelar [personal communication] February 1991.

9 THE FRAGILE STATE

1 Wanandi, Jusuf, (1993) 'Indonesia's National Agenda', paper delivered at Fifth Southeast Asia Forum, ISIS, Kuala Lumpur, 3–6 October, 1993, p.2.
2 Interviews with young abstainers (*golput*) on streets of Jogyakarta by the author 7-9 June 1992.
3 Emha Ainun Najib, interview, 10 June 1992.
4 Interview with General L. B. Murdani, 3 May 1993.
5 Crouch, H. (1992) 'The Succession Issue in Indonesia' [draft made available to the author].
6 Interview with General L. B. Murdani, 3 May 1993.
7 Personal communication, 1 May 1993.
8 *Straits Times* (Singapore) 18 June 1993.
9 KISS: 'Ke istana sendiri sendiri'; to the palace one-by-one.
10 Nasution met Suharto at a gathering of Abri senior officers on 26 July, 1993 – their first meeting in 20 years. Eyewitnesses to the encounter at the Merdeka palace said that after exchanging pleasantries – including comparing notes on their respective prostrate conditions, Nasution started to take out a piece of paper on which he had written a few points. At this point, Suharto excused himself and never came back. Later Nasution told reporters that 'nothing happened' and that 'There is no hope... what I hoped for is still far away.'
11 Pour, Julius (1993) *Benny Moerdani: Profile of a Soldier Statesman.* Yayasan Kejuangan Panglima Besar Sudirman, Jakarta.
12 *Detik*, 22–28 September 1993.
13 Personal Communication, 25 October, 1993.
14 Interview with General Sumitro, 24 September 1993.
15 Suharto, cited in *Tempo*, 9 October, 1993.
16 *Indonesian Business Weekly,* 15 October, 1993, p.11.
17 *Tempo*, 16 October, 1993, pp.30–1.
18 Op. cit, p.39.
19 Comments by Major General Sembiring Meliala, a DPR member and serving officer, cited by Reuters, 27 October, 1993.
20 Personal communication with Professor Juwono Sudharsono, 25 September 1993.
21 Interview with Abdurrahman Wahid, 23 September 1993.
22 Santoso, Amir, (1993) 'Implementasi Hak-Hak Manusia Dalam Perspectif Pembangunan Politik Indonesia', paper prepared for Centre of Information and Development Studies, Jakarta.
23 Suharto, National Day Address, 16 August 1993.
24 *Jakarta Post*, editorial, 19 August 1993.

INDEX